Petitions and Strategies of Persuasion in the Middle Ages

YORK MEDIEVAL PRESS

York Medieval Press is published by the University of York's Centre for Medieval Studies in association with Boydell & Brewer Limited. Our objective is the promotion of innovative scholarship and fresh criticism on medieval culture. We have a special commitment to interdisciplinary study, in line with the Centre's belief that the future of Medieval Studies lies in those areas in which its major constituent disciplines at once inform and challenge each other.

All enquiries of an editorial kind, including suggestions for monographs and essay collections, should be addressed to: The Academic Editor, York Medieval Press, Department of History, University of York, Heslington, York, YO10 5DD (E-mail: pete.biller@york.ac.uk)

Details of other York Medieval Press volumes are available from Boydell & Brewer Ltd.

Petitions and Strategies of Persuasion in the Middle Ages

The English Crown and the Church, c.1200–c.1550

Edited by
Thomas W. Smith
Helen Killick

THE UNIVERSITY *of York*

YORK MEDIEVAL PRESS

First published 2018

A York Medieval Press publication
in association with The Boydell Press
an imprint of Boydell & Brewer Ltd
PO Box 9, Woodbridge, Suffolk IP12 3DF, UK
and of Boydell & Brewer Inc.
668 Mt Hope Avenue, Rochester, NY 14620–2731, USA
website: www.boydellandbrewer.com
and with the
Centre for Medieval Studies, University of York

ISBN 978 1 903153 83 3

A CIP catalogue record for this book is available
from the British Library

This publication is printed on acid-free paper

Printed and bound in Great Britain by
TJ International Ltd, Padstow, Cornwall

FSC www.fsc.org
MIX
Paper from
responsible sources
FSC® C013056

Dedicated to the memory of Edward Killick

This book was produced with generous financial support from the School of History, University of Leeds

Contents

Contributors

Gwilym Dodd	University of Nottingham
Philippa M. Hoskin	University of Lincoln
Helen Killick	University of Reading
Helen Lacey	University of Oxford
Anthony Musson	Historic Royal Palaces
W. Mark Ormrod	University of York
Frederik Pedersen	University of Aberdeen
Matthew Phillips	Independent scholar
Kirsi Salonen	University of Turku
Thomas W. Smith	University of Leeds
Shelagh Sneddon	University of York

Foreword

W. Mark Ormrod

This collection of essays on petitioning in secular and ecclesiastical courts during the later Middle Ages bears testimony not only to the exceptionally rich body of archival evidence that survives for such processes but also to the intense interest that researchers have given to that material over the last decade and more. Very importantly, it seeks to address the place of petitioning within wider legal strategies and thus to pinpoint the role of 'professionals' in formulating and presenting the substance and context of the grievance of the plaintiff. In an earlier stage of thinking about this topic we may have been inclined to be misled by the apparent authenticity of the plaintiff's voice: not just because of the comparatively discursive nature of petitionary form but also because petitions were often made in the name of people who were comparatively marginalised by the usual formalities of legal process (peasants and women being notable cases in point) and whose predicaments sometimes make for very vivid narratives. To understand the ways in which experts at various levels imagined and composed the plaints of their clients such as to address the relevant points of law and/or to articulate the need for a resort to grace is not necessarily to call into doubt the more sensational aspects of some petitions. It does, however, serve as a salutary warning that the motives and aims of plaintiffs and their advisers were focused, purposeful and constructive. The hopeless conditions in which so many petitioners declared themselves were therefore part of a deliberate strategy of redemption and in this sense reflect not simply on the (undoubted) nastiness of the times but also on the remarkable confidence that later medieval society showed in the formal systems available to provide right for blatant wrongs.

A further feature of the studies represented in this volume is the way that such legal strategies crossed boundaries: those between Church and State, as well as those between princely jurisdictions. While the great majority of the case studies address material held in English archives, the process of petitioning needs to be thought of as a much more general European phenomenon, and one that was international in its potential reach. Studies of petitions to the papacy remind us that all parts of Latin Christendom needed to develop structures and communication systems that allowed private parties to access the grace of the curia. More generally, the access that petitioning provided to English royal prerogative courts was not simply enjoyed by the denizen subjects of the king; those from the dependent dominions of the crown and people of alien status were also accepted as petitioners in parliament, in the council and in the chancery. This international dimension is especially important to bear in mind in relation to a period when ideas of sovereignty are so often seen as placing ring fences round royal jurisdictions. To be a good lord in the Middle Ages was not simply about providing remedies for one's direct subjects; it was also about protecting the stranger and demonstrating to the world at large the breadth and efficacy of one's judgments.

Whither late medieval petitionary studies now? There are numerous topics that remain open either to re-consideration or to wholly new investigation, and this collection points the way to many of them – most especially, in terms of the fruitful results of treating the secular and the ecclesiastical arms as two parts of a single whole. Among the host of other possibilities, one may perhaps venture that the time has come for a deeper appreciation of collective petitioning in late medieval England. The representational mania that is a regular part of modern life – support this cause; sign this petition – is not, as so often assumed, the simple result of a technological change that makes electronic subscription so easy. It is the contemporary manifestation of a much longer tradition that finds its origins in the corporate activities of manors, vills, parishes and towns during the Middle Ages. We now need to establish the beginnings and meanings of the kinds of 'popular' petitioning that leave a clearer archival mark in the early modern period: not only petitions claiming to voice the ideas of the 'commons' but also those to which individuals subscribed as a conscious expression of the will to bring about action and change. Contemporary society is experiencing a significant ideological conflict, in which democratic principles about majority rule for the common good appear to be giving way increasingly to the assertion of individual rights and liberties. To understand the extent and the limitations, the situations and the valences, of both individual and common petitioning in the late Middle Ages is therefore to reflect upon the actual degrees of consensus and consent that may (or may not) have underpinned collective action in the past. Who prevails? It is a question that many people in late medieval English society found both real and unnerving. And it is a question to which petitions can provide some very valuable answers.

Acknowledgements

Special thanks go to Matthew Phillips, who played a key role in the conception and early gestation of this project; without him, this book would not exist. We are grateful to the contributors for delivering their chapters on time and thereby making the editing of this volume such a smooth and enjoyable process. At York Medieval Press and Boydell & Brewer Pete Biller, Caroline Palmer, Rob Kinsey and Rebecca Cribb have been such a pleasure to work with, and we are indebted to them for their kind support and encouragement. We would like to thank Mark Ormrod for writing the foreword and for his invaluable guidance in the final stages of editing. Our thanks go to the anonymous reviewer for incredibly helpful, thorough and thoughtful feedback, which has been crucial in developing the volume.

We are very grateful to the School of History at the University of Leeds for generously supporting the publication of this volume.

Abbreviations

CCR	*Calendar of Close Rolls*, 47 vols, PRO Texts and Calendars (London, 1900–63)
CFR	*Calendar of Fine Rolls*, 22 vols, PRO Texts and Calendars (London, 1911–62)
CFR Henry III	*Calendar of Fine Rolls of the Reign of Henry III preserved in The National Archives*, ed. P. Dryburgh and B. Hartland, 3 vols to date (Woodbridge, 2007–); <http://www.finerollshenry3.org.uk/content/calendar/calendar.html> [accessed 3 January 2018]
CIM	*Calendar of Inquisitions Miscellaneous*, 7 vols, PRO Texts and Calendars (London, 1916–68)
CIPM	*Calendar of Inquisitions Post Mortem*, 20 vols, PRO Texts and Calendars (London, 1904–95)
CPR	*Calendar of the Patent Rolls*, PRO Texts and Calendars (London, 1891–).
PROME	*The Parliament Rolls of Medieval England*, ed. C. Given-Wilson et al., 16 vols (Woodbridge, 2005); <http://www.sd-editions.com/PROME/home.html> [accessed 4 January 2018]
SR	*Statutes of the Realm*, ed. A. Luders et al., 11 vols (London, 1810–28)
TNA	The National Archives, Kew

Introduction: Medieval Petitions and Strategies of Persuasion

Thomas W. Smith and Helen Killick

In 2009 Mark Ormrod, Gwilym Dodd and Anthony Musson broke new ground in the study of supplications in the Middle Ages with their edited volume *Medieval Petitions: Grace and Grievance.*[1] Inspired by the completion of an AHRC-funded project to catalogue, digitise and study the SC 8 series of 'Ancient Petitions' preserved in The National Archives at Kew, *Medieval Petitions* tapped a rich vein of scholarship on supplications in medieval England and at the papal curia and helped to open up a field of study that has continued to flourish in the following decade.[2] Broadly, there exist two strong traditions of research on petitions to the English crown, on the one hand, and ecclesiastical, specifically papal, petitions, on the other.[3] Since 2009 a number of works have pushed the field in new directions. New research on petitions to the crown has illuminated aspects of petitioning such as supplications for royal pardon,[4] women's petitions,[5] multiple-clause

[1] *Medieval Petitions: Grace and Grievance*, ed. W. M. Ormrod, G. Dodd and A. Musson (York, 2009). This contributed further to the important studies on medieval supplications in *Suppliques et requêtes: Le gouvernement par la grâce en occident (XIIe–XVe siècle)*, ed. H. Millet (Rome, 2003), which adopted a broader European focus.

[2] The SC 8 series can be accessed at: <http://discovery.nationalarchives.gov.uk/details/r/C13526> [accessed 15 January 2018].

[3] For a comprehensive survey of the historiography on medieval petitions published before 2012, see B. Bombi, 'The Roman Rolls of Edward II as a Source of Administrative and Diplomatic Practice in the Early Fourteenth Century', *Historical Research* 85 (2012), 597–616. For the historiography since 2009, see below.

[4] H. Lacey, *The Royal Pardon: Access to Mercy in Fourteenth-Century England* (York, 2009); W. M. Ormrod, 'The King's Mercy: An Attribute of Later Medieval English Monarchy', in *La légitimité implicite: Le pouvoir symbolique en Occident (1300–1640)*, ed. J.-P. Genet, 2 vols (Paris, 2015), vol. II, pp. 321–35; W. M. Ormrod, 'Pardon, Parliament and Political Performance in Later Medieval England', in *Prowess, Piety and Public Order in Medieval Society: Studies in Honour of Richard W. Kaeuper*, ed. C. M. Nakashian and D. P. Franke (Leiden, 2017), pp. 301–20.

[5] W. M. Ormrod, 'Needy Knights and Wealthy Widows: The Encounters of John Cornewall and Lettice Kirriel, 1378–1382', in *The Medieval Python: The Purposive and*

petitions,[6] petitions of complaint,[7] the language of petitioning and the drafting process,[8] as well as more general aspects of the processes and mechanisms of petitioning.[9] These interpretative studies have also been supplemented by the publication of new documents in the form of the early common petitions

Provocative Work of Terry Jones, ed. R. F. Yeager and T. Takamiya (New York, 2012), pp. 137–49; C. Beattie, 'Your Oratrice: Women's Petitions to the Late Medieval Court of Chancery', in *Women, Agency and the Law, 1300–1700*, ed. B. C. Kane and F. Williamson (London, 2013), pp. 17–30; J. Goldberg, 'Echoes, Whispers, Ventriloquisms: on Recovering Women's Voices from the Court of York at the End of the Middle Ages', in *Women, Agency and the Law*, ed. Kane and Williamson, pp. 31–42.

6 G. Dodd, M. Phillips and H. Killick, 'Multiple-Clause Petitions to the English Parliament in the Later Middle Ages: Instruments of Pragmatism or Persuasion?', *Journal of Medieval History* 40 (2014), 176–94.

7 M. Phillips, 'Church, Crown and Complaint: Petitions from Bishops to the English Crown in the Fourteenth Century' (unpublished PhD thesis, University of Nottingham, 2013); S. L. Walker, 'Tyranny, Complaint and Redress: The Evidence of the Petitions presented to the Crown, c. 1320–35' (unpublished PhD thesis, University of Nottingham, 2013).

8 W. M. Ormrod, 'The Language of Complaint: Multilingualism and Petitioning in Later Medieval England', in *Language and Culture in Medieval Britain: The French of England, c. 1100–c. 1500*, ed. J. Wogan-Browne with C. Collette, M. Kowaleski, L. Mooney, A. Putter and D. Trotter (York, 2009), pp. 31–43; G. Dodd, 'The Rise of English, the Decline of French: Supplications to the English Crown, c. 1420–50', *Speculum* 86 (2011), 117–50; G. Dodd, 'Writing Wrongs: The Drafting of Supplications to the Crown in Later Fourteenth-Century England', *Medium Ævum* 80 (2011), 217–46; G. Dodd, 'Kingship, Parliament and the Court: The Emergence of "High Style" in Petitions to the English Crown, c. 1350–1405', *English Historical Review* 129 (2014), 515–48; H. Killick, 'Treason, Felony and Lollardy: A Common Petition in the Hand of Richard Osbarn, Clerk of the Chamber of the Guildhall, 1400–c. 1437', *Historical Research* 89 (2016), 227–45.

9 See the various chapters in *La supplication: discours et représentation*, ed. L. Albert, P. Bruley and A.-S. Dufief (Rennes, 2015); G. Dodd and S. Petit-Renaud, 'Grace and Favour: The Petition and its Mechanisms', in *Government and Political Life in England and France, c. 1300–c. 1500*, ed. C. Fletcher, J.-P. Genet and J. Watts (Cambridge, 2015), pp. 240–78; G. Dodd, 'Petitions from the King's Dominions: Wales, Ireland and Gascony, c. 1290–1350', in *The Plantagenet Empire, 1259–1453: Proceedings of the 2014 Harlaxton Symposium*, ed. P. Crooks, D. Green and W. M. Ormrod (Donington, 2016), pp. 187–215; M. A. González, 'Political Dissent in Towns and Cities in Castile and León, expressed through Complaints and Petitions to the Crown (Thirteenth–Fourteenth Centuries)', in *Disciplined Dissent: Strategies of Non-Confrontational Protest*, ed. F. Titone (Rome, 2016), pp. 65–88; J. Braekevelt, 'Popular Voices within Princely Legislation: Assessing the Discourse of Flemish Petitions and Burgundian *Narrationes*', in *The Voices of the People in Late Medieval Europe: Communication and Popular Politics*, ed. J. Dumolyn, J. Haemers, H. R. O. Herrer and V. Challet (Turnhout, 2014), pp. 149–66; J. Haemers, '*Ad petitionem burgensium*: Petitions and Peaceful Resistance of Craftsmen in Flanders and Mechelen (13th–16th Centuries)', in *Los grupos populares en la ciuda medieval europea*, ed. J. Á. S. Telechea, B. A. Bolumburu and J. Haemers (Logroño, 2014), pp. 371–94; J. Haemers, 'Governing and Gathering about the Common Welfare of the Town: The Petitions of the Craft

presented to the English parliament.[10] In the separate scholarly tradition on ecclesiastical supplications, new work has explored petitions regarding marriage,[11] petitions for papal trade licences,[12] the impact of petitioning on papal crusade diplomacy,[13] the roles of proctors[14] and more general aspects of petitioning.[15] A particularly fruitful avenue of research explores supplications to the papal penitentiary, which is illuminating many new aspects of medieval life and the Church.[16] The publication of new documents has also expanded the source base

Guilds of Leuven, 1378', in *La comunidad medieval como esfera pública*, ed. H. R. O. Herrer (Seville, 2014), pp. 153–72.

10 *Early Common Petitions in the English Parliament, c. 1290–c. 1420*, ed. W. M. Ormrod, H. Killick and P. Bradford (Cambridge, 2017).

11 P. Ostinelli, 'Wege zur richtigen Ehe: Suppliken in Ehesachen aus dem lombardischen Raum (zweite Hälfte des 15. Jahrhunderts)', in *Kirchlicher und religiöser Alltag im Spätmittelalter: Akten der internationalen Tagung in Weingarten, 4.–7. Oktober 2007*, ed. R. Götting, S. Fees and A. Meyer (Ostfildern, 2010), pp. 205–19; L. Schmugge, 'Eheprozesse aus dem Erzbistum Trier vor der römischen Pönitentiarie (1455–1500)', in *Christliches und jüdisches Europa im Mittelalter: Colloquium zu Ehren von Alfred Haverkamp, Trier 2007*, ed. L. Clemens and S. Hirbodian (Trier, 2011), pp. 167–87; K. Salonen, 'Impediments and Illegal Marriages: Marriage Petitions to the Apostolic Penitentiary during the Pontificate of Pius II (1458–1464)', *Quaderni storici* 49 (2014), 533–63.

12 M. Carr, 'Crossing Boundaries in the Mediterranean: Papal Trade Licences from the *Registra Supplicationum* of Pope Clement VI (1342–1352)', *Journal of Medieval History* 41 (2015), 107–29.

13 T. W. Smith, *Curia and Crusade: Pope Honorius III and the Recovery of the Holy Land, 1216–1227* (Turnhout, 2017).

14 M. Spadaccini, *Libri, libelli e procuratori: analisi di un codice giuridico* (Turin, 2016).

15 P. N. R. Zutshi, 'The Roman Curia and Papal Jurisdiction in the Twelfth and Thirteenth Centuries', in *Die Ordnung der Kommunikation und die Kommunikation der Ordnungen, 2. Zentralität: Papsttum und Orden im Europa des 12. und 13. Jahrhunderts*, ed. C. Andenna (Stuttgart, 2013), pp. 213–27; P. D. Clarke, 'Petitioning the Pope: English Supplicants and Rome in the Fifteenth Century', in *The Fifteenth Century XI: Concerns and Preoccupations*, ed. L. Clark (Woodbridge, 2012), pp. 41–60; P. D. Clarke, 'Central Authority and Local Powers: The Apostolic Penitentiary and the English Church in the Fifteenth Century', *Historical Research* 84 (2011), 416–42; P. D. Clarke, 'Canterbury as the New Rome: Dispensations and Henry VIII's Reformation', *Journal of Ecclesiastical History* 64 (2013), 20–44; T. W. Smith, 'Papal Executors and the Veracity of Petitions from Thirteenth-Century England', *Revue d'Histoire Ecclésiastique* 110 (2015), 662–83; T. W. Smith, 'English Episcopal *Acta* and Thirteenth-Century Petitions to the Pope', *Archives* 40 (2014), 16–22.

16 K. Salonen and L. Schmugge, *A Sip from the 'Well of Grace': Medieval Texts from the Apostolic Penitentiary* (Washington, DC, 2009); L. Schmugge, 'Le suppliche nell'Archivio della Penitenzieria Apostolica e le fonti in partibus', in *La Penitenzieria Apostolica e il suo archivio*, ed. A. Saraco (Vatican City, 2012), pp. 33–61; L. Schmugge, 'Mainzer Suppliken in der Apostolischen Pönitentiarie (1449–1503)', in *Trier – Mainz – Rom: Stationen, Wirkungsfelder, Netzwerke, Festschrift für Michael Matheus zum 60. Geburtstag*, ed. A. Esposito and H. Ochs (Regensburg, 2013), pp. 129–48; K. Salonen, '"*Ex magno devotionis fervore* ...": Danish Cistercians and the Apostolic Penitentiary in the Later Middle Ages', in *Monastic Culture: The Long Thirteenth Century, Essays*

for this strand in the form of late medieval petitions to the penitentiary, as well as papal supplications from the University of Paris.[17]

Despite common themes and the rich comparative possibilities, however, these two scholarly traditions have often remained separate, primarily because the Church and the crown had their own discrete – and extremely complex – systems of petitioning. Recently, however, a number of scholars have pioneered approaches that traverse the boundaries in the attempt to combine the two strands. Through her work on the fourteenth-century Roman Rolls in The National Archives, Barbara Bombi is pointing the way in the study of the interface between royal and papal supplicatory systems.[18] Bombi's research into the professional proctor Andrea Sapiti, who presented English royal petitions to the Avignon papacy in the early fourteenth century, tackles head-on the point at which royal chancery practices and the *stilus curiae* of the papal chancery met. The comparison of supplications in the Roman Rolls with Sapiti's register reveals how the English crown sent him petitions for adaptation and rewording in the correct style acceptable to the Roman curia.[19] The interface between the English crown and the papacy as judicial systems and founts of grace, then, was embodied in the person of Sapiti. Similarly, Gwilym Dodd and Alison K. McHardy have also contributed to broader approaches to the study of medieval petitions with their edition of

in Honour of Brian Patrick McGuire, ed. L. Bisgaard (Odense, 2014), pp. 284–96; É. Lusset, 'La fama et l'infamia des clercs réguliers d'après les suppliques adressées à la penitencerie apostolique au XV siècle', in *Faire jeunesses, rendre justice*, ed. A. Destemberg, Y. Potin and E. Rosenblieh (Paris, 2015), pp. 25–35.

17 *Supplications from England and Wales in the Registers of the Apostolic Penitentiary, 1410–1503*, ed. P. D. Clarke and P. N. R. Zutshi, 3 vols, Canterbury and York Society 103–5 (2013–15); *Repertorium Poenitentiariae Germanicum: Verzeichnis der in den Supplikenregistern der Pönitentiarie vorkommenden Personen, Kirchen und Orte des Deutschen Reiches*, ed. L. Schmugge, 11 vols to date (Tübingen, 1998–); *Rotuli Parisienses: Supplications to the Pope from the University of Paris*, ed. W. J. Courtenay and E. D. Goddard, 3 vols (Leiden, 2002–12).

18 B. Bombi, *Studies in Medieval Diplomacy: Anglo-Papal Relations in the Fourteenth Century* (Oxford, forthcoming); Bombi, 'The Roman Rolls of Edward II'; B. Bombi, 'Andrea Sapiti: His Origins, and his Register as a Curial Proctor', *English Historical Review* 123 (2008), 132–48. One can also point to earlier work which sought to compare and contrast papal and royal diplomatic, such as P. Chaplais, *English Diplomatic Practice in the Middle Ages* (London, 2003); J. E. Sayers, 'The Typology of English Royal Documents before 1200', in *Typologie der Königsurkunden: Kolloquium der Commission Internationale de Diplomatique in Olmütz, 30. 8.–3. 9. 1992*, ed. J. Bistricky (Olomouc, 1998), pp. 189–200; J. E. Sayers, 'The Influence of Papal Documents on English Documents before 1305', in *Papsturkunde und europäisches Urkundenwesen: Studien zu einer formalen und rechtlichen Kohärenz vom 11. bis 15. Jahrhundert*, ed. P. Herde and H. Jakobs (Cologne, 1999), pp. 161–200.

19 Bombi, 'Andrea Sapiti', 141–8. His register is edited in *Il registro di Andrea Sapiti, procuratore fiorentino presso la curia papale nei primi decenni del XIV secolo*, ed. B. Bombi (Rome, 2007).

late medieval *Petitions to the Crown from English Religious Houses*, which also sheds lights on the connection between ecclesiastical and secular institutions through petitionary processes.[20] Such research, which crosses the diplomatic boundaries and examines more broadly the supplicatory cultures extant in the Middle Ages, represents an exciting new direction for the study of medieval petitions, and the present volume is structured to promote such a reading (see below).

The study of medieval supplications has enjoyed a great resurgence because of the value of these sources for the social, ecclesiastical, diplomatic and political history of the medieval West, as well as the study of manuscripts and language. In particular, they offer different perspectives on those most familiar institutions of medieval history, the crown and the Church. They shed new light on exactly how those institutions operated and how medieval people, from all social strata, engaged with them. Using petitions as a starting point for research, rather than the official documents they resulted in, helps to shift the historian's perception: they allow the scholar to pursue a 'bottom-up' approach to secular and ecclesiastical institutions of government traditionally considered from 'top-down' perspectives. The present volume contributes to this approach by picking out a key thread from the history of petitioning, the legal strategies employed by supplicants, and following it through royal, parliamentary, ecclesiastical and papal supplications in order to trace how petitioners interacted with the organs of secular and ecclesiastical government in the Middle Ages. In so doing it brings into sharper focus the figure of 'the medieval supplicant', which included ordinary women and men, clergy, prelates and nobles. Examination of their petitions offers insights into how members of each of these groups plotted their petitionary strategies, how much and what kind of legal knowledge they possessed (or had access to), and their agency in expressing individuality in their petitions while simultaneously conforming to the expectations of the *stilus curiae*.

By examining a broad range of petitioners and supplicatory processes, the present book also seeks to bring the two research strands, royal and ecclesiastical petitions, closer together. It was a conscious decision not to erect artificial dividing lines between the chapters by dividing the book into two parts on the crown and the Church. Rather, the structure of the book is shaped in a way that encourages a holistic reading, transitioning from royal and parliamentary petitions in the opening chapters (Chapters 1–5) through essays that consider royal petitions from ecclesiastical prelates (Chapters 6–8) to petitions submitted by laity and clergy to the Church and the papacy (Chapters 9–11). It is hoped that, by locating work on royal and parliamentary petitions in the context of ecclesiastical supplications – and vice versa – the book will offer

[20] *Petitions to the Crown from English Religious Houses, c. 1272–c. 1485*, ed. G. Dodd and A. K. McHardy, Canterbury and York Society 100 (2010).

the opportunity for scholars to traverse the traditional divisions between the secular and ecclesiastical justice systems and to inspire research into the broader supplicatory cultures that existed in medieval Europe.

In Chapter 1 Gwilym Dodd explores how lexical choice, in particular the use of English, formed the tone and content of fifteenth-century parliamentary petitions. In so doing, Dodd tackles a tension in the historiography that exists between two schools of thought: one that sees English as a simple replacement for French as the language of petitioning as a matter of course, and another that interprets the selection of English as a deliberate supplicatory strategy pursued by petitioners as a means of increasing the persuasive power of their request. Dodd demonstrates that the use of English in the parliamentary petitions cannot be neatly aligned with one of these arguments to the prejudice of the other, and carefully traces how English could conform to the more rigid stylistic forms of Anglo-Norman petitions while also being deployed to express the authentic and individual voice of the supplicant.

Language also forms a central focus in Chapter 2, by Helen Lacey, in which she scrutinises petitions for royal pardon in the fourteenth century in order to assess the vocabulary and strategies deployed in the drafting of these supplications and how petitioners chose to present their stories in these texts. Here, the power of persuasion was key, and Lacey demonstrates how applicants for royal pardon stated the mitigating factors in their cases, reminding the king of their military service or pleading on grounds of charity. Lacey also moves beyond the texts and explores who was involved in procuring the petitions and what performances were involved in their presentation. She demonstrates how high-ranking patrons, especially queens, were key interlocutors between petitioners and the king and how they wielded important influence in the decision of the crown to grant mercy. Performance also played a central role in petitioning for pardon, and Lacey excavates fascinating details from the sources that reveal the important symbolism of 'crying mercy' and the religious connotations that underpinned royal petitions, neatly demonstrating the ecclesiastical context that informed secular supplicatory culture.

In Chapter 3 Helen Killick addresses the question of the identity of the scribes responsible for writing petitions, and in particular the debate over whether petitioners enlisted the services of those in their local vicinity or travelled to Westminster in order to have their complaints drawn up centrally. Palaeographical analysis reveals several well-known metropolitan scribes, such as Chaucer's scribe Adam Pinkhurst and the privy seal clerk and poet Thomas Hoccleve, to have authored petitions, yet evidence of the personal connections between these men and their clients suggests that this occurred on an ad hoc basis rather than forming a substantial part of their scribal activities. Linguistic analysis of English-language petitions demonstrates that many of these documents display features associated with a particular regional origin, supporting the idea that the majority of petitions were drafted by provincial scribes; furthermore, it is estimated that surviving numbers of English-language petitions are far greater than previously thought. Killick examines how this evidence contributes to our understanding of the petitionary drafting process and its accessibility as a legal strategy.

The question of access to justice is also a central theme of Chapter 4, in which Anthony Musson examines how legal knowledge and language informed litigation strategies in petitions to the crown in the fourteenth century. His chapter reveals how supplicants had some knowledge of, and were liable to cite or draw upon, Magna Carta and other statutes when wording the texts of their petitions. Musson argues that disparate groups of petitioners – especially manorial tenants – used this legal knowledge over a long chronology to shape impressively coherent discourses centring on their rights and freedoms, and the abuse of those privileges by figures of authority. The deployment of the provisions of Magna Carta was sometimes inventive, at other times incorrect, but, as Musson argues, even when the petitions display misconceptions or misunderstanding of the law, the effort to cite previous statutes can tell us much about the attitudes and legal consciousness of fourteenth-century men and women.

In Chapter 5, an essay on Louis Beaumont, bishop of Durham (1317–33), and his petitions to the crown regarding the forfeitures of war, Matthew Phillips demonstrates how ecclesiastical prelates had to be skilful in navigating the secular justice system in order to achieve their ends. By examining two case studies, the first regarding the bishop's dispute with the king of Scotland over rights to ferry men and goods across the River Tweed and the second concerning his conflict with Sir Walter Selby over a manor held as a forfeiture of war, Phillips peels away the seemingly formulaic wording and tone of the bishop's supplications in order to tease out the multi-functional dimension of medieval petitions. He reveals the complex layers of meaning encoded within the supplications that become evident only when the texts are located within the historical context of their original presentation to the crown. Phillips illustrates how the bishop of Durham thought innovatively about petitions and the purpose to which they might be put, using his acute awareness of political developments to submit his petitions at the most opportune moments, or using them to play power games in the north of England by seeking remedy through the goodwill of the king.

Taking the question of forfeitures of war further, in Chapter 6 Shelagh Sneddon considers two petitions submitted to the king of England in 1328 by the abbots of the Scottish religious houses at Arbroath and Jedburgh, which sought the restoration of the abbeys' churches in England, lost through the misfortunes of war. Sneddon compares and contrasts the very different strategies employed by the abbots and draws out what they can tell us about the two houses during the First Scottish War of Independence. In so doing, she considers how questions of national and spiritual identity are represented in the supplications, and what effect the war had on them. As in Lacey's chapter, Sneddon also points to the use of religious content as a supplicatory strategy in royal petitions, drawing attention to the appeal to St Thomas Becket in Arbroath's petition – intended to remind the English king of the outcome of Henry II's conflict with the Church and to modify his behaviour accordingly. Ultimately, though, despite the careful wording of the two abbots' supplications, Sneddon concludes that the supplicatory strategies developed to recover lost churches in England could only achieve so much; it was the political context that played the deciding factor, which rendered the power of petition of Scottish abbots in a period of heightened Anglo-Scottish conflict uncertain.

Philippa M. Hoskin analyses the recovery of churches from a different angle in Chapter 7, which explores the English common law writ *de vi laica amovenda* petitioned for by clergy in response to lay invasion of their property. Developed as a means of helping the clergy to recover churches occupied by lay invaders, Hoskin uses the writ as a lens through which to examine much broader aspects of Church–State relations in the thirteenth and fourteenth centuries. Her chapter ties together the supplicatory cultures of the Church and crown, demonstrating how fluid were the demarcating lines between them: although the Church claimed legal authority over its property, it still required the power of the secular arm in order to enforce that authority – in the case of lay invasion, through *de vi laica amovenda.* Hoskin problematises the idea that lay invasion of churches was a manifestation of anti-clericalism, arguing instead that the disputes were more complex and revolved more around the highly valued rights of patronage and the sense of lay investment and ownership of the fabric of churches than any supposed defects in the pastoral care of the incumbent.

The question of ecclesiastical patronage and the right of advowson is explored on an international stage in Chapter 8, in which Thomas W. Smith analyses how English and Italian clergy made use of the papal supplicatory system as part of legal strategies to secure ecclesiastical benefices in thirteenth-century England. As part of a reconsideration of the character of the controversial system of papal provision, which led to the appointment of Italian clergy to foreign benefices throughout Europe, Smith examines the main strengths and weaknesses of the papal judicial and supplicatory system in the process. Chief among these was the power of the appeal, which proved a double-edged sword. Smith argues that English clergy proved themselves masters of petitionary strategy – ironically using the papacy's own supplicatory system against Italian providees – and picks out a number of instances of wily English clergy dragging Italian opponents through the courts with the aim of bleeding them dry of funds and exhausting their will to prosecute claims to benefices. He concludes that the system of papal provision and the supplicatory strategies employed in opposition to it were more complex than previous research has allowed.

Frederick Pedersen also explores ecclesiastical supplicatory strategies, but for a very different topic, in Chapter 9: marriage litigation in the fourteenth century. Drawing upon the rich records preserved in the York Cause Papers, Pedersen problematises the idea that court depositions can be used as true accounts of everyday life in the Middle Ages, since, like Musson, he argues that ordinary medieval people possessed a complex understanding of the law and that one can trace this in the source material. Through a wide reading of the available information about four marriage cases, and the context in which they played out, Pedersen shows how, far from being ill-advised, medieval litigants were able to access legal advice without difficulty and, in response to this advice, they shaped their narratives and their out-of-court behaviour as part of deliberate legal strategies. Rather than offering easy pickings for social historical approaches, then, Pedersen reveals that the testimony of petitioners went through a process of selection and verification informed by legal advisers, and cautions that such court cases involving ordinary medieval people must be read with care and placed in their wider legal, social and cultural contexts if they are to yield fruit for the historian.

In the final essay in this volume, Chapter 10, Kirsi Salonen also sheds new light on late medieval social and legal history and expands the scope of the book further by examining a new aspect of papal supplicatory culture: penitentiary petitions from killer clergy. Salonen explores the penitentiary records from the fifteenth and early sixteenth centuries in order to explain how clergy justified homicide in their supplications for absolution. Despite a strict ban on violence by members of the clergy, as Salonen notes, penitentiary documents reveal numerous petitions from clerics from all over Europe seeking pardon for their role in mortal violence. Through careful analysis of the wording of the petitions for absolution, Salonen traces the strategies that supplicants employed in the effort to clear their names. Like a number of the other studies in this book, Salonen draws attention to the role of professionals in the composition of the petitions and demonstrates that proctors provided their clients with crucial professional knowledge of the regulations of canon law and the different extenuating circumstances that guilty clergy needed to cite. Nevertheless, it is clear that, despite this expert advice, it was the petitioners themselves who remained responsible for deciding upon their own supplicatory strategies. Furthermore, Salonen also questions, like Pedersen, how far we can trust the accounts of the petitioners – on this point, though, the penitentiary records yield quite a different answer.

This volume harvests some of the fruits of a decade of research conducted into supplications since the publication of Ormrod, Dodd and Musson's *Medieval Petitions* in 2009; we hope that its chapters will inspire and help to point the way during the next decade of research into medieval petitions and strategies of persuasion. Taken alone, each of these chapters provides fresh insights into the petitionary strategies of the Middle Ages. But, as they demonstrate, the petitions themselves are only the tips of metaphorical icebergs, the visible parts of much larger strategies of persuasion that until now have been concealed. These essays offer readers a glimpse beneath the surface, exposing the motivations, lexical choices, personnel, legal advice and contemporary contexts that helped to shape the texts of the petitions and which contributed to the success or failure of their causes. Taken together, however, the volume breaks new ground in enabling supplications to the crown to be read alongside their ecclesiastical counterparts – which have tended previously to remain separate. It is hoped that this holistic angle will lead to the cross-fertilisation of the traditions, provoking new questions and the pursuit of new avenues of scholarship.

1

Blood, Brains and Bay-Windows: The Use of English in Fifteenth-Century Parliamentary Petitions*

Gwilym Dodd

In the course of the first half of the fifteenth century a decisive shift occurred in the language used to write petitions addressed to the king, his ministers and the Lords and Commons in parliament. In 1420 almost all such supplications were drafted in French, long associated as the language *par excellence* of petitioning. Over the next twenty years, however, English began to be used with increasing regularity. Elsewhere I have estimated that the scales tipped decisively in favour of the English language in the late 1430s, and specifically between 1435 and 1437.[1] From this point onwards it was the predominant language, while the use of French diminished. By the middle of the century, English was chosen as a matter of course. This change is to be found in each of the three main series of petitions, or bills, held in The National Archives: SC 8 (Special Collections: Ancient Petitions); C 1 (Court of Chancery: Early Proceedings); and E 28 (Exchequer, Treasury of the Receipt: Council and Privy Seal Records). In seeking to explain why the language of petitioning changed across the period, I have emphasised the complexity of the dynamics which underlay shifting contemporary attitudes to language, as well as the importance of placing the records in their proper administrative context. Ultimately, the linguistic conservatism of the clerks, scriveners or attorneys who were employed to write petitions, and which had hitherto acted as a seemingly unassailable bulwark against the spread of the vernacular, faltered in the second quarter of the fifteenth century as a result of a number of converging factors: the flourishing of English in a literary context; its broader acceptance as a *bone fide* language of the court; its adoption in some bureaucratic contexts, notably in letters issued under the signet seal; the laicisation of the writing classes; the onset of Henry VI's majority rule; and the increasingly inward-looking stance of the English

* My thanks to Lisa Liddy and Margaret Condon for their palaeographical assistance.

[1] G. Dodd, 'The Rise of English, the Decline of French: Supplications to the English Crown, c. 1420–1450', *Speculum* 86 (2011), 117–50.

political classes, brought about by their defeat in the Hundred Years War and the consequent severing of ties to the Continent.

In a volume of essays addressing the themes of rhetoric and persuasion in petitionary discourse, it seems especially apposite to consider how lexical choice, and in particular the use of English, shaped the tone and content of petitions, as well as the rhetorical possibilities available to those who drafted them. Measuring the impact of this momentous linguistic shift has received very little attention in published work, not just in a petitionary milieu, but in scholarship in general. This may be explained by the continuing focus of scholars on the literary context of linguistic choice, in which the possibilities of comparing like-for-like modes of English and French (and Latin) composition are relatively limited. Administrative records hold more promise because they were usually drafted according to a set formula and were often part of a long series of comparable documents stretching across an extended period of time. Petitions are especially, and perhaps uniquely, valuable in this respect for although they were written to conform to a widely held petitionary form – the *ars dictaminis*[2] – they were not overbearingly prescribed: there was still enough scope for the writer to put his or her individual stamp on the composition. Petitions are thus sufficiently standardised to make comparisons across the class of documents meaningful, but at the same time sufficiently open to the particular lexical and linguistic preferences of the drafter, and/or petitioner, to enable historians to discern distinct, individualised authorial input. It is difficult to find such a finely tuned balance in other types of document. In this discussion, the focus is on petitions presented in parliament. These hold particular interest because of the very public nature of the processes by which parliamentary petitions were expedited. By the fifteenth century, the Lords and Commons were often actively involved in passing judgement upon petitions, and increasingly petitioners addressed their complaints and requests directly to the Lords or Commons in the hope that they might intercede on their behalf with the king.[3] The involvement of this broader audience in the reception of cases brought into parliament throws into sharp relief questions about language-choice and the strategies of persuasion which petitioners adopted to solicit a favourable response.

Preliminary Considerations

There is no clear-cut answer to the question: how did the replacement of French with English impact on the petitionary culture of the fifteenth century?

[2] G. Dodd, 'Writing Wrongs: The Drafting of Supplications to the Crown in Later Fourteenth-Century England', *Medium Ævum* 80 (2011), 217–46.

[3] G. Dodd, *Justice and Grace: Private Petitioning and the English Parliament in the Late Middle Ages* (Oxford, 2007), pp. 174–87.

Indeed, one of the aims of this discussion is to address conflicting approaches to the status of English and its relationship with the French language. There are two distinct historiographical trends. On the one hand, there are arguments – and undoubted factors – which suggest that the transition to English was a more or less seamless process, and that the choice of French or English made no discernible impression on how cases came to be represented in parliament. This is an approach I have emphasised in my own work, in particular by highlighting the gradual nature of the shift from French to English across a thirty-year period from the start of Henry VI's reign.[4] I have argued that the leisurely pace of the transition indicates that little advantage accrued to the use of one or the other language and that the choice between the two was primarily a matter of individual preference rather than clear-cut persuasive strategy. The coexistence of the two languages in petitions presented between c. 1420 and c. 1450 thus points to the strength of a bilingual supplicatory culture.[5] This bilingualism was to a great extent facilitated by the close lexical and syntactical relationship that existed between the English and French languages. In an important contribution to the subject, William Rothwell warned that '[o]ur modern clear separation of one language from another must not be allowed to blind us to the reality of a medieval situation in which a cut-and-dried divide between languages did not exist'.[6] Thus, it was not the case that the English and French languages existed as entirely separated linguistic systems, but that they closely coalesced, such that 'the boundary [between French and] … English was harder to determine as the years went by, to such an extent that in many fifteenth-century records it is virtually impossible to state categorically whether a term is French or English'.[7] In this light, decisions about whether to write in French or English may have been rather less stark than we might imagine.

These points are further reinforced by the apparent indifference of the crown to the languages used in administrative and legal contexts. It used to be thought that the English language was a state-sponsored medium and that the king, and specifically Henry V, promoted the vernacular as part of a deliberate language policy.[8] It was an approach that emphasised the distinctive qualities of English and the political advantages that its adoption

[4] Dodd, 'Rise of English', 123–6.

[5] In fact, a *tri*-lingual writing culture prevailed at this time, for which see G. Dodd, 'Trilingualism in the Medieval English Bureaucracy: The Use – and Disuse – of Languages in the Fifteenth-Century Privy Seal Office', *Journal of British Studies* 51 (2012), 253–83.

[6] W. Rothwell, 'English and French in England after 1362', *English Studies* 6 (2001), 539–59 (quotation at 545).

[7] Rothwell, 'English and French in England after 1362', 555.

[8] The original proponent of this view was J. H. Fisher in two key works: 'A Language Policy for Lancastrian England', *Proceedings of the Modern Language Association* 107 (1992), 1168–80 and 'Chancery and the Emergence of Standard Written English in

could bring to the crown. But the theory founders for lack of evidence: there was no wholesale 'vernacularisation' of royal records and nothing to suggest anything approaching a 'policy', let alone a concerted attempt, to introduce linguistic standardisation.[9] Although signet letters converted to English in 1417, this was an isolated phenomenon and did not extend to other types of record which the king might have used to communicate his linguistic preferences to the wider realm. For example, letters issued under the privy seal or the statutes that were promulgated after each parliament continued to be written in French.[10] Against the notion that the king's subjects might still have taken their linguistic cue from the crown we might cite a petition presented by the prior of Bath in 1418.[11] The prior addressed his petition to Henry V and complained that the mayor and Commons of Bath were continuing to ring the bells of the town's churches at inopportune times of the day, in spite of a signet letter sent to them by the king ordering an end to such activity. The prior had a copy of this letter and cited it in full within the text of his petition. The letter he copied was written in English, in line with the new language of the signet office; but the remainder of his petition was drafted in French. Self-evidently, the king's choice of English for his signet letter had no impact on the prior's choice of French for his petition. The case also demonstrates the ease with which those who drafted such documents could move from one language to another. 'Codeswitching', at least in some contexts, underlined the interchangeability and equivalence of English and French.[12]

This, then, is one approach. Another approach is to place emphasis on the distinctiveness of the two languages and the deliberate and conscious choices that were made when deciding whether to use one or the other. This

the Fifteenth Century', *Speculum* 52 (1977), 870–99, both reprinted in J. H. Fisher, *The Emergence of Standard English* (Lexington, KY, 1996), chaps 1 and 2.

9 See M. Benskin, 'Chancery Standard', in *New Perspectives on English Historical Linguistics: Selected Papers from 12 ICEHL, Glasgow, 21–26 August 2002*, vol. II: Lexis and Transmission, ed. C. Kay, C. Hough and I. Wotherspoon (Glasgow, 2004), pp. 1–39; and most recently, T. W. Machan, 'Snakes, Ladders, and Standard Language', in *Imagining Medieval English: Language Structures and Theories, 500–1500*, ed. T. W. Machan (Cambridge, 2016), pp. 54–77.

10 For the language of fifteenth-century legislation, and especially the linguistic relationship between the official chancery statute roll and the unofficial commercially available copies, see D. Rowland, 'The End of the Statute Rolls: Manuscript, Print and Language Change in Fifteenth-Century English Statutes', in *The Fifteenth Century XI: Concerns and Conceptions*, ed. L. Clark (Woodbridge, 2012), pp. 107–25.

11 TNA, SC 8/176/8781. An earlier petition from the prior is SC 8/302/15089, printed in *Petitions to the Crown from English Religious Houses, c. 1272–c. 1485*, ed. G. Dodd and A. K. McHardy, Canterbury and York Society 100 (2010), no. 131, pp. 158–60.

12 J. Wogan-Browne, 'General Introduction: What's in a Name: the "French" of "England"', in *Language and Culture in Medieval Britain: The French of England, c. 1100–c. 1500*, ed. J. Wogan-Browne with C. Collette, M. Kowaleski, L. Mooney, A. Putter and D. Trotter (York, 2009), pp. 1–13, at pp. 5–8. For discussion and further references, see Dodd, 'Trilingualism', 256–9.

perspective refutes the idea that language choice could ever be neutral.[13] Perhaps the most obvious consideration is that by the fifteenth century, French had ceased to be widely spoken or understood. In 1362 Edward III famously enacted the Statute of Pleading, which ordained that henceforth legal debates and arguments in the king's courts should be conducted in English so that 'the said laws and customs would be learned and known and better understood in the language used in the said realm'.[14] It has been suggested that from early in the fourteenth century the Commons in parliament would have spoken English to each other and that the parliamentary Lords finally abandoned French in favour of English by the end of the century.[15] From about the mid-fourteenth century French began to be replaced by English as the language for teaching Latin in grammar schools.[16] Indeed, linguistic analysis by Richard Ingham indicates that French had ceased to be a mother tongue by the last quarter of the fourteenth century, even for the clerks who wrote up the parliament rolls.[17] The language was thus becoming increasingly specialised and elitist.[18] By the fifteenth century French was generally used either in literature or for learning, or in administration and the law.[19] Its continued vitality in a legal context was a testament to the technical and authoritative meaning and prestige it gave to legal process.[20] It was also especially suited

13 *Multilingualism in Later Medieval Britain*, ed. D. A. Trotter (Cambridge, 2000), p. xxx; *Multilingualism in Medieval Britain (c. 1066–1520): Sources and Analysis*, ed. J. A. Jefferson and A. Putter (Turnhout, 2013).

14 *SR*, vol. I, pp. 375–6. For discussion, see W. M. Ormrod, 'The Use of English: Language, Law, and Political Culture in Fourteenth-Century England', *Speculum* 78 (2003), 750–87.

15 Ormrod, 'Use of English', 778. Useful discussion of language use in the fourteenth century may be found in W. Rothwell, 'Henry of Lancaster and Geoffrey Chaucer: Anglo-French and Middle English in Fourteenth-Century England', *The Modern Language Review* 99 (2004), 313–27.

16 N. Orme, 'Schools and Languages in Medieval England', in *Language in Medieval Britain: Networks and Exchanges, Proceedings of the 2013 Harlaxton Symposium*, ed. M. Carruthers (Donington, 2015), at pp. 152–67, pp. 156–60.

17 R. Ingham, 'The Transmission of Later Anglo-Norman: Some Syntactic Evidence', in *The Anglo-Norman Language and its Contexts*, ed. R. Ingham (York, 2010), pp. 164–82, esp. p. 177.

18 Ormrod, 'Use of English', 764–7.

19 For the use of French in literary contexts in the fifteenth century, see R. F. Yeager, 'John Gower's French and his Readers'; J. Marvin, 'The Vitality of Anglo-Norman in Late Medieval England: The Case of the Prose *Brut* Chronicle'; and S. Downes, 'A "Frenche booke called the Pistill of Othea": Christine de Pizan's French in England', all in *Language and Culture*, ed. Wogan-Browne et al., pp. 135–45, 303–19, 457–68. In administrative and legal contexts, see P. Brand, 'The Languages of the Law in Later Medieval England', in *Multilingualism in Later Medieval Britain*, ed. Trotter, pp. 63–76.

20 G. E. Woodbine, 'The Language of English Law', *Speculum* 18 (1943), 395–436; J. H. Baker, 'The Three Languages of the Common Law', in idem, *The Common Law Tradition: Lawyers, Books and the Law* (London, 2000), pp. 225–46; Brand, 'Languages

to the linguistic ornamentation of the court,[21] and continued to hold sway as the foremost language of letter writing, because it was regarded as the best medium for polite correspondence.[22] But it was now a specialist language used by a relatively small segment of society. For its part, English emerged as an acceptable mode of official writing because it lent authenticity to the words it recorded, and because it was, straightforwardly, the most effective means of communicating in an increasingly Anglophone society. Work on the earliest vernacular texts to engage with governmental and legal processes suggests that English was chosen deliberately and consciously for the clarity with which it represented the views of their and the rhetorical power it lent to their words.[23] As the main vernacular language, English had a particular association with sedition, until it began to be accepted more widely within the medieval 'Establishment'.[24] Recently, renewed emphasis has been placed on Henry V's regard for the English language and his 'conscious choice of English for certain instruments and memoranda'.[25] These perspectives suggest that, if not by design then by effect, the appearance of English-language petitions altered the nature of petitioning itself, as the complaints were now articulated in a language that was understood by all parties involved in the petitionary process.

Part of the complexity in working through these conflicting perspectives lies in identifying who actually wrote petitions and who was intended to read them. So long as petitions continued to be written in French we might safely

of the Law'; Rothwell, 'English and French in England after 1362'; and P. Brand, 'The Language of the English Legal Profession: The Emergence of a Distinctive Legal Lexicon in Insular French', in *The Anglo-Norman Language and its Contexts*, ed. R. Ingham (York, 2010), pp. 94–101.

[21] G. Dodd, 'Kingship, Parliament and the Court: The Emergence of "High Style" in Petitions to the English Crown, 1350–1405', *English Historical Review* 129 (2014), 515–48.

[22] *Anglo-Norman Letters and Petitions from All Souls MS 182*, ed. M. D. Legge, Anglo-Norman Text Society 3 (Oxford, 1941); A. Putter, 'The French of English Letters: Two Trilingual Verse Epistles in Context', in *Language and Culture*, ed. Wogan-Browne et al., pp. 397–408.

[23] G. Dodd, 'The Spread of English in the Records of Central Government, 1400–1430', in *Vernacularity in England and Wales, c. 1300–1550*, ed. E. Salter and H. Wicker (Turnhout, 2011), pp. 225–66, at pp. 254–7. See also, H. Lacey, 'Pragmatic Literacy and Political Consciousness in Later Medieval England', *Cahiers électroniques d'histoire textuelle du Laboratoire de Médiévistique Occidentale de Paris* 5 (2012), 38–70, esp. 64–6; and E. A. McVitty, '"My name of a trewe man": Gender, Vernacularity, and Treasonous Speech in Late Medieval England', *Parergon* 33 (2016), 91–111, esp. 96–100, 103–5.

[24] N. Watson, 'Censorship and Cultural Change in Late-Medieval England: Vernacular Theology, the Oxford Translation Debate, and Arundel's Constitutions of 1409', *Speculum* 70 (1995), 822–64; M. Vale, 'Language, Politics and Society: The Uses of the Vernacular in the Later Middle Ages', *English Historical Review* 120 (2005), 15–34.

[25] M. Vale, *Henry V: The Conscience of a King* (New Haven, CT, 2016), p. 115.

assume that they were overwhelmingly products of the clerks, scriveners or attorneys who wrote them. Their use of French well into the fifteenth century denoted an important distinction between the linguistic values and assumptions which underpinned the process of *writing* a petition and the discussions, representations and decisions that were conducted *orally* – and in English – once the petition had been presented. In the Francophone writing culture of the fourteenth and early fifteenth centuries the role of clerks, scriveners and attorneys as intermediaries between the petitioner and the adjudicating bodies in parliament loomed large, for the petitioner relied on them to translate his or her complaint into a specialist French-language discourse. Moreover, once it had been handed in, the contents of the petition were presumably read out loud and translated back into English, by clerks or lawyers, for the benefit of those who were charged to deal with the case. It is reasonable to assume that, once English began to be used in petitions, there was greater scope for petitioners to influence how the circumstances of their complaint or request came to be articulated in written form, and that the desire to write petitions in a way that might connect more directly with those who were to pass judgement on them might have become stronger. A key question, then, is the extent to which the onset of English in petitions reduced the reliance of petitioners on the expertise of clerks, scriveners and attorneys? Is there evidence to suggest that petitioners no longer actually needed the services of such professionals and began writing out petitions themselves? Did the distinction between writing and oral legal cultures, so long demarcated by the different languages used, now begin to break down once English was employed all through the petitionary process?

Useful work on the question of agency has been done in relation to the use of the courts by women in the fifteenth and sixteenth centuries. It is to be noted, however, that even in the context of vernacular writing, scholars have been at pains to stress the continued vital input of legal counsel, emphasising the value placed by contemporaries in having formal deposition conform to the legal norms and linguistic conventions of the day. In his work on the Elizabethan court of Requests Tim Stretton has gone so far as to suggest that readers ought just to focus on 'the story-telling, rather than the story-teller' because he regarded attempts to separate the voice of the litigant from that of her attorney as a futile exercise.[26] Other work offers a more positive outlook. In her analysis of a chancery bill presented by Johanne Bawde in c. 1480 Cordelia Beattie noted a number of features that strongly suggest, as she puts it, 'Johanne's key role not only in the events that the bill narrates but also in the construction of the bill'.[27] Elsewhere, Beattie suggests that 'the Chancery

[26] T. Stretton, *Women Waging Law in Elizabethan England* (Cambridge, 1998), p. 19.

[27] C. Beattie, 'Your Oratrice: Women's Petitions to the Late Medieval Court of Chancery', in *Women, Agency and the Law, 1300–1700*, ed. B. Kane and F. Williamson (London, 2013), pp. 17–29, 164–9 (quotation at p. 28). Useful additional context is

clerk or lawyer who drew [the bill] up was not in complete control of its narrative'.[28] Although the issue of language choice is not directly addressed, there is implicit in this discussion an acceptance that the use of the vernacular significantly aided the litigant's ability to influence the narrative of her own circumstances. Looking beyond the agency of the 'professional' to identify the voice of the petitioners is clearly a difficult proposition. An informal vernacular writing style did not necessarily denote the retreat of a scribe's influence, for recent work has emphasised the professional versatility of a medieval 'man of letters' and his ability to adjust 'his language to fit the occasion'.[29] But the very possibility that petitioners could dictate the content and tone of their complaints, which the use of English in petitions now provided, raises important questions about the relationship between attorneys and their clients and about the balance to be struck between choosing to have a petition written in accordance with the stylistic norms of conventional supplicatory discourse, on the one hand, or having it exhibit all the individualism, eccentricity and colour of a free-standing composition, on the other hand.

Curial Prose

What, then, was a conventionally worded petition? If English-language petitions used language and rhetoric in a manner clearly different to French-language petitions, how might we measure this divergence? By c. 1420, when English began to appear in parliamentary petitions, supplicatory discourse had evolved quite strikingly over the course of the previous hundred years. In the early fourteenth century petitions were usually written perfunctorily, employing language (i.e. Anglo-Norman French) in a very measured and unembellished way. From the middle of the fourteenth century, and particularly from c. 1370, however, the lexical structure of petitions underwent a significant change. In the place of the concise, laconic prose of the

provided by J. Bailey, 'Voices in Court: Lawyers' or Litigants'?', *Historical Research* 74 (2001), 392–408; and J. Goldberg, 'Echoes, Whispers, Ventriloquisms: On Recovering Women's Voices from the Court of York in the Late Middle Ages', in *Women, Agency and the Law*, ed. Kane and Williamson, pp. 31–41, 169–71.

[28] Beattie, 'Your Oratrice', p. 22.

[29] S. Horobin, 'The Nature of Material Evidence', in *Imagining Medieval English*, ed. Machan, pp. 147–65 (quotation at p. 152). See also Linne Mooney's analysis of the career of Adam Pinkhurst, in L. R. Mooney, 'Chaucer's Scribe', *Speculum* 81 (2006), 97–138; and H. Killick, 'Treason, Felony and Lollardy: A Common Petition in the Hand of Richard Osbarn, clerk of the Chamber of the Guildhall, 1400–c. 1437', *Historical Research* 89 (2016), 227–45. For the continued vital input of the professional scribe or scrivener in the writing of petitions, see F. Dabhoiwala, 'Writing Petitions in Early Modern England', in *Suffering and Happiness in England 1555–1850: Narratives and Representations, a Collection in Honour of Paul Slack*, ed. M. J. Braddick and J. Innes (Oxford, 2017), pp. 127–4.

early fourteenth century a more elaborate and convoluted mode of writing appeared that provided a distinct model for clerks and attorneys to follow. This writing style has been described as curial prose. In a ground-breaking discussion on the subject John Burnley demonstrated that curial prose style had its roots in French-language administrative documents.[30] Much of the evidence he drew on was taken from the fourteenth-century parliament rolls. Curial prose had a number of clearly distinguishing features, which Diane Bornstein summarises as follows: 'It was characterized by the use of formulaic expressions, terms of reference (*dessusdit, le dit, cette dit*), introductory phrases, Latinate words, elaborate explanations, legal phrases, synonyms (particularly doublets), reliance on the passive voice, and a grave, ceremonious tone.'[31] We might add to this an observation by Burnley that has special relevance to this discussion, that the 'congratulatory aspect of the administrative curial style is most apparent ... in open letters and petitions, where information content may be very sparse, but the establishment of mutual attitudes or relative status is all important'.[32] Here, as an example, is a private petition presented by Margaret Cornish on behalf of her husband in 1426:

> Au Roi noster tressoveraigne seignur, et as autres seignurs espirituelx et temporelx d'icest present parlement supplie treshumblement vostre povere et continuell oratrice Margaret la femme du Thomas Cornyssh de Woxebrigge el Countee de Midd': qe come le dit Thomas fuit par graunt malice et enmite, endite de ceo qe le dit Thomas et Nicolas Herford, de mesmes les ville et counte laborer, le joesdy proschein devaunt le fest de l'invention de Seint Crois, l'an de vostre regne tierce, le cloos \d'un/ Alice Scolecroft a Woxebrigge entra, et quatres berbes pris.vi. s.viij. d. des biens et chateux \d'un/ Johan Martyn, illeoqes trovez felonousement emblast; pur quele felonie, le dit Thomas par conspiracie de ses enemys fuit convict et dampnez, al suit du roi. Le quel gracious Roi, al supplication del tresgracious roigne sa mier, pardona au dit Thomas, sibien la dite felonie, come l'execution del juggement a cele cause rendu ou a rendre; la quele pardon, sibien par les trespuissantz princes les dukes de Bedford et de Gloucestr', et autres tresgracious seignurs du counsaill, est ratifiez et confermez. Qe please sibien au roiall mageste, come vous, tresgraciouses seignurs, pur endorser ceste bille, et l'ein deliverer al prive seall, pur faire brief al chaunceller d'Engleterre, d'ent faire la chartre de pardon, et ce pur Dieu et en oevere de charite.

[30] J. D. Burnley, 'Curial Prose in England', *Speculum* 61 (1986), 593–614. In fact, the origins of curial prose can be found in Latin documents produced by the clerks of the Roman curia, for which see J. Rasmussen, *La Prose Narrative Française du XVe siècle: Étude esthétique et stylistique* (Copenhagen, 1958), pp. 22–44.

[31] D. Bornstein, 'French Influence on Fifteenth-Century English Prose as Exemplified by the Translation of Christine de Pisan's *Livre du Corps de Policie*', *Mediaeval Studies* 39 (1977), 369–86 (quotation at 370–1).

[32] Burnley, 'Curial Prose', 595.

[To our most sovereign lord king, and to the other lords spiritual and temporal in this present parliament, your poor and unceasing petitioner Margaret, the wife of Thomas Cornish of Uxbridge, in Middlesex, most humbly petitions: whereas the said Thomas was, by great malice and enmity, indicted on the charge that, the said Thomas and Nicholas Herford, labourer of the same town and county, on Thursday before the feast of the Invention of the Holy Cross, in the third year of your reign [26 April 1425], entered the close of one Alice Scolecroft at Uxbridge, and feloniously stole four sheep worth 6s 8d from the goods and chattels of one John Martin found there; of which felony, the said Thomas, by the conspiracy of his enemies, was convicted and condemned at the king's suit. Which gracious king, at the supplication of the most gracious queen, his mother, pardoned the said Thomas both of the said felony and the execution of the sentence given or to be given in this case; which pardon is ratified and confirmed by both the most mighty princes the dukes of Bedford and of Gloucester, and other most gracious lords of the council. May it please both the royal majesty and you, most gracious lords, to endorse this bill, and to deliver it to the privy seal to issue a charter of pardon thereupon, and this for God and by way of charity.][33]

In this short request are to be found some of the classic features of curial prose style: synonyms (*malice et enmite; convict et dampnez; ratifiez et confermez*); formulae (e.g. the opening and concluding clauses); the use of the passive voice (*le dit Thomas … fuit convict*); cohesive devices (*le dit, Le quell*); legalistic phraseology (e.g. *endite, felonousement, suit*); and elaborate ceremonial and deferential vocabulary (*tressoveraigne seignur; povere et continuell oratrice; gracious roi; tresgracious roigne; trespuissantz princes; roiall mageste*). One other key characteristic of petitions written in French was their measured and controlled tone. This example is useful because it illustrates how efficiently language was used to describe a grave miscarriage of justice. The scribe wastes no time detailing how and why Thomas Cornish came to be wrongly convicted of theft; it was deemed sufficient simply to note that he had been the victim of a conspiracy by his enemies. The overall linguistic construction of the petition is conservative, concise, predictable and matter-of-fact. The rhetoric, such as it is, is limited, and seems in fact to be used more as matter of form rather than as part of any clear persuasive strategy.

Given that the most famous practitioner of curial prose style was William Caxton, it should come as no surprise to find that many of the linguistic characteristics of French-language petitions transferred straightforwardly into an English-language context.[34] In this respect, it is important to stress that clerks and attorneys were just as capable of writing in a controlled, formal and ornamental style when they used English as when they used French.

33 *PROME*, parliament of 1426, item 26.

34 N. F. Blake, 'Caxton and Courtly Style', *Essays and Studies* n.s. 21 (1968), 29–45; N. Davis, 'Styles in English Prose of the Late Middle and Early Modern Period', in *Langue et Littérature: Actes du VIIIe congrès de la Fédération internationale des langues et littératures modernes* (Paris, 1961), pp. 165–84, esp. pp. 175–7 for the influence of the French language on English.

Chaucer demonstrated this when he translated the *Tale of Melibee* into English, and in the process *amplified* the curial style that was to be found in the original French text.[35] By far the greater proportion of the English-language petitions that survive in TNA series SC 8 actually conform closely to the linguistic conventions to be found in French-language petitions. Here, to illustrate a typical example, is the first half of a petition presented in 1455 by William Tyrell:

> Besecheth mekely William Tyrell late of Raureth in the counte of Essex the yongger squyer þat where he was endityd at Thaxstede in the seid counte the saturday next after alhalowyn in the yere of the kyng owre soverayn lorde þat nowe is xxxi be fore John Prisot John Markham and other late justice of oyer and determiner there of þat that he the iii[de] day of july with other the yere of the reigne of owre seid soverayn lorde þat nowe is xxviij at Stratford Langthorn and other placys within the counte of Essex in diversis conventiculis un lawfull in the maner of werre arreyed and armyd to grete nowmbre gaderid hem and made insurreccion and the deth and distruccion of the seid kyng owre soverayn lorde then and there ffalsly and traytously ymagenyd circuid and compassid and werre ayenst the kyng owre soverayn lorde ayenst the dewete of her liegeaunce then and there ffalsly and traytously areysid into the finiall distruccion of owre seid soverayne lorde ayenst theire liegeaunce. The which enditement was laborid procurid and conspirid by diverses personis untrewly disposid for males hadde ayenst youre seid suppliaunt withowtyn cause or demerit of youre seid suppliaunt as gode knoweth.[36]

Many of the classic elements of curial style are evident in this supplication, including generous use of lexical couplets and triplets (*arrayed and armyd; deth and distruccion; ffalsly and traytously; ymagenyd circuid and compassed; laborid procured and conspired*), cohesive devices (*the seid; owre seid;* [*t*]*he which; youre seid*) and standard legalistic formulae (*the kyng owre soverayn lorde; then and there; in the maner of werre arrayed and armyd*). It has all the hallmarks of a conventionally worded petition. Above all, like the French example, it provides little more than a summary of the petitioner's plight. No information is given to explain why the petitioner had been wrongly accused of treason, and no effort is taken to discredit Tyrell's accusers. There is nothing in this petition to mark it out as unusual and, with the possible exception of the interesting phrase 'dewete of her liegeaunce', the vocabulary is unremarkable and entirely predictable. One strongly suspects that the condensed nature of the prose indicates that the details of this case, as in many other cases brought before parliament, came to be rehearsed orally, and that the main purpose of the petition was procedural rather than rhetorical.

35 D. Bornstein, 'Chaucer's "Tale of Melibee" as an Example of the Style Clergial', *The Chaucer Review* 12 (1978), 236–54.
36 SC 8/144/7177.

English – New Linguistic Opportunities?

In this section I present evidence to suggest that the composition of petitions in English provided new opportunities to offer description that was, in its detail, vividness and colour, of a quite different level to that traditionally found in petitions. It is worth repeating that the following examples should not be taken as representative of English-language petitions in general, but are selected cases in which the vocabulary is especially and unusually distinctive: even among the overall body of English-language petitions they constitute a minority. But their existence suggests that attitudes to the composition of petitions had, in some instances, begun to change. Take, for example, a petition presented to parliament by Roger Woodcock at some point between 1448 and 1451. Woodcock's narrative outlined the persecution he had suffered at the hands of Richard Tregoys, and it left little to the imagination. Tregoys was accused of having:

> bonde the heed of the seide Roger with abowestreng so faste that the same bowestreng by strengthe of the seide byndyng brak and afterward the same day the seide Richard Tregoys toke a nother streng and bonde the heed of the seide Roger till that streng brak and after that in the same day the seid Richard Tregoys toke a fraylyng courde[37] and sore bonde the seid Roger aboute the heed in so moche that the blod came oute atte his eyen and nose and thenne with the ende of the same cord bonde his handes be hynde hym and boffet hym a borcte his chekys and with a knyf kut of his lyft ere a yenst the kyng pees to his uttermyst schame disfiguring and undoing ... .[38]

Woodcock's purpose in presenting his petition was not to summarise but to enumerate in detail the various outrages that he claimed had been committed against him. Even more gruesome was the petition presented by the Commons in 1443 against John Carpenter of Brydham, husbondman. Only fifteen days after their marriage Carpenter was said to have told his sixteen-year-old wife, Isabell, that they were to go on pilgrimage. But on arriving in the town of Stoughton in Sussex:

[37] According to N. Cox and K. Dannehl, *Dictionary of Traded Goods and Commodities 1550–1820* (Wolverhampton, 2007), *British History Online* <http://www.british-history.ac.uk/no-series/traded-goods-dictionary/1550–1820/frailing-cord-frocking> [accessed 21 March 2018], a frailing cord is most likely to have been a cord used for threshing corn.

[38] SC 8/148/7365. A commission of oyer and terminer was issued on 24 July 1452 to investigate the alleged crimes of Tregoys and his associates: *CPR, 1446–52*, p. 585. There is useful discussion of Tregoys, though not this particular case, by H. Kleineke, 'Why the West was Wild: Law and Disorder in Fifteenth-Century Cornwall and Devon', in *The Fifteenth Century III: Authority and Subversion*, ed. L. Clark (Woodbridge, 2003), pp. 75–93.

> there in a woode he smote the said Isabell his wiff on the hede, that the brayne wende oute, and with his knyff yaf her many other dedly woundes, and streped hir naked oute of hir clothes, and toke his knyff and slytte hir bely from the brest doune, and toke hir bowels oute of hir body, and loked if she wer with child; and thus the said John murdered horribly his wyff.[39]

Of a rather different order was the petition presented by Philip Okeover between 1446 and 1457. It described crimes against Okeover's property, rather than his body. The sheriff of Staffordshire and Derbyshire, William Cokyn of Ashbourne, together with a hundred 'mysdoers and riottes persones', were alleged to have:

> come to the seid maner and ther and than brake uppe the dores bay wyndowes and other wyndowes of the seid maner with foormes[40] trestillez[41] and tabull dorment[42] and brende them there and by the seid fire rostid parcel of the seid deere takyn in the seid parke in dispyte of youre seyd besecher and ther huntyd and distroyed the seid parke and brake down the pales therof … . On the day of the Conception of oure lady last paste come to the seid parke and there and then huntyd all the daye and drowen downe the most part of the pale of the seid parke ther then kyllyd all the dere ther ine to the noumbre of vi^{xx} and laste in the seid parke but v dere alyve and so hit is utterly distroyed to the grete hurtte and utterly shame and undoyng of youre seid besecher.[43]

Here, then, are the blood, brains and bay-windows; but other English-language petitions display equally fascinating and unexpected details. In c. 1439 the prior of Plympton described the various macabre acts performed by the inhabitants of Plympton on the corpse of the prior's servant Gerard Jonson.[44] We join the narrative after the townsmen had 'horribilly toke uppe the seid ded body out of his grave':

> And aftur the same dede body was so violently takyn uppe thei bette hit and leid opon hit with ther wepyns, and so horribly fared with hit that hit is not \ones.../ … or declare. And then thei bere hit forth with a thre men song hevelowe, rumbelowe,[45] and threwe hit in to a myre with inne the seid church yerd, and made on of the seid misgoverned people to stond ther

[39] SC 8/26/1281; *PROME*, parliament of 1433, item 43. Printed in *An Anthology of Chancery English*, ed. J. H. Fisher, M. Richardson and J. L. Fisher (Knoxville, TN, 1984), pp. 235–6.

[40] I.e. benches without backs.

[41] I.e. stands for trestle tables.

[42] I.e. non-moveable tables.

[43] SC 8/132/6597.

[44] SC 8/135/6740; printed in *Petitions to the Crown from English Religious Houses*, ed. Dodd and McHardy, no. 135, pp. 165–6 (discussion at pp. xxxvii–xxxviii).

[45] Middle English Dictionary: both 'hevelowe' and 'rumbelowe' are defined as 'a sailor's cry'.

> above to resceyve offuryng, holding his typette[46] in hie hondes. And then all the riotouse people offred silver to hym and kyssed his hond, in dirisione of the blessed custome of the church, and then wente to the ale and drank hit.

Similar sensationalism is conveyed in the details of the petition presented by the inhabitants of King's Langley, this time against members of a local religious house.[47] The townsmen had a litany of complaint to relay about their troublesome neighbours, including the damage the monks had caused to a common wood by their 'multitude of catell', but by far the most scandalous charge was that 'the same freres [i.e. brothers] resorten to suspect persones and to myslyveng women of their bodyes, to the great displeasure of Almyghty God and great shame to the religion'. The vivid detail of a complaint presented in 1426 by English merchants trading with Flanders helped to convey the unpleasantness of their ordeal. On 2 January 1426 they had been imprisoned by the townsmen of Middleburgh 'amonges felons and manquetters'. They had been kept there for nine days and nights, during which 'none of þair frendis nor welwilling myght speke with þaim'. Finally, they had been compelled by 'suche persones as dide þaim turment' to 'delyvere þair keyes and yeve knowleche of alle þair goodis',which were subsequently stolen.[48]

In other cases, detail was embedded within fairly standard narrative prose. Take, for example, the petition of four Londoners presented in 1440.[49] They had been imprisoned for speaking 'diveres presumtuose wordes and langwage' to the officers presiding over the execution of the Lollard Richard Wyche. Although they claimed to have submitted to the correction of the bishop of London, the petitioners still languished in gaol and asked for remedy because of their poverty and, as they put it, the 'unkounyng grete sorowe and hevynesse of ther wyves'. Or the petition of Ralph Blenerhayset, who made various complaints against John Hawe that included the theft of a horse 'of price of xx mark of the seid besecher that he had left ther to rest and tobe cheriset vnto his hasty goyng ouer the see'.[50] Or the petition of Agnes Bermythier, widow of Thomas Bermythier, who complained that Thomas Berkeley had so threatened her that if she sued against the killers of her husband she 'shall be slayn or kypte in soche ward as she shall never come

46 Middle English Dictionary: 'An ornamental piece of cloth, usu. long and narrow, worn separately covering the shoulders or as part of a hood, the sleeves.'

47 SC 8/345/E 1324; printed in *Petitions to the Crown*, ed. Dodd and McHardy, no. 213, pp. 270–1.

48 SC 8/126/6265; an edition of this petition is in *Bronnen Tot de Geschiedenis van den Handel met Engelond, Schotland en Ierland*, ed. H. J. Smit, vol. I (Den Haag, 1928), pp. 620–1.

49 SC 8/251/12528.

50 SC 8/96/4762.

to hire own howse nor se non of here fryndys'.[51] Or the petition of William Bultell, who made a complaint against the abbot of Waltham, providing a vivid description of his personal circumstances: he claimed to be 'an old man & impotent & nigh blynd and [his wif] lyth continuell bedrede and now have they no good to lyve bi'.[52] Or the petition of Ralph Bassett, who complained in c. 1449 of attacks on his house, pointing out that 'youre seid besecher darenot in no wise be at home in his on house which shulde be his grete defence and tuition'.[53] Or the petition of Thomas Squire, who claimed that he had been threatened by the servants of Richard Makeney to the effect that 'yf he may be founde in hys hows to be hewe as final as fleysshe to the potte'.[54] Occasionally petitions used language that illuminated contemporary attitudes or world views. In a petition presented by a group of scholars in 1447 the city of London was described as the 'commune concours of this lond' and their complaint against the dearth of properly qualified school masters was described as a state of affairs that went 'aynst all vertue and ordre of well puplik'.[55]

A number of rape or attempted rape cases were enrolled on the parliament roll and contained especially vivid descriptions of the fate apparently to befall the victims. In 1445 the Commons petitioned the king asking him to rescind a pardon granted to John Bolton for the murder of Isabell Bakeler. In the narrative we learn that Bakeler had spurned Bolton's advances, as a result of which:

> he vilanisly toke of here all the attire of her hed, and also her clothis of her body, otake her smokke, and yet sche wold never assent unto his unlefull desire, but at all tymes kept her a gode womman; and atte the last be cause he cowde not have his desire of here, he there atte the same tyme felonesly sloeth and murdred here, and kutte her throte twies, and twies stiked her thurgh her pappes and sides with a dagger, wher uppon she died.[56]

In 1437 two petitions were presented by Isabell, widow of John Boteler, complaining of abduction and forced marriage.[57] In the first petition, the account was limited to a brief summary of events, in which her attacker, William Pulle, was alleged to have led her naked 'except hir kirtyll and hir smoke ... into the wylde and desolate places of Wales'. In the second petition the account was more detailed. It was specified that Pulle and his accomplices had come to Isabelle's house at Bewsey (Cheshire) 'at v of þe clokke in þe

[51] SC 8/96/4800.
[52] SC 8/84/4186.
[53] SC 8/96/4795.
[54] SC 8/307/15339.
[55] *PROME*, parliament of 1447, item 19.
[56] *PROME*, parliament of 1445, item 42.
[57] *PROME*, parliament of 1437, items 14 and 15.

mornyng' and, having 'toke and ravysshed' her, she was taken to the parish church of Bidston on the Wirral peninsula. Once there:

> itt was \asked/ of hir by þe prist, if shoo wolde agree \her to have/ the said William Pulle to husbond, and sho saide, nay never by hir wille; wheruppon þe said William, manassed hir that she solde be dede, but sho walde sey þe wordes of matrimonye, and theruppon þe prest agayns hir will wedded þaym; whiche weddyng by cohercion so done, þe said William ledde and droghe þe said Isabell, agayn to þe said Birkhede þe same Tuysday, and there putte hir in a stronge chaumbre till nyght; and þen þere þe said William, felonousely and flesshly knewe and ravysshed þe said Isabell.

A slightly different perspective, at least from the point of view of the presiding priest, was given by Henry Beaumont in a petition of 1453 that made complaint against Edward Lancaster, who was accused of the rape and forced marriage of his mother, Joan, in breach of the marital contract she had with Charles Nowell.[58] Beaumont paints a vivid picture of what happened to his mother. Lancaster and his accomplices, numbering over forty men who were 'arraied in the maner of werre ... as felons of our said soverain lord ... the seid Johane there and than fonde with force and armes felonesly ravisshed'. She was then put on a horse behind one of his men 'and bonde her fast to hym with a towell'. She was taken to a church, whereupon,

> a preest of his assent was redy to wedde and mary the said Edwarde Lancastre and her togidre; and whan the said preest wold have hir to sey the wordes of matrimony, she wold not sey hem, for she said \that she was/ another mannes wyf, and therupon the seid Edward manaced hir hidously, to bete and to lede hir out of this land into Scotlond, but she wold sey as the preest bad hir; and than she asked the preest how [he] durst take upon hym for to wedde hem togidre, without that they had be lawfully askid in the chirche, after the cours of the lawe, and he seid þat he durst doo noon otherwise for fere and dought of his \dethe/; and so she was ayenst her will by cohercion wedded unto hym.

Such petitions were carefully constructed stories leading the reader – or audience – through the various stages of the petitioner's woes, before finishing with the circumstances in which they now found themselves. They were written to stimulate the interest of the reader. The detail added colour, individuality and an air of authenticity to the events being recounted, for they helped form a picture of how and why the supplicant came to be in his or her predicament. One of the best such narratives was presented in 1455 by John

[58] SC 8/28/1362; *PROME*, parliament of 1453, item 72. The petition led to the enactment of a statute against forced marriage: *SR*, vol. II, 367–8 (c. ix). On 8 February 1453 a commission of oyer and terminer was issued to investigate the alleged crimes committed against Joan: *CPR, 1452–61*, p. 60.

Radford, who demanded that those implicated in the murder of his cousin Nicholas Radford, for whom John was executor, be brought to justice.[59] The petition is a masterful demonstration of persuasive rhetoric. It shows story-telling, in the context of petition writing, at its most effective. John introduces his cousin as 'oon of the moste notable and famous apprentice of your [i.e. the king's] lawe in this youre realm of England'. He then provides an account of the murder of Nicholas Radford, which is as captivating as it is shocking. On 24 October 1455, at midnight, Thomas Courtney, son of the earl of Devon, arrived at Radford's house at Uppecote in Devonshire with over a hundred other 'riotouse person'. Radford, who was in bed, awoke 'and herynge a grate noise and sturynge about his said place, arose and opened his wyndowe of his chamber' to see what was going on. There then follows an account of the dialogue that took place between Radford and Courtney, in which the latter persuaded Radford to come down to him, having declared 'I promise you as I am trewe knight and Gentylman þe shal be save bothe of youre body and of youre godes.' But this was a trick. While Radford was held in conversation, Courtney's men ransacked his house. They found his 'wyffe in her bed, sore sike as she hathe ben this ij yere and more, and rolled her oute of her bedd'. Radford was then led away and brutally murdered a short distance from his house: 'and then and there the said Nicholas Philippe with a glaive smote þe said Nicholas Radford a hideous dedlye stroke overthwarte the face, and felled him to the grounde, and ... yaf him a noder stroke upon his heade behind that the brayne felle oute of heade'. Even in death, however, Radford could not escape the depravations of his persecutors: Henry Courtenay, brother of Thomas, and other accomplices, took Radford's body out of its coffin 'and rolled him oute of hys shete in ye whiche he was wound; and there and then caste the bodye alle naked into þe pytte'. They then hurled stones upon 'his bodye and heade, and it horribly brake and quashed, having no more compassion no pite than though it hadde be a Jewe or a sarrison'.

Graphic detail might catch attention and elicit empathy and sympathy. One suspects that these intentions lay behind a petition presented in 1472 by Joan Glyn, widow of John, who had been viciously attacked and murdered by Thomas Clemens.[60] John Glyn was a respected member of Cornish society,

[59] SC 8/138/6864. The petition is printed and discussed by G. H. Radford, 'Nicholas Radford, 1385(?)–1455', *Reports and Transactions of the Devonshire Association* 35 (1903), 251–78, at 264–8. For Radford's career, see J. S. Roskell et al., *The House of Commons, 1386–1421*, 4 vols (Stroud, 1992), vol. IV, pp. 168–70. The dispute and its context are surveyed by M. Cherry, 'The Struggle for Power in Mid-Fifteenth-Century Devonshire', in *Patronage, the Crown and the Provinces*, ed. R. A. Griffiths (Gloucester, 1981), pp. 123–44, esp. pp. 136–7; J. R. Lander, 'Henry VI and the Duke of York's Second Protectorate, 1455 to 1456', *Bulletin of the John Rylands Library* 43 (1960), 46–69, esp. 59–65; and R. L. Storey, *The End of the House of Lancaster* (Stroud, 1966, repr. 1999), pp. 168–73.

[60] SC 8/29/1439; *PROME*, parliament of 1472, item 38.

a skilled local attorney, a JP and deputy steward of the duchy of Cornwall. In January 1470 the proceedings of the duchy court at Liskeard had been interrupted by Thomas Clemens, who had previously occupied Glyn's office. Motivated, it was said, by 'olde malice and envye', Clemens had almost twenty of his servants and associates make 'a grete assaute' on Glyn and his servants. Particular note was made of the fact that the malefactors violently tore and ripped into small pieces various court rolls of the courts of the said duchy – described as 'the kynges courte of the maner of Leskerde' – and a purse of black leather containing eight marks in money was said to have been cut from Glyn's girdle. Glyn was then led away and imprisoned in Liskeard castle. Here he was kept 'by the space of v oures and more, so that noon of his frendes myght come where he was to releve hym with drynk, or staunche his bloode [from the wounds he had suffered during the assault], to thentent that he shuld have bled to deth, except they suffered a preste to come to shryve and howsell hym'. But worse was to come. On 29 August 1472 Clemens's henchmen

> lay in a waite of the said John Glyn, and then and there, at iiij of the clok in the mornyng, hym felonsly and horribly slewe and murdred, and clove his hede in iiij parties, and gave hym x dede woondes in his body, and when he was dede they kutte of oon of his legges, and oone of his armes, and his hede from his body, to make hym sure. And over that, then and there, his purs, and xxij li of money nombred, a signet of golde, a grete signet of sylver in the same purs conteyned, a double cloke of musterdeviles, a swerd, and a dagger, to \the/ value of vi marcs, of the goodes and catelx of the said John Glyn, felonsly fro hym they robbed, toke and bare awey.

An attack on 'the kynges hye way', early in the morning, against a defenceless man of the law who was savagely assaulted and killed and whose body was then subjected to dismemberment and whose possessions were 'feloniously' stolen was a powerful picture of anarchy and lawlessness, deliberately and skilfully aimed to cause outrage among those who heard the tale.[61]

Explanations

The most obvious explanation for the idiosyncratic nature of the examples given in the previous section is that they convey in a far less 'filtered' manner than conventional petitions the real-life details of the petitioners' circumstances. The tendency we have observed for parliamentary complaint to be rendered into type-cast narrative, circumscribed by formulaic summaries and

[61] TNA, C 1/59/107 is a chancery bill presented by Glyn's youngest son, John, against John Fortescue, late sheriff of Cornwall, for failing to arrest Thomas Clemens and his associates. This suggests that their crimes went unpunished.

a reserved or measured tone, is to a greater or lesser extent absent in these cases. This suggests a higher level of input into the compilation of the petitions by the supplicants themselves. Either they, or the clerks or attorneys they employed, took the decision to present the complaint in a way that enhanced, rather than obscured, the very individual nature of the petitioners' plight. So who did make this decision? Are these colourful phrases, passages and narratives windows into the creative mental worlds of the clerks and attorneys who wrote the petitions, or are they the authentic testimony of the petitioners themselves, faithfully conveying in their own words the full horror of their own personal experiences or of those close to them? In some instances the guiding hand of expert counsel may be detected. The narratives of the alleged rape and forced marriage of Isabella Boteler and Joan Beaumont contain some notably individualised detail, but they also follow an established and fairly standardised rape discourse, in which they are cast as hapless victims coerced into marriage against their will.[62] On the other hand, it is hard to envisage that the particulars of the awful fate to befall Isabell Carpenter, or the dreadful injuries inflicted on John Woodcock or the scandalous circumstances of Nicholas Radford's murder were merely products of the fertile imaginations of the clerks or attorneys who drafted these cases. When the petition of Christine Brok, asking for the king's assistance in a dispute over her husband's will, ended with a plea 'for the love of Ihu' – a highly unusual invocation – it seems more likely that this reflected the language choice of the petitioner than of the clerk or attorney she had employed.[63]

A couple of cases suggest a clearer connection between the level of colour and detail incorporated into a petition and the input of 'professional' counsel. In the late 1420s and early 1430s a number of petitions were presented in parliament requesting free passage along the River Severn for merchants trading along its route. In 1427, 1429 and 1431 the crown was entreated on this matter by common petitions. All three complaints were written in French and all displayed the classic characteristics of a heavily filtered narrative: the most that could be said of the perpetrators of wrongdoing was that they were disrupting the flow of river traffic 'pur graund malice et orgoile, q'ils ount de ceo q'ils ne serront pursuiez par la commune ley, pur ascun chose ou offence fait en Gales et les autres ditz lieux previlegies' ('on account of the great arrogance and strength which they have because they will not be

[62] B. A. Hanawalt, *'Of Good and Ill Repute': Gender and Social Control in Medieval England* (Oxford, 1998), chap. 8 ('Whose Story was this? Rape Narratives in Medieval English Courts'); K. M. Phillips, 'Written on the Body: Reading Rape from the Twelfth to Fifteenth Centuries', in *Medieval Women and the Law*, ed. N. J. Menuge (Woodbridge, 2000), pp. 125–44; K. M. Phillips, 'Four Virgins' Tales: Sex and Power in Medieval Law', in *Medieval Virginities*, ed. A. Bernau, S. Salih and R. Evans (Toronto, 2003), pp. 80–101; C. Dunn, *Stolen Women in Medieval England: Rape, Abduction, and Adultery, 1100–1500* (Cambridge, 2013), chaps 2 and 3.

[63] SC 8/190/9489.

pursued by the common law for anything or offence committed in Wales and the other said privileged places').[64] In 1429 the bailiffs, burgesses and commons of the town of Tewkesbury presented a petition that articulated a very similar complaint to that found in the common petitions; in fact, it is very likely to have been the inhabitants of Tewkesbury whose lobbying of MPs had prompted the common petitions in the first place.[65] But their own 'private' petition looked very different. Not only was it written in English,[66] but the language and narrative were noticeably more forthright and descriptive. The perpetrators were described as a 'grete multitude of peple, and rowtes of the communes of the same forest [of Dean], and of the hundredes of Bledislowe and Wesebury, with greete ryot and strengthe in maner of werre, as enemys of a straunge lande'. Upon finding the petitioner's vessels on the river:

> the men of the same trowes[67] cast over the borde, and diverse of hem drowned, and the hausters [i.e. hawsers] of the same trowes cutte atwayne, and maneshud the owners of the saide goodes, and the saide trowmen, that they sholde not be so hardy to carye no maner of vitaille by the seide streme up ne doune, for lorde ne lady.

Finally, the petitioners expressed the hopelessness of their situation by remarking that 'the saide forest and hundredes been large cuntrees, and wylde of peple, and negh adjoynaunt to Wales, and alle the communes of the same forest and hundredes, of oon affinite in malice and riot, settyng no prise by þe lawe'. The two styles of petitions are plain to see. One is clipped and bureaucratic; the other is emotive and personalised. The difference is probably to be explained by the origins of the two narratives: while the common petition is likely to have been compiled by the clerk of the Commons, who rendered the 'raw narrative' into formal, polished bureaucratic prose style, the private petition, written perhaps by a clerk from Tewkesbury itself, more faithfully represented the sentiments of the petitioners themselves.

To be clear, my suggestion is not that colourful language was *uniquely* characteristic of either the private petition or the use of the English language. My argument is that such language tended to be used more readily in English-language private petitions because the scope for the petitioner's voice to be heard more clearly in supplications increased when their own language was used, and when the subject of the complaint was of a more personal or individual nature. In contrast, common petitions, whether they were written in French or in English, tended to be more linguistically conservative. This should come as no surprise, as common petitions expressed the will of the

64 *PROME*, parliament of 1427, item 44. See also, *PROME*, parliament of 1429, item 44; and parliament of 1431, item 38.

65 *PROME*, parliament of 1429, item 30.

66 Except for the opening address, which was articulated in French.

67 Middle English Dictionary: 'A flat-bottomed vessel for transporting goods, a barge.'

political community and often formed the basis of remedial legislation. As such, a high level of formality and exactitude could be expected to have attended their compilation. For the most part, what we read on the parliament rolls, therefore, is not the unmediated voice of the political community but the linguistic formulation of chancery clerks charged by MPs to render their requests into language befitting the occasion of parliament.[68] From 1363 MPs had their own clerk whose remit would most certainly have been dominated by the task of writing up their requests.[69]

In only two instances is it possible to identify common petitions that seemed to have represented exceptions to this rule. The first is the oft-cited common petition of April 1414, in which MPs voiced their concern that the original meaning and intention of their requests was being subverted by the process that saw common petitions turned into statutory legislation.[70] Although the complaint did not refer to the intervention of the clerks, it is significant that the request was articulated in English at a time when all other common petitions were written in French. The language, as well as the self-reflective and discursive tone of the complaint, suggest that the petition articulated the unmediated voice of MPs in parliament.[71] The second example is a common petition presented in November 1449 accusing William Tailboys of the murder of Lord Cromwell.[72] The petition is emotive and highly rhetorical: it is, in effect, a demand that the king take action. It begins with the pointed observation 'that the honour, welthe and prosperite, of every prynce reynyng uppon his people, stondith moost principally upon conservation of his peas'. The great giveaway is that highly unusual use of the personal pronoun in reference to the petitioners themselves: 'we your comons of this your roialme'. This suggests a deliberate and self-conscious attempt to establish the authentic authorial voice of the request in order to underline the strength of feeling that lay behind it. These rare examples emphasise the extent to which common petitions would ordinarily have passed through the lexical filter of the royal bureaucracy.

But let us return to the question of the choice between English and French languages. It is important to stress that the French language was also capable of being used in a less formal or controlled linguistic environment, like English. The fact that it usually was not reflected not the limitations of the language but the way it was used by the writers of petitions. When French

68 W. M. Ormrod, 'On – and Off – the Record: The Rolls of Parliament, 1337–77', *Parliamentary History* 23 (2004), 39–56, esp. 43–8.

69 A. F. Pollard, 'The Clerical Organization of Parliament', *English Historical Review* 57 (1942), 31–58, at 36.

70 *PROME*, parliament of April 1414, item 22 (X).

71 W. M. Ormrod, 'The Language of Complaint: Multilingualism and Petitioning in Later Medieval England', in *Language and Culture*, ed. Wogan-Browne et al., pp. 31–43, esp. pp. 40–1.

72 *PROME*, parliament of November 1449, item 56.

was used, the content of the petition tended to conform more directly with the dictates of traditional curial prose style;[73] but not always. In 1393 Richard Stermesworth presented a French-language petition to the king and council in which he complained about the mayor of Northampton, John Fox, who was said to have used royal power to permit Lollards to preach freely in the town.[74] There are some fascinating details and pointed opinions, all articulated in French. These included the claim that the townspeople were so enamoured with their mayor that they looked upon him as though he were a prophet with an angel's tongue; the observation that vulgar people who had become infected with Lollardy were received in the town as if they too were prophets; an account of several dramatic showdowns in the church of All Saints, Northampton, in which mass had effectively been hijacked by Lollard preachers; and the guile of the preachers who borrowed furred hoods and habits to wear during their sermons so that the common people would think them important clergymen. Stermesworth's petition provides a comprehensive account of the invidious spread of heresy within an urban community. It is so exhaustive, in fact, that it reads less as a conventional petition and more as personal testimony. It is fundamentally a blow-by-blow account of what happened, rather than a summary of the petitioner's main points of grievance. As such, it has a lot in common with some of the English-language cases already mentioned.[75]

Could the greater use of such detail in fifteenth-century English-language petitions indicate a subtle shift in the purpose that these supplications were

[73] P. Tucker, *Law Courts and Lawyers in the City of London, 1300–1550* (Cambridge, 2007), p. 178 has observed that after the 1440s the only petitions written in French and presented to the Mayor's Court of London were those of apprentices at law: the rest were written in English.

[74] SC 8/142/7099; a nineteenth-century translation of the petition is published in *The Peasants' Rising and the Lollards: A Collection of Unpublished Documents Forming an Appendix to England in the Age of Wycliffe*, ed. E. Powell and G. M. Trevelyan (New York, 1899), pp. 45–50.

[75] Another highly unusual French-language petition is SC 8/97/4826, printed in N. Saul, *Knights and Esquires: The Gloucestershire Gentry in the Fourteenth Century* (Oxford, 1981), pp. 266–7. This was a complaint presented by the people of King's Barton near Gloucester in the 1330s against Sir Thomas de Bradeston. In unusual detail, the petitioners detailed the grisly murder by one of Bradeston's valets, Piers de St Comb, of his own wife. He was said to have burned her alive in bed and buried the body in his garden for seven weeks before attempting to dispose of it in the River Severn. Lady Bradeston was accused of collusion by harbouring de St Comb, and the petitioners lamented the fact that if Sir Thomas had not been so close to the king or powerful in his locality, a thousand petitions would be presented against him (*pur tant come sire Thomas est si pres del Roi, mes apres le Roi avera mile billes sur ly et les soens si de lour poer fuissent osteez*), and that, whereas at court he behaved like a little saint, in his own country he was like a raging lion (*le dit sire Thomas se port en court come un seinturel et en son pays com un lyon rampaunt*). This type of expressive and figurative language was highly unusual in fourteenth-century supplications.

intended to serve? What was the aim of all this colour and detail if it was not regarded by the petitioner and/or those who counselled him/her as serving a worthwhile function? Some years ago I wrote about the case of Thomas Paunfield, who presented a petition in November 1414 complaining about the depredations of Barnwell Priory (Cambridgeshire).[76] Paunfield presented a standard petition, written in French, as well as a much lengthier English-language account of his circumstances.[77] I argued that this second document was conceived not as a conventional petition but as legal testimony. The rhetorical force of this testimony lay in the fact that it presented in exhaustive detail, and apparently in Paunfield's own words, the 'facts of the case', undistorted by clerical filters. This case study has an important bearing on the current discussion, as it suggests a way of understanding how the employment of English in petitions might have changed the function of petitioning itself. In 1414 the French language still monopolised the composition of petitions, so a clear distinction existed between petitions (written in French and usually providing only an outline of the case) and personal testimony (written in English, and offering a more comprehensive account of what had happened). It is my contention that once English began to be used in the petitions themselves the lines between the two began to blur. It seems to have happened most commonly in petitions complaining about acts of violence and intimidation: virtually all the passages cited in this discussion have been drawn from petitions of this nature. In cases that were especially contentious, or notorious, there was evidently a greater tendency for English-language petitions to push the voice of the petitioner to the foreground, and for the petitioners to provide more personalised testimony in support of their case.

It is possible to link these conclusions to a broader legal context. In his consideration of supplicatory language, Mark Ormrod suggested that the written petition acted as a substitute for the oral pleading that took place in the king's common law courts.[78] His arguments derived from the fact that, at least until the enactment of the Statute of Pleading in 1362, the French language was used both for petitioning and for pleading, so contemporaries would have seen the petition as a written extension of the arguments made by lawyers in the courtroom. Nevertheless, as Ormrod notes, this linguistic connection was severed once pleading in the king's courts began to be

[76] G. Dodd, 'Thomas Paunfield, the "heye Court of rightwisenesse" and the Language of Petitioning in the Fifteenth Century', in *Medieval Petitions: Grace and Grievance*, ed. W. M. Ormrod, G. Dodd and A. Musson (York, 2009), pp. 222–41.

[77] SC 8/23/1143A and SC 8/23/1143B; printed in *Anthology of Chancery English*, ed. Fisher et al., pp. 198–204.

[78] Ormrod, 'Language of Complaint', pp. 35–8. There is also useful discussion of the close relationship between orality and textuality in J. M. Gellrich, *Discourse and Dominion in the Fourteenth Century: Oral Contexts of Writing in Philosophy, Politics, and Poetry* (Princeton, NJ, 1995), pp. 3–7, 26–7.

conducted in English after 1362, and it was not until the second quarter of the fifteenth century, when petitions began to be written in English, that the link was restored. While there is much to be said for this explanation, there is room for refinement. To understand the particular legal characteristics of the petition it is necessary to make a distinction between the 'count' or 'declaration', on the one hand, and the oral argument between the parties to suit, on the other hand: both stages in legal process can be described as 'pleading'.[79] While Ormrod likened the petition to pleading in general, it may in fact be more apposite to align it specifically with the 'count'. This was the formal declaration which initiated legal process.[80] It was in the 'count' that the circumstances of the plaintiff and the nature of his or her grievance was presented to the court. Exactitude and brevity were hallmarks of the count, just as they were in conventional petitions. The fact that the count, in Latin, was described as the *narracio*, which was also the term used in the *ars dictaminis* to describe the principal persuasive element to be found in the composition of letters and petitions, is highly suggestive of the shared meanings and functions of these two contexts.[81]

If we characterise the petition in these more precise terms, it makes better sense of a number of different aspects of the petitionary form. First, from the early thirteenth century the count was usually delivered in the third person to reflect the fact that serjeants-at-law were presenting the facts of a case to the court on behalf of their clients.[82] Petitions were similarly written in the third person, probably also to emulate some of the legal values underpinning mesne process.[83] Second, if we accept that the petition was closely aligned with the 'count' in mesne process, we are no longer faced with the curious separation of linguistic practice that the Statute of Pleading apparently heralded, for, while legal debates were conducted in English after 1362, the formal 'count' almost certainly continued to be delivered in French.[84]

[79] T. F. T. Plucknett, *A Concise History of the Common Law*, 5th edn (London, 1956), pp. 399–418.

[80] P. Brand, *The Origins of the English Legal Profession* (Oxford, 1992), pp. 38–40. For examples of 'counts' in contemporary pleading manuals, see *Brevia Placitata*, ed. G. J. Turner, Selden Society 66 (London, 1951), *passim*; and *Novae Narrationes*, ed. S. F. C. Milsom, Selden Society 80 (London, 1963), *passim*.

[81] J. H. Baker, *The Order of Serjeants at Law* (London, 1984), p. 8; M. Camargo, 'Toward a Comprehensive Art of Written Discourse: Geoffrey of Vinsauf and the *Ars Dictaminis*', *Rhetorica* 6 (1988), 167–94, esp. 177. On the application of the *ars dictaminis* to petitions, see Dodd, 'Writing Wrongs', 224–7.

[82] Brand, *Origins*, pp. 54–5.

[83] For the role of the serjeant-at-law and his relationship with a litigant, see P. Brand, 'Inside the Courtroom: Lawyers, Litigants and Justices in England in the Late Middle Ages', in *The Moral World of the Law*, ed. P. Coss (Cambridge, 2000), pp. 91–112, esp. p. 95.

[84] Baker, 'Three Languages of the Common Law', p. 243; Ormrod, 'Use of English', 773.

The close correlation between petitioning and the count would therefore make better sense of the continued use of French in petitions well into the fifteenth century. And finally, and for the present purposes most importantly, it provides a firmer institutional context for the more discursive, personalised discourse to be found in some English-language petitions. This 'colour' did not represent a loosening of the legal framework of the petition, or a lowering of the linguistic standards of its compilation. Rather, it represented the oral testimony and arguments that the litigant might have brought into the court room as part of the debates that followed the formal declaration or count. When petitions were written in a looser, less formal style they therefore connected to that aspect of legal culture that placed value on the evidential power of the written vernacular.[85] My argument, then, is that the petition continued to represent an 'oral document' – but this discourse, where it developed a more idiosyncratic and personalised aspect, was understood in legal terms to represent more the testimonial aspect of legal pleading than the traditional, formalised declaration.

Concomitantly, it is possible that the use of English changed how petitions were handled in parliament. Whereas previously, as we have seen, the content of a French-language petition would probably be translated for the benefit of those charged to consider its content, the onset of English-language petitions provided an opportunity for petitioners to 'connect' with their audience more directly. In a French-language environment there would have been greater onus on the aural testimony of the petitioner as a means of obtaining additional relevant detail pertinent to a case that was not given in the petition. There is plenty of evidence to show that in the fourteenth century petitioners were routinely called upon in person before the king and council to explain their circumstances or the nature of their complaint.[86] Employing English in petitions offered a means of circumventing this process, or at least of speeding it up. One notable feature of many English-language petitions is their impressive length. This suggests that some petitioners were taking the opportunity of setting down in writing what might previously have been presented in speech as their own personal testimony. It is even possible that some petitions composed in English were written not to be read out loud but to be read as written script by those present in parliament. In these circumstances one could perhaps afford to be more long-winded and verbose.

By the fifteenth century it was common for many private petitions to be presented to MPs to win their backing and endorsement, before being

[85] See above n. 22, and H. Wicker, 'The Politics of Vernacular Speech: Cases of Treasonable Language, c. 1440–1453', in *Vernacularity in England and Wales*, ed. Salter and Wicker, pp. 171–97, at pp. 183–5.

[86] E.g. SC 8/13/623; 13/631; 31/1529; 45/2227; 53/2650; 59/2910; 84/4166; 88/4367; 95/4732; 257/12849.

dispatched to the king and the Lords for adjudication.[87] Concomitantly those which were addressed and presented directly to the king and/or Lords were often sent to the Commons for their approval.[88] The content of petitions was therefore coming to be considered by a much broader audience, including representatives of the provincial gentry and urban elites. This may have given additional impetus behind the choice of some of the more colourful passages in the examples I have considered, and a tendency in some cases towards expressions of moral outrage and personal indignation. One wonders, for example, whether the trouble taken by Philip Okeover to specify that it was not just his windows, but his *bay*-windows, that had been broken by William Cokyn was an appeal to the gentlemanly sensibilities of an audience whose members might have appreciated the finer things in life.[89] The claim by Henry Beaumont and his co-petitioners that Edward Lancaster had threatened to abscond with his mother to Scotland unless she consented to marry him, as though one could hardly imagine a worse fate, was presumably aimed at rousing the chivalric indignation and racial prejudices of the English gentry gathered in parliament.[90] The detailed descriptions of the horrific murders of Nicholas Radford and John Glyn may also have struck a chord with MPs, many of whom served, like Radford and Glyn, as attorneys and/or local commissioners. Graphic descriptions of horrendous crimes indicated a preponderance for sensationalism in an age when the outcome to a petition now depended to a greater extent on swaying parliamentary opinion. In short, the use of English enabled the petitioner to speak the language of those who passed judgement on cases, both literally and figuratively.

With the greater involvement of the parliamentary community in the adjudication of petitions one would expect some cases to make an impression on the men who attended the assembly. Evidence to show this is difficult to come by, but in one instance it is very plain to see. This was the murder of Nicholas Radford on 23 October 1455. We have noted already that the petition was presented in parliament by Radford's cousin and executor John Radford.[91] This, and a more general complaint about lawlessness in Devon presented by the Commons,[92] were alluded to in a writ dated to 23 January

[87] Dodd, *Justice and Grace*, pp. 179–87.

[88] Dodd, *Justice and Grace*, pp. 174–9.

[89] Detailed discussion of the increasing popularity of bay-windows – or oriels – is provided by M. Wood, *The English Medieval House* (London, 1965), chap. 7.

[90] On anti-Scottish sentiment within England, see C. J. Neville, 'Local Sentiment and the "National" Enemy in Northern England in the Late Middle Ages', *Journal of British Studies* 35 (1996), 419–47; A. J. MacDonald, 'John Hardyng, Northumbrian Identity and the Scots', in *North-East England in the Later Middle Ages*, ed. C. D. Liddy and R. H. Britnell (Woodbridge, 2005), pp. 29–42; A. Ruddick, *English Identity and Political Culture in the Fourteenth Century* (Cambridge, 2013), pp. 143–7.

[91] See above, pp. 26–7.

[92] TNA, C 49/30/14; *Rotuli Parliamentorum*, 6 vols (London, 1767–77), vol. V,

1456,[93] which might logically suggest that both petitions were presented early in 1456. In fact, it is more likely that they were presented in the autumn of 1455.[94] Moreover, given the fact that John Radford's complaint focused only on the immediate circumstances of his cousin's murder and not on the subsequent theft of Sir Nicholas's goods and property by the earl of Devon and his son,[95] it also seems reasonable to conclude that his petition was drafted and presented very soon after the incident had occurred. The timing is important because on 28 October the details of this notorious incident were recorded in a letter written by John Gresham to John Paston at Norwich.[96] In his correspondence Gresham explains that the details of the murder were 'told to my Lord Chaunceler this fornoon'. This would be consistent with parliamentary procedure, where the chancellor often took the lead in cases brought by private petitioners before the assembly. The point of interest is the close correlation between the contents of the petition and the details of Gresham's letter. Gresham picked out all the salient details set out by John Radford in his petition, *viz*: that Nicholas Radford had been tricked into conversing with Courtenay while his chamber was ransacked by Courtenay's servants; that he had been forced to accompany Courtenay on foot despite protesting his old age and infirmity; and that he had been brutally stabbed to death only a short distance from his house. Gresham's purpose was to provide a summary of the incident for his friend, but in one place – where Courtenay ordered his servant to make a horse ready for Nicholas Radford, only to find that all the spare horses were being used to carry the loot away – the correlation of the two accounts is so close as to suggest that Gresham may have heard, or even read, John Radford's petition at first hand. Gresham's letter therefore provides evidence to show how the wording of a petition could directly influence wider public opinion. His account also suggests an appetite for the sort of graphic, almost tabloidesque, detail that some petitions now contained. If John Radford's purpose was to create a stir within, and beyond, parliament, Gresham's letter is evidence that he succeeded. The use of English to communicate the scandalous details of this scurrilous crime must surely have aided John in this endeavour.

no. 8, p. 332. This petition was amongst a number that were not enrolled on the parliament roll for this assembly.

93 Radford, 'Nicholas Radford', 278.

94 On 13 November 1455 the Commons requested that Richard, duke of York be made Protector in view of the king's incapacity. The recent disturbances in Devon were explicitly mentioned as a reason to appoint a Protector: *PROME*, parliament of 1455, item 31.

95 Storey, *End of House of Lancaster*, p. 170.

96 *The Paston Letters*, ed. J. Gairdner, 6 vols (London, 1904), vol. III, pp. 48–9.

Conclusion

Towards the start of this discussion I noted the tension that exists in the way that the use of the English language has been portrayed in scholarship. On the one hand, there is the view that the written English of the fifteenth century was a readily compatible substitute for French, so that when French was replaced by English this required no serious reflection on the part of the writer about the consequences of their language choice, in terms of either comprehension or administrative process. On the other hand, there is a tradition that sees English as a language that possessed distinctive characteristics, so that its employment must have entailed conscious deliberation by those who chose to use it. Now, at the end of the discussion, it becomes clear that petitions exclusively align English with neither one nor the other of these alternative standpoints: the language could both emulate and conform to the formal stylistic norms of conventional Anglo-Norman petitions, but it could also be used to articulate the authentic, idiosyncratic and individualised voice of the petitioner. The majority of petitions, however, fall into the first of these categories, which is one reason to explain why the shift from French to English was so gradual. The example of John Fox's petition shows that French also had the capacity to be used in a more informal petitionary prose style, but, because English was a universal idiom and also the language of the petitioners themselves, English-language petitions showed a much greater tendency to adopt these idiosyncratic lexical structures. I have identified cases involving disputes or violent crime as especially prone to such trends. The personalised nature of some of these narratives suggests direct input on the part of the petitioner. It is unlikely, however, that the services of professional scribes or attorneys were entirely dispensed with. Just as the advent of English-language pleading signalled no reduction in the demand for the services of legal professionals in the common law courts, so too we should be careful not to assume that the advent of English-language petitions heralded a new era of self-help and accessibility in supplicatory culture.

Adjudication on petitions remained overwhelmingly an oral/aural process, but the expansive, almost encyclopaedic, nature of some English-language petitions suggests that earlier conventions that had determined the way petitions were written and which had placed special emphasis on brevity and precision had given way to a more comprehensive, thorough-going writing style. The impressive range of vocabulary and lexical construction suggests no anxiety on the part of the writers of these petitions about the limitations of written English to communicate meaning to a broad audience.[97] This

[97] See above n. 8; and N. Davis, 'The Language of the Pastons', *Proceedings of the British Academy* (1954), 119–44. Davis showed that the use of English by members of the Paston family could vary considerably without impeding communication. See also K. Heikkonen, 'Regional Variation in Standardization: A Case Study of

underlines the point that the development of a workable (as a distinct from an absolute) written standard was a prerequisite, rather than a consequence, of the emergence of English-language petitions from the 1420s.[98] I have suggested that some petitioners were now using petitions as a form of written testimony. In many of the cases that I have brought to light the rhetorical strength of the narrative lay in their detail and graphic description. Petitions were written in this way not because this necessarily increased the chances of a final, successful conclusion but because, in the fifteenth-century parliament, the petitionary process now frequently involved an intermediate stage of public scrutiny by the Lords and/or Commons before final judgement was rendered by the king and his ministers. I have argued that the involvement of a broader audience in the adjudication of petitions encouraged more creative writing styles. Some examples show an impressive literary aptitude. John Radford's petition is nothing less than a *tour de force* in storytelling, with a narrative replete with drama, dialogue, scandal and outrage. But such cases are rare. This suggests that it was the truth of the allegation or claim which a petitioner brought to parliament, rather than the language used, the detail offered or the rhetoric employed, that still really mattered. Generally speaking, style did not yet count for more than substance. While some petitioners opted to spice up their petitions with polemic, the majority of supplicants were content to let the facts do the talking.

Henry V's Signet Office', in *Sociolinguistics and Language History: Studies Based on the Corpus of Early English Correspondence*, ed. T. Nevalainen and H. Raumolin-Brunberg (Amsterdam, 1996), pp. 111–27.

[98] See *The Beginnings of Standardization: Language and Culture in Fourteenth-Century England*, ed. U. Schaefer (Frankfurt am Main, 2006), esp. 'Introduction' (pp. 3–24) and 'Epilogue' (pp. 183–200). For an important distinction between a 'standardized language', and a 'standard language', see Machan, 'Snakes, Ladders, and Standard Language', pp. 66–8.

2

Petitioners for Royal Pardon in Fourteenth-Century England

Helen Lacey

Over the course of the fourteenth century approximately 38,000 letters patent of pardon were issued from the royal chancery, and numbers were increasing across the period, despite the dramatic fall in population after the Black Death in mid-century.[1] This compares with approximately 800 petitions for (or relating to) pardon that survive in the collections of The National Archives.[2] Thus barely 2 per cent of the pardons known to have been issued can be matched with a surviving written petition for pardon. Of course, it is unlikely that all written petitions have survived, and in some instances it is clear that there never was a written petition; supplicants or their representatives appealed for mercy in person. More usually, individuals who hoped for pardon received one on the recommendation of a trial judge after appearing in court.[3] Indeed, it is important to note that these petitions do not represent the norm. It was more usual for a trial judge to recommend pardon in consideration of clear mitigating factors, and by the fourteenth century recognised procedures had been established for judges to recommend pardon and for the chancellor to grant one as a matter of course (*de cursu*) rather than involve the king directly by petitioning for his mercy (*de gracia*). But, for some people, taking the initiative themselves and petitioning for pardon seemed the most prudent course of action. They might do so if they feared arrest or if they were indignant at a 'malicious accusation' against them and sought to clear their name. If they were in prison awaiting trial or had already been outlawed they might seek a patron to act on their behalf rather than wait and trust in the lengthy and costly legal process. Sometimes they argued that they deserved

[1] H. Lacey, *The Royal Pardon: Access to Mercy in Fourteenth-Century England* (York, 2009), p. 1.

[2] TNA, SC 1 and SC 8 have been surveyed here. This, of course, does not represent an exhaustive search and other fourteenth-century petitions for pardon might well be found in other collections of TNA.

[3] Pardons could arise out of trial proceedings, or by circumventing the king's courts entirely. See Lacey, *Royal Pardon*, part I; T. A. Green, *Verdict According to Conscience: Perspectives on the English Criminal Trial Jury, 1200–1800* (Chicago, IL, 1985).

pardon; on other occasions they admitted guilt, but appealed to the king to show mercy. For those who did decide to have a petition drawn up there were conventions to follow; by the fourteenth century a discrete culture of petitioning for pardon can be discerned.

As far as they can be dated at all, the petitions for pardon are skewed to the first half of the fourteenth century. Approximately three-quarters of them date to before 1350. This mirrors the overall trend for petitions, with the heaviest concentration in the same period.[4] All were written in Anglo-Norman French, as was the convention.[5] By far the majority of petitions for pardon were submitted by men, but there were female petitioners too, acting on their own or alongside male relatives.[6] A few petitioners were foreigners.[7] Some were submitted by interest groups or in the name of the Commons.[8] Overwhelmingly, petitions for pardon concerned debts to the crown or issues concerning land transactions. Thus the petitioners were broadly of middling social status; an involvement in monetary or land transactions largely excluded the lowest social orders. In most cases, the crown ordered further investigation of the claims of the petitioner. This article focuses on the vocabulary and strategies deployed in the drafting of the petition itself.[9] This allows us to examine the way supplicants presented themselves, or at least their stories, in the petitions. Furthermore, it is possible to understand something about the processes that went on behind the scenes, such as the people involved in procuring these petitions, the journeys that were made and the performance sometimes involved in the presentation of the petitions – essentially the 'supplicatory culture'. It is these practical aspects of petitioning that will be examined first.

Procurement of the Petition

The first concern for those individuals who decided to petition for pardon would have been the cost of the documents. Letters patent of pardon usually

[4] See G. Dodd, 'Parliamentary Petitions? The Origins and Provenance of the "Ancient Petitions" (SC 8) in the National Archives', in *Medieval Petitions: Grace and Grievance*, ed. W. M. Ormrod, G. Dodd and A. Musson (York, 2009), pp. 12–46, at p. 12.

[5] See the chapters by G. Dodd and H. Killick in this volume for further discussion of language choices.

[6] For example, see below, pp. 55–60.

[7] For example, SC 1/60/35.

[8] See W. M. Ormrod, 'Murmur, Clamour and Noise: Voicing Complaint and Remedy in Petitions to the English Crown, c. 1300–c. 1460', in *Medieval Petitions*, ed. Ormrod et al., pp. 136–7.

[9] French petitions for pardon are far more voluminous than the English examples discussed here: C. Gauvard, *'De grace especiall': Crime, etat et société en France à la fin du Moyen Age* (Paris, 1991); N. Z. Davis, *Fiction in the Archives: Pardon Tales and their Tellers in Sixteenth-Century France* (Stanford, 1987).

cost 18s 4d, in addition to which supplicants would in all likelihood have needed to pay a professional county lawyer or scribe to draw up the petition for them.[10] The cost alone might have encouraged them to seek the help of a patron. For others, circumstances made the services of an intermediary essential. If they were in custody awaiting trial, or evading arrest, or outlawed, it was imperative to seek the help of someone who could act as an intercessor.[11] Overall, of the extant fourteenth-century petitions for pardon, only a minority (c. 9 per cent) named an intermediary. This is comparable to the overall figure for pardons that mentioned a patron (c. 12 per cent). The petitions include patrons familiar from the overall run of pardons.[12] Queens, military commanders and high-ranking royal officials stand out.[13] In particular, military commanders who were serving overseas are well represented, as the distance from Westminster made a written petition necessary. Of the fourteenth-century queens, Isabella of France is mentioned both as queen and later as queen mother. Queen Anne is also mentioned. Towards the end of the century both Princess Joan and Alice de Holland, countess of Kent, were also both mentioned as patrons.[14] Women, and particularly queens, had

[10] The cost of a pardon could be remitted by the king, usually on grounds of poverty. See H. Killick's chapter in this volume and also G. Dodd, *Justice and Grace: Private Petitioning and the English Parliament in the Late Middle Ages* (Oxford, 2007), p. 306; T. S. Haskett, 'County Lawyers? The Composers of English Chancery Bills', in *The Life of the Law: Proceedings of the Tenth British Legal History Conference, Oxford 1991*, ed. P. Birks (London, 1993), pp. 9–23. See also L. R. Mooney and E. Stubbs, *Scribes and the City: London Guildhall Clerks and the Dissemination of Middle English Literature, 1375–1425* (York, 2013). N. Z. Davis argues that scribes who might also be versed in fictional narratives would recognise a good pardon story: Davis, *Fiction in the Archives*, p. 16.

[11] N. D. Hurnard, *The King's Pardon for Homicide before A.D. 1307* (Oxford, 1969), p. 34, n. 3.

[12] See Lacey, *Royal Pardon*, chap. 3 and Appendix 4.

[13] Queen Anne (2); Queen Isabella (2) and 'Isabella of France, queen mother' (1); Princess Joan (1); A[lice] de H[olland], countess of Kent, lady Wake (1); Henry of Grosmont, duke of Lancaster (5); Walter de Bentley, lieutenant of Brittany (8); William de Montague, earl of Salisbury (1); John de Wingfield (1); Robert de Ufford, earl of Suffolk (1); Ralph de Stafford, baron Stafford (3); earls of Northampton, Warwick, Suffolk and Huntingdon (1); Walter Langton, treasurer (1); Wulstan Bransford, bishop of Worcester; chancellor (1); Michael de la Pole, earl of Suffolk, chancellor (1); Hugh le Despenser, earl of Winchester (1); Hugh de Hastings (1); Edward [Balliol], king of Scotland (1); Robert Morley, marshal of Ireland, admiral of the northern fleet (22); William de Bohun, earl of Northampton (6), John de Hastings, lord of Abergavenny (1); Michael de Poynings (4); Edward, prince of Aquitaine and Wales (3); Laurence de Hastings, earl of Pembroke (1); William Latimer (1); Thomas, earl of Lancaster (3); Henry de Lacy, earl of Lincoln (2); Roger Damory (1); Robert de Tawton, archdeacon of Durham, keeper of the privy seal (1); Richard fitz Alan, earl of Arundel (1); John de Beauchamp (1); Thomas de Drayton (1).

[14] Joan of Kent also attempted to promote reconciliation between the king and his uncle John of Gaunt and pleaded with Richard to show mercy to her second son,

an important role as intercessors for pardon. Recent scholarship has done much to elucidate this area; John Carmi Parsons, for example, discussed the evocation of Marian intercession and its association with earthly queenship in thirteenth-century texts. Importantly, Joanna Laynesmith has argued that this role was fading in importance by the fifteenth century. However, queens continued to emphasise the human qualities of kings, particularly by providing a voice of mercy and domesticity.[15]

Among the military commanders, Robert Morley, marshal of Ireland and admiral of the northern fleet, features prominently. In July and August 1342 he was named as patron in twenty-one petitions requesting pardon for men serving as mariners and one who provided a ship for the fleet.[16] These were part of preparations for the earl of Northampton's expedition to Brittany in August 1342.[17] Another patron was Edward Balliol, significantly styled 'king of Scotland'. He wrote to the chancellor, Robert Stratford, on 1 July 1337, requesting the proclamation of a pardon granted to his 'valet'.[18] The previous year Balliol had been useful to Edward III, advising him on tactics in his campaign against David II's Scottish army. However, by 1337 Edward III's attention was increasingly being taken up with France and Balliol had started to be side-lined, eventually resigning his claim to the crown and kingdom of Scotland in 1356.[19] Here, though, in 1337, his ability to ask grace of Edward III attests to their close working relationship. The role of these influential patrons in the pardoning process was somewhat controversial and various attempts were made at least to regularise the procedure, but their influence continued to be felt throughout the century.[20]

On rare occasions, petitions for pardon were actually addressed to someone other than the king. Whether the intention was for the recipient then to intercede with the king or whether the petitioner thought that the person they

John Holland, earl of Huntingdon, who had murdered Ralph Stafford. It was Richard's recalcitrance in the face of her entreaty which, according to Walsingham, hastened her demise. No written petitions I have found mention Eleanor of Castile, Margaret of France, Philippa of Hainault or Isabella of Valois, but from the evidence of the pardons themselves it is clear that they were all prolific patrons.

15 J. C. Parsons, 'The Queen's Intercession in Thirteenth-Century England', in *The Power of the Weak: Studies on Medieval Women*, ed. J. Carpenter and S.-B. MacLean (Urbana, IL, 1995), pp. 147–77.

16 SC 1/41/66; SC 1/39/81; SC 1/40/16; SC 1/40/17; SC 1/40/18; SC 1/40/11B; SC 1/40/11A; SC 1/40/13; SC 1/40/11; SC 1/40/12; SC 1/40/14; SC 1/40/11C; SC 1/38/35; SC 1/40/15; SC 1/40/13A; SC 1/40/15A; SC 1/39/157; SC 1/40/20; SC 1/40/13B; SC 1/60/84; SC 1/40/14A; SC 1/40/19.

17 See below, pp. 52–3.

18 SC 1/45/230.

19 B. Webster, 'Balliol, Edward (b. in or after 1281, d. 1364)', in *Oxford Dictionary of National Biography*; online edn, January 2008 <http://www.oxforddnb.com/view/article/1206> [accessed 26 September 2017].

20 See Lacey, *Royal Pardon*, chap. 4.

addressed could grant pardon in their own right is unclear. In these cases recipients were queens or chancellors, or, in one instance, Piers Gaveston, Edward II's notorious favourite.[21] The latter petition, dating from the summer of 1310, was also unusual because the supplicant was requesting pardon after surviving attempted execution by hanging.[22] In routine cases, chancellors could issue pardons without consulting the king, so petitioners were right to think that addressing a petition directly to the chancellor might meet with success. However, queens or favourites such as Gaveston could not authorise pardons; their power lay in their role as intercessors with the monarch.

Prominent patrons were not the only ones to act as intermediaries in the pardoning process. On occasion, acquaintances of a supplicant might be willing to stand surety as a 'mainpernor', to guarantee their future good conduct.[23] They were liable to be fined themselves if the pardoned individual subsequently reoffended. A more clandestine role in securing pardons might be played by those willing to provide forged documents, at the right price.[24] Indeed, in one such case from 1305, a person accused of acquiring a forged royal pardon came before the court of king's bench and, during the trial, incidental details of the procedures for obtaining pardon were laid out. The defendants demonstrated their knowledge of the petitioning process, the importance of procuring charters and writs and the journeys that might be involved. At the centre of the case was a man called William of Truro, who had been arrested and kept in York prison because he was accused of procuring a 'certain false charter of pardon' for homicide in the name of another man. William's version of events was that the charter had been handed to him by the man named in the pardon, one Thomas Trewyder of Fowey, and by John Pervet of Lostwithiel. They had asked him to carry it to the king's chancery on their behalf and, once there, obtain a writ of pardon. Here, William distinguishes between the 'carte' of pardon and the 'breve' of pardon, the former being a document with the great seal attached, the latter being the royal order to issue the pardon, which would have been written out in chancery, recorded

[21] SC 1/42/110; SC 1/39/66; SC 1/36/193; SC 1/28/51; SC 1/30/43. There are a few other instances of pardons issued because the condemned person survived hanging: see Lacey, *Royal Pardon*, p. 69.

[22] SC 1/30/43. Petitioners also corresponded with the keeper of the privy seal: in 1304 Edward, prince of Wales, requested a writ to the keeper of the privy seal to issue a warrant for a pardon. In 1348 Ralph le Cause wrote to William de Bohun, earl of Northampton, requesting his seal to the bill for a pardon to be sent to the keeper of the privy seal: SC 1/63/81; SC 1/42/9.

[23] The concept appeared in vernacular literature such as Piers Plowman, where mainprise is offered during the Trial of Wrong, and in Chaucer's *Tale of Melibee*, where the criminals take friends with them to court to stand as guarantors. In 1336 a statute stipulated that any person who had been pardoned should find sureties or their charters would be void. See Lacey, *Royal Pardon*, p. 77 and below p. 53.

[24] See below, p. 46.

on the patent rolls and then sent to the local sheriff to proclaim.[25] The intention was for William to return to Cornwall with the (forged) charter *and* the writ (the latter probably a much smaller document with only a tiny dab of wax, possibly even the foot of the seal attached) and present them to the sheriff.[26] This part of William's story suggests that it was not unheard of for intermediaries to be involved in the process of procuring a pardon, sometimes by undertaking journeys to the chancery on behalf of the supplicant.

William's version of events was endorsed by John Pervet when he handed himself in. In court, John was shown the offending charter and, after examining it, he claimed that it was the pardon of his uncle, Thomas Trewyder. Thomas had told John that he had obtained the lord king's peace and asked John to present the charter in the county court (thus demonstrating his awareness of the procedures for 'proclaiming' pardons). John claimed that he had duly taken the pardon to the county court, but had been told by the sheriff that he would not validate it without the king's writ. It was at this point, John claimed, that he and his uncle sought out William, because they knew he was about to set out for London on his own business, and handed him the charter so that he could obtain a writ for them. John's testimony therefore supported William's claim that he was merely an innocent go-between and William was duly freed. John then went on to implicate another man, Stephen, goldsmith of Winchelsea. Stephen, he said, was present when the charter of pardon was made, and had even lent Thomas 18s for the purpose. Stephen was duly summoned, but testified that he had never seen the charter before and had nothing to do with the case. He claimed that he was merely a business associate of Thomas; they were partners in a certain ship. He had, he acknowledged, lent Thomas the money in order to accomplish certain business in the same ship, but not for the purpose of suing out a charter. Stephen surrendered for trial and was found innocent. Finally, in 1309 John was tried and released after the jurors found him innocent. Thomas, the subject of the petition, had subsequently been outlawed. The mention of lending money to purchase a pardon and the possible involvement of several intermediaries in order to travel to London, obtain the writ and get the pardon proclaimed by the sheriff in the county court are all laid out in this case.[27]

[25] In another case from c. 1326, Thomas le Whyte stated that his wife, Eve la Bruth, had been imprisoned in Salisbury for trespass, despite having a pardon 'with a writ to the Sheriff of Wiltshire to proclaim the King's peace': SC 8/297/14810.

[26] Many thanks to Paul Dryburgh, Principal Records Specialist (Medieval Records) at The National Archives, for his expert advice on this point.

[27] Difficulties in the journey to collect a pardon were not uncommon. If the supplicant had to travel from abroad, rough seas might delay their progress. In c. 1300 Hemelin le Bel petitioned that he was imprisoned in Guernsey castle by the bailiff because of a false accusation of theft. He was released but he could not make it to the assize in time because of rough seas and was sent back to prison. The bailiff forced him to abjure until he received the king's command. Bel requested that he might have a pardon 'in

This was not an isolated case of forgery; for supplicants who were desperate enough, 'false pardons' could be purchased from forgers who were able to replicate the king's seal. In 1301 a man called Richard de Haumon was found to have purchased a false pardon for robbery. Richard had then managed to secure an authentic pardon for both offences (robbery and obtaining forged letters) by serving with the army in Scotland.[28] In a high-profile case from 1307, William Ferrers accused Walter Langton of producing a forged letter of pardon for champerty, 'concocted without the king's knowledge'.[29] In 1345 Edward III's government took the step of appointing three commissioners to arrest men who 'stay in secret places in divers parts of the realm with counterfeits of the king's great and little seals and daily seal with the counterfeit great seal letters patent of pardon of felonies'.[30] Most supplicants, however, avoided such illicit routes. For them, the next step, after paying for the drafting of a petition and/or enlisting a patron to act on their behalf, was to decide on the wording of the petition itself.

Persuasion

The drafting of a petition was a collaborative process. Few supplicants would have actually authored the petitions themselves, so the extent to which decisions over language and style of expression were taken by the scribe (probably often a county lawyer) is an important if unanswerable question. Certainly many petitions for pardon exemplify knowledge of precise legal terms: 'with force and arms' was commonly used to ensure the case was categorised as trespass, even if the 'force' was a fiction. Overall, these petitions tended to be short and to the point. Unlike their French counterparts, they did not usually weave intricate 'pardon tales' from which historians such as Natalie Zemon Davis have gleaned so much. However, we can still learn from the techniques that Davis employed to examine the crafting of the narrative in petitions for pardon. Davis explained that she wanted to examine variations in these stories according to teller and listener and to see how they interacted with contemporary habits of explanation, description and evaluation. Davis also wanted to contextualise these stories in terms of the existing 'structures' in the minds and lives of the sixteenth-century participants: 'possible story

principali' because of the banishment and this was granted: SC 8/201/10009; see also P. Brand, 'The Travails of Travel: The Difficulties of Getting to Court in Later Medieval England', in *Freedom of Movement in the Middle Ages: Proceedings of the 2003 Harlaxton Symposium*, ed. P. Horden (Donington, 2006), pp. 215–28.

28 *CPR, 1292–1301*, pp. 615, 618; *CPR, 1301–1307*, p. 40; *Calendar of Chancery Warrants preserved in the Public Record Office* (London, 1927), p. 142; Hurnard, *The King's Pardon for Homicide*, p. 304.

29 M. Prestwich, *Edward I* (London, 1988), p. 550.

30 *CPR, 1343–1345*, p. 589. See Lacey, *Royal Pardon*, p. 52.

lines determined by the constraints of the law and approaches to narrative learned in past listening to and telling of stories or derived from other cultural constructions'.[31] These petitions had to tell stories that would be plausible enough to elicit a sympathetic reaction. After all, as Davis put it, 'seeking mercy rather than justice had its risks'.[32] Asking for pardon often meant admitting to some transgression – taking part in a homicide, for instance – rather than simply denying all knowledge. This could put the supplicant in jeopardy if the plea for mercy was dismissed. The authors of these petitions, then, needed to convince the crown of the extenuating circumstances surrounding their case, or of their sincere contrition, in order to receive mercy.

One rare English petition that does compare with Davis's 'pardon tales' in its carefully woven narrative is that of Geoffrey de Worsley, written sometime in the early 1380s.[33] It was actually a common petition, in which the 'Commons of England' expressed support for Worsley's predicament. The Commons would have endorsed this petition in order to persuade the 'triers' of the petitions to single it out for discussion in parliament, rather than set it aside to be heard by a select group of lords. However, no discussion of this case can be seen in parliament rolls. The petitioners sought pardon for Worsley 'in certain important matters':

> they state that he was long established in the estate of esquire and of knight to the king's father, from whom he took his knighthood at the battle of Spain [Najera], and to the king's grandfather and to the king in his wars, in which he was taken and not ransomed nor released before this hour, suffering great harm, and is in debt and has no movables. Lately Geoffrey and one of the daughters and heirs of Thomas de Felton were married for his advancement, and for years the marriage continued for the great trust he had in his servant Thomas Pulle, in times that he went overseas in the king's service, assigning to Thomas attendance upon his wife for safety while he was absent. Pulle has been false and traitorous to his master and dishonoured his wife in his absence, and roused the wife to falsely make a divorce, by which falseness and treason Geoffrey has lost advancement, marriage and a great heritage, as is openly known since their meeting at Reading at the last council in the dispute that erupted between them in which Thomas was wounded, of which injury he was healed (as it seemed to many), and subsequently espoused the said wife, [but] now Thomas is dead and his friends wish to impeach Geoffrey that he died from the said injury.[34]

31 Davis, *Fiction in the Archives*, p. 4.

32 Davis, *Fiction in the Archives*, p. 11.

33 SC 8/103/5109. For Worsley's military career and reversal of fortunes, see R. C. Ambühl, 'The English Reversal of Fortunes in the 1370s and the Experience of Prisoners of War', in *The Soldier Experience in the Fourteenth Century*, ed. A. Bell and A. Curry with A. Chapman, A. King and D. Simpson (Woodbridge, 2011), pp. 193–5.

34 Quotation from TNA catalogue SC 8/103/5109. Printed in full in *Early Common*

The first concern of the petitioners was to establish Worsley's reputation. His long-established social status and military prowess were seemingly crucial to persuading their audience that he deserved pardon. He was not just a knight but a knight to the king's father and grandfather. He was not just knighted but knighted on the battlefield at a specific battle, the 'battle of Spain' [Najera, 3 April 1367]. The specificity of this point helps to persuade the audience of the veracity of the account, although it might have been a detail included to give the 'illusion of actuality'.[35] However, this is a story of an honourable knight fallen on hard times. His long suffering as prisoner of the king's enemies is explicitly related to his debt and lack of possessions. The petition then moves on to his marriage to 'one of the daughters and heirs of Thomas de Felton' (the woman herself not identified by name). The fact that the marriage was explicitly 'for his advancement' does not seem to be regarded as shameful. Worsley's servant, Thomas Pulle, then enters the narrative. The marriage continued 'because of the great trust' he had in his servant to protect his wife while he was overseas. However, in contravention of this trust, Pulle was 'false and traitorous to his master' (emphasising the particularly shocking transgression of the deference owed to his superior). Pulle 'dishonoured' Worsley's wife in his absence, with the implication that honour was a particularly precious status in women. Pulle 'roused [her] to falsely make a divorce', an act that was not only false but even treasonous. Worsley's wife is here the passive instrument of Pulle's manipulation. Thus Pulle was responsible for Worsley's 'lost advancement, marriage and a great heritage'. This echoed the well-known tropes of the treacherous servant and the cuckolded husband.[36] Moreover, this was a case that turned on reputation: 'as is openly known'; 'known by many'; 'as it seemed to many'. Worsley had been dishonoured before his peers. All of this contextual information justified Worsley's actions when he encountered Pulle at the last great council at Reading: a dispute had erupted and in the heat of the moment Pulle had been wounded. Finally, the crux of the petition; Worsley deserves pardon because Pulle did not die of the wound Worsley inflicted. Pulle's friends were trying to claim that Worsley, the distinguished war veteran, the wronged husband and master, had inflicted a wound that proved fatal. Thus the time that had elapsed between the wound Worsley admitted he inflicted and Pulle's death was crucial to his defence. Indeed, concepts of time are carefully expressed in the petition; key events

Petitions in the English Parliament, c. 1290–c. 1420, ed. W. M. Ormrod, H. Killick and P. Bradford (Cambridge, 2017), p. 184.

35 D. Pearsall argues that details such as these provided 'authentic touches', the air of something witnessed, not invented, although on the other hand it might have been a detail included to give the 'illusion of actuality': D. A. Pearsall, 'Interpretative Models for the Peasants' Revolt', in *Hermeneutics and Medieval Culture*, ed. P. J. Gallacher and H. Damico (New York, 1989), p. 67.

36 Davis, *Fiction in the Archives*, pp. 95–6.

such as battles are used as memorable dates and Worsley's reputation is established over a long period.[37]

Worsley's wife, not mentioned by name in the petition, was not accorded agency of her own. Unusually, however, it is possible to compare Worsley's supplication for pardon with his wife's account of events. Mary Felton married Worsley in 1376 in Leamington Priors, Warwick, and, as Worsley freely admitted in his petition, the marriage offered him social advancement, as Mary was one of three sisters who would inherit part of their father's (Thomas Felton's) substantial estate. However, according to Mary, on the death of her father in 1381 it was her husband who sought an annulment of their marriage in the ecclesiastical courts in Chester.[38] She claimed that she was divorced 'upon a fained ground' and was then forced by her husband 'through fear' into a convent.[39] Apparently, Worsley sought annulment on grounds of bigamy; Mary, he claimed, had gone through a marriage ceremony with another man, Sir Thomas Breton, in the chapel of her father's house in Candlewick Street in London. Breton had died in 1380 in Aquitaine and thus was still alive when Mary had married Worsley. Worsley won the case and Mary became a recluse in the Abbey of St Clare without Aldgate.[40] He soon remarried, to an heiress called Isabel de Lathom, and they had a daughter, Elizabeth. We only know that Mary Felton disputed Worsley's version of events because of what she did after his death. Between the annulment in 1381 and Geoffrey's death in 1385, Mary had remained a minoress in the Abbey of St Clare.[41] However, when Geoffrey died in March 1385, Mary absconded

37 Medieval methods of recollecting the timing of events are discussed in P. J. P. Goldberg, 'Gender and Matrimonial Litigation in the Church Courts in the Later Middle Ages: The Evidence of the Court of York', *Gender & History* 19 (2007), 43–59.

38 'Townships: Worsley', in *A History of the County of Lancaster: Volume 4*, ed. W. Farrer and J. Brownbill (London, 1911), pp. 376–92, n. 26, <http://www.british-history.ac.uk/vch/lancs/vol4/pp376-392> [accessed 19 September 2017]. This cites the source for the divorce as Ellesmere Deed no. 268. Most of the Ellesmere collection was sold to the Huntingdon Library after the publication of the Victoria County History volume. This deed cannot now be identified.

39 TNA, E 135/6/74 (n. 45).

40 Elizabeth Makowski demonstrates that the archdeacons of Chester would have heard the case. Unfortunately, the records have not survived. See E. Makowski, 'The Curious Case of Mary Felton', in *Monumenta Iuris Canonici, Series C: Subsidia, Biblioteca Apostolica Vaticana* (Vatican City, 2016), p. 736. Many thanks to Elizabeth for sharing her research with me. See also: S. M. Butler, *Divorce in Medieval England: From One to Two Persons in Law* (New York, 2013), pp. 76–8; W. G. Davis, *The Ancestry of Mary Isaac, c. 1549–1613, Wife of Thomas Appleton of little Waldingfield, co. Suffolk, and Mother of Samuel Appleton of Ipswich* (Portland, ME, 1955), p. 315.

41 Her mother, Joan, was busy as executrix and there are several references to Joan's dealings in the close and patent rolls. In these documents Mary was referred to as a minoress: Makowski, 'Mary Felton', pp. 737–8; *Manuscripts of Rye and Hereford Corporations, Royal Commission on Historical Manuscripts Thirteenth report, part 4*, ed. W. Page and W. J. Hardy (London, 1892), p. 424.

from the abbey. On 16 November 1385 a royal order was issued to John de Morewell, the king's serjeant-at-arms, to arrest Mary, 'an apostate vagabond sister', and deliver her to the abbess of the Sisters Minoresses for punishment.[42] Mary responded with a plea of non-profession. Elizabeth Makowski notes that this was an extremely unusual course of action for a woman to pursue.[43] Evidence that Mary Felton made such a plea comes from a writ sent from the crown to the bishop of London, Robert Braybrooke, requiring him to decide on the veracity of Mary's claim.[44] Braybrooke was to send his decision to the chief justice of the court of common pleas, Robert Bealknap, as Mary had a lawsuit pending in that court. In that suit, Mary contended that one John Sturmy had unjustly deprived her of profits from the manor of Kirby Bedon (Kirbybiden), Norfolk. Sturmy countered by claiming Mary had been a professed nun and thus ineligible to claim the profits. According to Mary, however, she had never been a professed nun because she had entered the convent under duress.[45] Braybrooke appointed a commission to look into the case.[46]

Alongside her new husband, John Curson, Mary continued to pursue her case for inheritance through the court of common pleas.[47] As her case dragged on it drew in other squabbling relatives. Robert Worsley, Geoffrey's relative and guardian to his daughter Elizabeth, petitioned parliament to complain that Mary was trying to disinherit Elizabeth (Robert planned a marriage between his son and Elizabeth).[48] In this petition there is also a reference to Mary's actions after she fled from the convent. Mary, it states, had petitioned the pope, who then issued a commission of enquiry in five different counties.[49] Makowski identified the episcopal findings in the case, along

[42] *CPR, 1385–1389*, p. 86.

[43] Makowski, 'Mary Felton', p. 738.

[44] Dated 8 November 1386: *Registers of the Bishops of London, 1304–1660* (Brighton, 1984), reel 2, 408.

[45] SC 8/146/7276; Makowski, 'Mary Felton', p. 740, n. 46.

[46] Makowski identified the commission Braybrooke appointed on 5 December 1386: John Appleby, Doctor of Laws and William Sondeye, licentiate in the laws and 'our commissary general'; Makowski, 'Mary Felton', p. 740. The records of the London commissary court for the fourteenth century are no longer extant.

[47] E 135/6/74 image 2.

[48] SC 8/146/7276. See biographical entries for Robert Worsley and John Curson in *The History of Parliament Online*, <http://www.historyofparliamentonline.org/volume/1386–1421/member/worsley-robert-1402>; <http://www.historyofparliamentonline.org/volume/1386–1421/member/curson-sir-john-1415> [accessed 4 January 2018].

[49] The seventeenth-century antiquarian Peter Leycester stated that: 'After the death of Sir Geoffrey Worseley, Mary came out, and proved she entered for fear, and that she was divorced upon a fained ground, and proved Elizabeth to be illegitimate: and the pope confirms her return to secularity'; G. Ormerod, *The History of the County Palatine and City of Chester*, ed. T. Helsby, 2nd edn (London, 1882), vol. I, p. 345. See

with the original royal writs, which were finally issued in 1392. Braybrooke certified that Mary 'was a secular and had never been otherwise'.[50] Thus this case gives an unusual insight into the complex matrix of relations that lay behind one petition for pardon. Worsley's petition for pardon for the wounding of one of his servants had a hidden context that emerged after his death when his wife sought redress through the courts. While the narrative written on his behalf gave one version of the reasons for divorce, Mary Felton begged to differ.

In more prosaic petitions than that of Geoffrey Worsley, the case for pardon simply stated self-defence or misadventure as the justification. Alternatively, the petitioner might admit to the offence, but beg the monarch for pardon on grounds of charity or in return for military service.[51] In 1385 one petitioner, John de Felsted, an usher in the exchequer, sought pardon for killing in self-defence. He was detained in the Fleet prison but managed to secure the aid of Adam Ramsey, esquire, in petitioning for pardon. Felsted claimed that he had been instructed to guard the door of the exchequer against 'a certain chaplain' who had gone mad and was wandering around Westminster Hall. The affair escalated when the chaplain reacted to being denied entry by beating Felsted severely with his staff and Felsted defended himself by striking the chaplain with his dagger. The chief baron of the exchequer responded to the incident by removing Felsted from office and imprisoning him in the Fleet. Felsted's petition asked the king 'through Adam Ramsey' to pardon him the contempt and to 'grant him his letters, mentioning this pardon, to the chief baron and his companions, that he might have his office back as before'. The king granted the request.[52] In another self-defence case from 1302, Benedicta Choffyn of Guernsey requested pardon for the death of Owar, her husband, whom she killed with a knife when he was beating her. She then fled to Normandy. The response in this case demonstrated an ambivalence towards domestic violence: initially the response was that '[i]t is unworthy to grant grace in this case', but the king agreed that the bailiff

also J. S. Roskell, *The Knights of the Shire for the County Palatine of Lancaster, 1377–1460* (Manchester, 1937), p. 75.

50 E 135/6/74 (n. 45); Makowski, 'Mary Felton', p. 741.

51 In response to a petition in the parliament of 1309, complaining about the ease with which pardons were obtained, it was stated that 'the king wills that henceforth no pardon for felony should be granted, except in the cases where it used of old to be granted, that is to say, if a man kills another by misadventure, in self-defence, or in madness, and this is found by the record of the justices': SC 8/294/14698. See Lacey, *Royal Pardon*, pp. 22–4.

52 SC 8/255/12746; *CPR, 1385–1389*, p. 12. In one case from 1335, a woman petitioned for pardon on behalf of her husband, whom she claimed had killed in self-defence: SC 8/99/4922. See also: SC 8/226/11293, *CPR, 1350–1354*, p. 249; SC 8/253/12605, *CPR, 1385–1389*, p. 516; SC 8/249/12437, *CPR, 1396–1399*, p. 427; SC 8/255/12746, *CPR, 1385–1389*, p. 12; SC 8/90/4500, SC 1/40/106; SC 8/55/2742; *CPR, 1317–1321*, p. 508.

should 'certify him of the matter' at the next parliament. A pardon was in fact issued to the petitioner for the death of her husband and her abjuration on 26 October 1302.[53] Death by misadventure, or 'mischance', was also given as a reason for seeking pardon. On one occasion, John de Shropshire of Ireland requested that he be granted a charter of pardon for the death of Simon Utlauch in the vill of Boey, 'which was by mischance, since he has served in the king's wars in Scotland'. Pardon was granted under the king's Irish seal.[54]

Sometimes petitioners sought pardon on grounds of charity, if they were poor and destitute with children to provide for. In one such example from 1302, Alice de la Chapele sought pardon for taking 'thirty-five sheaves of all kinds of grain of the king's share which sheaves were almost of no value'. She was a native of Guernsey but had been made to abjure the islands for the theft. She asked 'by way of charity and mercy that grace be given her in the matter of this abjuration because she took them because of poverty and to feed her child'.[55] The king replied to the keeper of the Channel Islands, Otto de Grandison, with instructions to inform him of the circumstances of the case without delay. In another petition for pardon, the supplicant, John de Barton, claimed that he had been 'totally ruined' and had 'nothing for him or his wife and children to live on'. His neighbours, he said, had indicted him of homicide, arson and theft and he had been outlawed. The petition was presented during the period when the young Edward III had just acceded to the throne, and the response to the petition seems to have come from those surrounding the king rather than from Edward himself: 'Concerning the pardon of the felonies the king ought not to do this, but concerning the outlawry, let this petition be delivered to [Richard de] Bury that he show the king, and say his will so that if the outlawry be pardoned, that he surrender and stand to the law.'[56]

Several petitioners reminded the king of their military service to the crown. Although pardons on grounds of military service and for no other

[53] SC 8/278/13872; *CPR, 1301–1307*, p. 69. Defence of another person was also claimed, for instance in 1354 Richard Gunny of Frismarsh, a valet, requested pardon for the death of John Constable. Gunny had been indicted for the death, but claimed that it had happened following an argument when Constable pursued him to kill him. Gunny's servant, Richard Pynder, saw that his master could not escape alive and shot at Constable with an arrow that killed him. Gunny had witnesses affix their seals to attest that the death was not his desire: SC 8/227/11341, *CPR, 1354–1358*, p. 76.

[54] SC 8/74/3682; SC 8/329/E922; *CPR, 1292–1301*, p. 497.

[55] *PROME*, Original Documents: Edward I Parliaments, Petition 2, item 1.

[56] SC 8/268/13388. Mercy was also extended to pregnant women. See Lacey, *Royal Pardon*, p. 69. In one unusual case Christine, widow of Thomas Scot, potter of London, petitioned Isabella of France, queen mother, for a pardon for her husband's murderer: SC 1/42/110.

reason were always a fairly small percentage of the total number of pardons granted, they were perceived to be an abuse of the royal prerogative of mercy.[57] Despite this, military service continued to be cited as a factor in petitions for pardon throughout the fourteenth century.[58] John Gernoun of Walsworth petitioned in 1336 because he had received a pardon of various felonies 'for his service to the king in the Scottish wars'. However, he heard news of a statute that required all recipients of pardon to come before the sheriff and coroners with the names of sureties to their future good conduct. John was concerned because during the time the statute was made public he was in Scotland on the king's service. The response was that his case should be brought to the attention of Gernoun's commander, Edward de Kendale. Meanwhile Gernoun was excused his surety until the following Whitsun, and he was allowed to submit the names of his guarantors into chancery without their seals.[59] While 'military pardons' were never eradicated, some attempt was made to verify that those who received pardons conditional on military service actually turned up to fight. On 14 January 1343 Peter Gretheved, the chancellor and chamberlain of the king in Scotland, wrote to Robert Parving, chancellor, to certify that men given conditional pardons had arrived to do their service.[60] False claims to have served the king in his wars also came to light. On one occasion in 1334, a group of supplicants requested the annulment of a pardon on such grounds. The petitioners were tenants of Queen Philippa in High Peak and they complained that Roger de Wendesley had escaped prison and gathered together a band of robbers who committed robberies and ambushes in the region 'among others, on the day of the king's victory at Berwick [Halidon Hill], he tied Randolph de Lokwode up, naked, until he made fine with him in 80 marks'. Wendesley then purchased a general pardon at York, 'contrary to the ordinance that such pardons are only to be available to those who were in the king's company in his wars – which he never was'. The response was to allow them writs of oyer and terminer

[57] See Lacey, *Royal Pardon*, pp. 100–6.

[58] SC 8/333/E1026; SC 8/305/15227; SC 8/103/5109; SC 8/254/12679; SC 8/228/11378; SC 8/297/14830A; SC 8/106/5283; SC 8/346/E1382; SC 8/74/3682; SC 8/144/7189; SC 8/48/2379; SC 8/245/12248; SC 8/281/14009; SC 8/181/9042; SC 8/181/9043; SC 8/182/9089; SC 8/188/9379; SC 8/185/9212; SC 8/190/9477; SC 8/185/9213; SC 8/310/15497; SC 8/260/12997; SC 1/28/134; SC 1/40/179; SC 1/39/17; SC 1/39/147; SC 1/50/1; SC 1/39/146; SC 1/39/144; SC 1/39/145; SC 1/40/7; SC 1/42/34; SC 1/40/146; SC 1/40/108; SC 1/39/148; SC 1/41/43; SC 1/42/195. Also see n. 16 above.

[59] SC 8/48/2379; *Rotuli Scotiae in turri Londonensi et in domo capitulari Westmonasteriensi asservati*, ed. D. Macpherson et al., 2 vols (London, 1814–19), vol. II, pp. 421–3. See n. 23 above.

[60] SC 1/39/154.

to bring their accusations before the justices.[61] Petitioners living in Ireland or on the borders with Scotland and Wales sometimes claimed the losses inflicted as a result of fighting as grounds for pardon of debts owed to the crown.[62] So too did inhabitants of English-held regions on the continent. On such occasions the crown's willingness to receive petitions for pardon from its overseas subjects was of course a political act. In two cases petitioners asked pardon for having been in the obedience of Edward III's enemy, the king of France. They subsequently returned to their 'true obedience' and asked Edward's pardon for having offended him.[63]

These petitions also highlight the fact that the supplicants could be groups representing a whole community, not simply individuals. Merchants such as the 'weavers of the city of York' or the 'merchants of the Bardi', the 'Liege merchants' or the 'burgesses of Scarborough' might present a petition to lobby the crown about their business interests.[64] Religious institutions such as the 'clergy of Carlisle diocese', the 'prior and convent' or simply the 'religious of England' might put forward a petition for pardon, usually concerning land transactions or debts.[65] The clergy might also be grouped with the secular, in petitions such as that from 'The clergy and poor people of Cheshire'.[66] Family members might petition for pardon on behalf of one of their own: 'All the kin of Tewdwr ap Grono Vethan', for instance.[67] The 'Chancellor and Scholars' of Cambridge and Oxford universities both petitioned for pardon – for malicious accusations of the townspeople and for exemption from the poll tax, respectively.[68] So too did the citizens of Dublin

[61] SC 8/51/2516.

[62] SC 8/32/1566; SC 8/7/317; SC 8/215/10749; SC 8/106/5283; SC 8/238/11857; SC 8/32/1565; SC 8/84/4170.

[63] SC 8/215/10742; SC 8/216/10752; SC 8/266/13283. Even within England inhabitants of the palatinates were not straightforwardly under the jurisdiction of the king in matters of grace. In one instance, the 'people of the liberty of Durham and Norhamshire' petitioned the king and council requesting a copy of the pardon granted to the people of Northumberland for debts owed to the crown, 'as the liberties are within the county'. However, the council did not feel competent to pass judgment on the matter 'because this grace was made to the people of that county, the council does not dare to extend it to the people of the bishop [of Durham] without advising the king'. The king did subsequently pardon them, but was careful to make the grant separate from that given to Northumberland: SC 8/44/2169; *CPR, 1330–1334*, p. 528. See also SC 8/105/5230.

[64] SC 8/108/5371; SC 8/193/9643; SC 8/79/3928; SC 8/139/6949; SC 8/34/1652.

[65] SC 8/34/1683; SC 8/54/2698; SC 8/264/13192; SC 8/52/2588; SC 8/20/994; SC 8/233/11621; SC 8/131/6522; SC 8/94/4698; SC 8/71/3530; SC 8/186/9287; SC 8/239/11914; SC 8/278/13889; SC 8/225/11245; SC 8/184/9164; SC 8/150/7483; SC 8/54/2687; SC 8/45/2226.

[66] SC 8/311/15505.

[67] SC 8/238/11855.

[68] SC 8/183/9101; SC 8/132/6575.

and of York.[69] Many petitions were put forward in the name of the 'People of' and given place.[70] Alternatively they might be styled the 'Community of the realm' or the 'Commons of England', to emphasise their political status in a parliamentary setting.[71] Citizens of towns and cities or manorial tenants such as the 'Poor tenants of the demesne lands of Newcastle Lyons' might also petition.[72] These were strategic decisions, of course, designed to emphasise the collective will behind a petition or to evoke the solidarity of the political community.

Only a small minority of petitions for pardon came from women. Seventeen of the petitions related to land transactions or debts owed to the crown, concentrated in the late 1320s and early 1330s, a period when the dominance of the Despenser family at court had come to an end and the extent of their illegal and heavy-handed land dealings began to unravel. The lands and debts referred to in these petitions suggest that the women were of relatively high social standing. One of the petitions, dating from the early years of Richard II's reign, was made by William and Alice Windsor.[73] Alice was more commonly known as Alice Perrers, the former mistress of Edward III. The petition requested pardon for William and protection against 'all other things which could harm him through Alice'. It also notes that judgement had been made against Alice as a single woman, but that she was in fact William's wife at that time, thus alluding to the clandestine marriage that took place sometime between 1373 and 1376. Overall, women were proportionally much more successful in securing pardon. Only one woman, petitioning on behalf of her husband, who stood accused of murder, was denied a pardon outright.[74] However, this success rate probably reflects the nature of the offences in question, rather than a gender bias *per se*.

69 SC 8/106/5283; SC 8/206/10258.

70 SC 8/95/4725; SC 8/32/1563; SC 8/32/1566; SC 8/32/1565; SC 8/54/2685; SC 8/54/2686; SC 8/215/10732; SC 8/123/6116; SC 8/65/3218; SC 8/165/8209; SC 8/129/6436; SC 8/63/3133; SC 8/11/506; SC 8/141/7046; SC 8/99/4927; SC 8/337/15941; SC 8/242/12057; SC 8/171/8520; SC 8/64/3199; SC 8/41/2036; SC 8/82/4086; SC 8/12/594; SC 8/341/16076; SC 8/78/3856; SC 1/54/130.

71 SC 8/294/14698; SC 8/108/5398; SC 8/103/5109; SC 8/124/6157; SC 8/342/16132; SC 8/261/13003; SC 8/64/3189; SC 8/257/12809; SC 8/147/7342; SC 8/80/3959; SC 8/18/855; SC 8/79/3947; SC 8/53/2626; SC 8/194/9688; SC 8/162/8087; SC 8/130/6490.

72 SC 8/212/10585; SC 8/58/2866; SC 8/44/2179; SC 8/125/6206; SC 8/274/13655; SC 8/156/7783; SC 8/341/16100; SC 8/229/11407; SC 8/140/6953; SC 8/86/4263; SC 8/86/4264; SC 8/75/3705; SC 8/118/5888; SC 8/86/4296; SC 8/51/2516; SC 1/18/87.

73 SC 8/146/7265. See W. M. Ormrod, 'Who Was Alice Perrers?', *The Chaucer Review* 40 (2006), 219–29, at 222; W. M. Ormrod, 'The Trials of Alice Perrers', *Speculum* 83 (2008), 366–96.

74 SC 8/52/2586.

Petitioning to Deny Pardon

Another interesting subset of petitions are those that sought to deny pardon to someone else or to challenge a pardon given to someone who had wronged them. The supplicants are usually women, who presented themselves as victims of force and intimidation at the hands of men.[75] In doing so, these women drew on established stereotypes of the helpless widow or the virtuous maiden. However, they might also be represented as strong-willed when their course of action could be deemed virtuous. In one such case from October 1381, Lettice Crioll, widow of Sir John Crioll, petitioned parliament in an attempt to ensure Sir John de Cornwall was not granted a pardon for his 'detestable wickedness' towards her.[76] Moreover, she wanted writs to be delivered to all the sheriffs of England to arrest Cornwall and imprison him, to deny him passage overseas and to deny him any petition.[77] The reason for this strong stance was Cornwall's campaign of violence against Lettice, which she described in her petition. Cornwall, she alleged, had entered her manor (Westenhanger castle in Kent) 'in the habit of a friar' and 'stripped her servants of their clothes' and then allowed into the castle forty armed men who 'held her in torment' for four hours until she paid him. Cornwall's duplicity and immoral character are clearly established in his willingness to disguise himself in religious garb and strip her servants. Furthermore, she claimed that he had since returned on a number of occasions over the previous four years and assaulted her. Finally, he came to the castle at night with armed men and scaling ladders and pursued the petitioner into a river, where she remained in fear for four hours until she was 'as good as dead'. Believing she was dead, Cornwall stole twelve horses and saddlery, jewellery and other goods worth £1,000. Despite the fear and intimidation he exerted over her, she had initiated various suits against him and now petitioned the king to prevent him from receiving pardon. The petition repeats several times the extent of Lettice's despair and the severity of Cornwall's attacks on her. But the very existence of the petition itself also demonstrates that Lettice was sufficiently assertive to petition the king in order to see that her assailant was not pardoned.[78]

[75] Davis, *Fiction in the Archives*, p. 79.

[76] SC 8/55/2713.

[77] *CPR, 1381–1385*, p. 133 for the resulting commission. C. Coulson, 'Some Analysis of the Castle of Bodiam, East Sussex', in *Medieval Knighthood IV: Papers from the Fifth Strawberry Hill Conference, 1990*, ed. C. Harper-Bill and R. Harvey (Woodbridge, 1992), p. 100.

[78] Another woman, Margery de Treverbin, petitioned against the injustice of her attacker escaping punishment. She claimed that Thomas de Gevely had robbed her and raped her daughter Sibyl on more than one occasion, but that he escaped punishment because of protection from Henry de Beaumount. Gevely had already

In the case of Joan de Passele, she was too late to request that her opponent be denied pardon. Instead she petitioned for remedy, as pardon had been wrongfully granted to Margaret de Vescy, the woman 'with whom her husband had been living' at the time of his death in 1327.[79] Joan claimed to be the legitimate widow of Edmund de Passele, a knight and MP from East Sussex who served for two decades as one of the leading serjeants of the common bench.[80] The story was a complex one. In 1288 Edmund had first been married to Maud, with whom he had three sons.[81] Maud had died by 1318 and Passele is subsequently referred to as the husband of Margaret, the posthumous daughter of Thomas de Normanville. Margaret and Edmund had three sons and a daughter. Then, in February 1327, in good health and of sound mind, Edmund made his will, leaving all his goods to Margaret. Ten days later he was dead (writs to hold his inquisition post mortem were issued on 27 March).[82] After his death, various members of his family began a dispute over inheritance that dragged through the court of common pleas for twenty years. One of these 'family members' was Joan, who came forward in Easter term 1328 and claimed dower because, she said, she was Edmund's legitimate wife. The bishop of London was called on to assess Joan's claim and he endorsed her status as widow: she had indeed gone through a marriage ceremony with Passele at St Mary Magdalen, Old Fish Street, in London. The implication was that if Passele had actually ever married Margaret it was bigamous.[83] At some point after this Joan submitted her petition to the king and council, with her allegations against Margaret (whom she referred to as Margaret de Vescy and not Margaret Passele), and claimed to be Edmund's legitimate widow. But the most shocking claim in her petition was yet to come. She also alleged that Margaret had murdered Passele, as well as his eldest son by his first marriage, William, and third son, Edmund, allowing Margaret's children to inherit instead:

> To our lord the king and his council, Joan, who was the wife of Edmund de Passele, shows that whereas Margaret, who was the wife of William de [Basyng], lived a long time with the said Edmund in concubinage until he was charged by his confessors to return to the said Joan, who was his rightful wife, the said Margaret, perceiving that he did not wish either to marry her or to keep her in defiance of God and Holy Church, because she wished that her sons might enjoy the lands of the said Edmund, so the said Margaret had the said Edmund and William, his son and heir, feloniously

been pardoned, but Margaret requested 'that he might be received to answer to her, according to the law': SC 8/76/3756; *CPR, 1307–1313*, p. 362.

[79] SC 8/266/13293.

[80] *Oxford Dictionary of National Biography* (Oxford, 2004); online edn, January 2008, <http://www.oxforddnb.com/view/article/21506> [accessed 9 May 2017].

[81] Daughter and heir of John of Kitchenour. Their sons were William, who predeceased his father, John, and Edmund.

[82] *CIPM*, vol. VII, no. 32.

[83] TNA, CP 40/273, m. 1d.

> poisoned and then, as this could not be accomplished without shedding Christian blood, she had murdered Edmund his son, aged 13 years, and John Wallet, his servant, at Coulsdon in the county of Surrey as it appears in the indictment concerning it, taken and sent before the king, upon which a writ issued to take her body, and she came and gave herself up and was wrongfully mainprised, whereby it seems since then, that the principal [?] object has been attained and thus she falsely keeps the lands of the said Edmund, so that the said Joan, who is his rightful wife, cannot get her dower, not the rightful heir his inheritance, and goes threatening the said Joan of life and limb, and procuring a charter of pardon and a false peace-making, to acquit herself of this felony and of many others done, as well against our said lord the king as against other outside people, and this is well known and notorious in all the five counties round about and in many other places in the kingdom, of which the said Joan asks grace and remedy.[84]

Joan's petition adopted the language of sin, highlighting the 'concubinage', the fact that her husband had been 'charged by his confessors' to return to her, that for Edmund to persist in his relationship with Margaret would be 'in defiance of God and Holy Church' and that Margaret's plot could not be achieved 'without shedding Christian blood'. In contrast, Joan was the moral arbiter, the rightful but wronged wife. The petition also used precise legal terms: Edmund and William were 'feloniously' poisoned and Margaret was threatening Joan 'of life and limb'. Joan also accused Margaret of 'procuring a charter of pardon and a false peace-making', an interesting phrase to use and one that might have a number of connotations. Peace-making could involve a formal process, with ritualised elements of gift-exchange and gestures of submission.[85] Again, Joan's petition played on the importance of reputation, stressing that Margaret's crimes were 'well known and notorious in all the five counties round about and in many other places in the kingdom'.[86] Whether or not Margaret was widely regarded as a criminal, her neighbours in Pashley, East Sussex, would have been aware of ongoing disputes and violence surrounding her family.[87] John de Passele, Edmund's son and heir, complained in 1327 that Margaret's male relatives had trespassed on his lands and had assaulted his servant.[88] Joan's claim that Margaret procured the murder of Passele's young son Edmund and his servant John Wallet at Coulsdon in Surrey was validated by a jury of her peers, who were instructed

[84] SC 8/266/13293; translated by N. H. MacMichael, 'The Descent of the Manor of Evegate in Smeeth with Some Account of its Lords', *Archaeologia Cantiana* 74 (1960), 1–47, at 21. See also P. Coss, *The Lady in Medieval England, 1000–1500* (Stroud, 1998), p. 69.

[85] J. Benham, *Peacemaking in the Middle Ages: Principles and Practice* (Manchester, 2011).

[86] The king and council's response instructed her to sue for the death of her husband and at common law for her dower.

[87] *CCR, 1327–1330*, p. 182; *CCR, 1330–1333*, pp. 148, 295; *CPR, 1330–1334*, p. 315.

[88] *CPR, 1327–1330*, pp. 157, 556.

to inquire into the circumstances of the deaths in April 1329. They returned that Edmund and John, by the procuration of Margaret de Basing, had been 'wretchedly murdered' and robbed of woollen clothes to the value of 13s 4d by Adam Saule and Edward le Peleter. The jury also claimed that Margaret harboured the murderers after the act. In response, the king ordered the arrest of Margaret and the two alleged murderers and sent the case to king's bench.[89] However, when royal officers came to arrest Margaret, a large number of men turned up to rescue her and an altercation ensued. Apparently encouraged by Margaret, the gang 'insulted, assaulted, wounded and maltreated' the king's officers so that they fled in fear of their lives. In the commotion, one of the king's officers, Robert de Pelvesdon, a clerk whom the king had appointed to supervise the arrest, had been wounded by one of Margaret's sons with 'a certain sword of Cologne' so that he completely lost the use of his right hand. The hue and cry was raised but Margaret and her supporters evaded capture and fled into Kent. Meanwhile, one of the alleged murderers, Adam Saule, had been captured and held in Newgate prison. He came before gaol delivery at Newgate and was transferred to king's bench, where a jury from Coulsdon in Surrey acquitted him. The other alleged murderer had been outlawed and eventually, in Michaelmas 1330, Margaret surrendered herself to the Marshalsea prison. The case dragged on, but the outcome was acquittal for Margaret and for the men involved in the affray. The clerk whose hand had been badly wounded brought an appeal. Again the case dragged on and in the interval Margaret secured a pardon. In 1332 she produced the pardon in court and the case against her and her followers collapsed. Not to be deterred, Margaret then began her claims for Edmund's inheritance, which she pursued through the court of common pleas against Joan and John. In these inheritance disputes Joan and John always referred to Margaret by her first marriage, as 'Margaret, late the wife of William de Basynge'. Thus petitions for pardon and petitions to deny pardon were at the centre of disputes that had resonances throughout the local community and beyond.[90]

Performance

Written petitions for pardon would usually have been submitted to parliament and sorted by the receivers of petitions before being sent to the king or an officer of the crown for further consideration. However, there were rare instances in which a supplicant was able to gain an audience with the monarch to put their case forward in person. One supplicant, a woman

[89] TNA, KB 29/1, mm. 53d, 59; KB 27/278, rex, mm. 16d, 21; Kb 27/283, rex, mm. 7, 11d; KB 27/286, rex, mm. 16, 16d; MacMichael, 'The Descent of the Manor of Evegate', pp. 22–6.

[90] *CCR, 1330–1333*, p. 534.

called Alice Fournour, submitted a written petition stating that she had been 'promised grace' by the king in person on his last visit to York.[91] On another occasion, a woman called Margaret de la Chaumbre of Norwich submitted a written petition stating that she had been granted a pardon but had not received it. She asked the king 'to order his porters and other officers to permit her to have free entry to pursue before the King what he has granted her'.[92] This overlap between the written petition for pardon and the physical, spoken performance of supplication was reflected in the vocabulary of some petitions, where supplicants were said to 'cry mercy'.[93] For instance, when three men, 'formerly your merchants of the company of the Riccardi of Lucca', petitioned for pardon, they were said to:

> pray the most high and most noble king … that for God's sake and for pity you have pity and mercy on them and their company and their poor estate and that it will please you to pardon them your anger and ill-will and to restore them to your grace … and for that which the company is in arrears to you *we cry mercy* [my italics] … And for the sake of God and Our Lady and your soul remember if the company ever did anything that pleased you.[94]

The most high-profile supplicant to 'cry mercy' of the king was Henry Bolingbroke, when he begged for pardon in parliament on 31 January 1398.[95] The description of Bolingbroke's supplication before parliament evokes the physical aspects of the performance in kneeling before the king and begging for pardon. This physical demonstration of contrition was played upon:

> the duke of Hereford in full parliament, kneeling humbly before the king said to him, 'My liege lord, I know well that many uprisings, troubles and misdeeds have been perpetrated in your kingdom, to the offence of you and of your royal majesty, in which I have taken part amongst others … I now know and fully confess my offences and misdeeds in that matter; therefor, my lord, *I cry you mercy* [my italics], and ask you to pardon me.'

This description is comparable with the pleas for pardon recorded in the parliament rolls by John Holland in 1386 and the Appellants in 1398. In these descriptions, the physical appearance of the supplicant was dwelt upon. In

[91] Her late husband had apparently received four tuns of flour from members of the king's household when they last returned from Scotland. After his death, in great poverty, she was arrested and imprisoned for a year: SC 8/184/9174; *CPR, 1401–1405*, p. 412.

[92] SC 8/255/12707.

[93] Ormrod, 'Voicing Complaint', p. 138, n. 16; P. Brand, 'Petitions and Parliament in the Reign of Edward I', *Parliamentary History* 23 (2004), 14–38.

[94] SC 8/75/3733; *PROME*, Original Documents: Edward I Parliaments, Roll 12, Appendix no. 274.

[95] *PROME*, parliament of September 1397, item 67. See Ormrod, 'Voicing Complaint', p. 141, n. 36.

cases involving homicide the culprit would often be described as wearing clothes that symbolised their mourning for the deceased, and would perform physical actions to convey their remorse: throwing themselves to the floor, crying and wailing with regret. The presence of patrons willing to intercede on behalf of the supplicant was also important; women or churchmen might be favoured for this role. In some cases, the injured party – a relative of the victim in a homicide case, for example – would be persuaded publicly to forgive the felon in the king's presence. The audience who witnessed this scene of supplication were also important; the earnest entreaty of the supplicant would move them to pity, even to tears, according to some writers. The reported speech of the duke of Gloucester in begging for pardon from Richard II includes these stylised elements and the orthodox religious overtones of Christ's passion:

> I beseche my lyege and souverayn loord the Kyng, that he wyll of his heygh grace and benyngnytee accepte me to his mercy and his grace ... Besechyng to hys heygh lordeschipp that he wyll, for the passion that God soffred for all mankynde and for the compassion that he hadde of hys moder on the cros and the pytee that he hadde of Marye Maudelyne, that he wyll vouchesauf for to have compassion and pytee; and to accepte me unto his mercy and to his grace.[96]

These cases seem to have been mirrored by those in less exalted circles. In one case reported in the York Memorandum Book for 1390, a man called Robert Ellerbek, a mercer of York, had gained an audience before the mayor and civic dignitaries at the city chambers.[97] Ellerbek proceeded to beg mercy from one of the men present, one Ranulph del See, for killing his father. According to the record, Ellerbek entered the chamber with bare head and feet and prostrated himself before the feet of Ranulph. He then proceeded to beg pardon for killing his father, asking for it in the name of 'God and his son Jesus Christ, who gave his precious blood on the Cross to redeem all mankind'. Moved by his entreaty, the mayor and dignitaries present added their voice to the call for mercy. Ranulph agreed to endorse his request for pardon in honour of the soul of his father. It was clear, though, that forgiveness had to be given sincerely. Pardons could be nullified if it was later proved that forgiveness had been extorted under duress, and in some instances the supplicant would be required to perform an act of penance in return for pardon.[98] While few petitioners would actually have come before the monarch themselves to present their petition, the face-to-face scene of supplication was popular in literary descriptions, presumably because of the immediacy and drama that

[96] *PROME*, parliament of September 1397, item 7.

[97] *York Memorandum Book II*, ed. M. Sellers, Surtees Society 125 (Durham, 1914), pp. 30–1.

[98] SC 8/214/10683.

could then be conveyed, rather than the more mundane reality of the bureaucratic procedures of chancery.[99]

Conclusion

The overall impression must be that the decision to pardon was not an arbitrary one made by the monarch alone, but was for the most part authorised by the king or his representative after consultation with the council or parliament. One petition, for example, was addressed to the king, and it was noted that it had come into his presence, but it was endorsed with the statement that 'the council of parliament does not assent'.[100] It was also usual for the king and council to ask for further documentation (often trial records) before passing judgment on a particular case. Once a decision had been reached more writs would be sent out to relevant departments of government, notably the exchequer, to advise them of the action they should take now pardon had been granted. The basis on which the king made his decision is sometimes unclear; some simply state that they have been granted 'by the grace of the king' or that they are 'pardons of grace'. The use of such terms might suggest that kings took a vague, undefined approach to symbolic acts of pardon, concerned only to promote a general sense of munificent royal mercy allied with divine grace and forgiveness (particularly in high-profile cases, when the benevolent grant of a pardon would cast the monarch in a favourable light). However, in some cases a greater level of detail was recorded, which allows for a more nuanced examination of the reasons for granting, or denying, these petitions for grace, and a picture of established administrative procedures and longstanding custom emerges.

For the successful supplicant two hurdles remained: they had to pay for the document (unless the fee had been remitted, as happened on occasion) and they had to have the pardon 'proved' in court. There is also evidence of pardons drafted out but never handed over because of failure to pay the fee. Some were probably intended for individuals on military service who did not live to collect them from chancery.[101] Those in receipt of a pardon were expected to have them proclaimed in court, at which time anyone who wished to bring an appeal was invited to come forward. If no one came forward, final peace could be proclaimed. In one case from Edward II's reign it was noted that final peace was proclaimed by the marshal, who received 2s for carrying out the service. In addition, every clerk was to receive a pair of gloves, and 2s was payable to the chief clerk.[102]

[99] See Lacey, *Royal Pardon*, pp. 40–3.
[100] SC 8/52/2595.
[101] Writs of the privy seal warranting the issue of pardons can be found in TNA, C 81.
[102] *The Eyre of Kent: 6 & 7 Edward II, A.D. 1313–1314*, ed. and trans. W. C. Bolland,

While this article has focused on royal pardons, it is of course true that the same ideological basis informed contemporary notions of religious pardons, 'indulgences'.[103] Fourteenth-century monarchs initiated the granting of royal mercy to mark events in the Church calendar. Royal pardons began to be distributed to mark Good Friday, for example, at least from the beginning of Richard II's reign. Good Friday was a day particularly associated with ideas of mercy, because of Christ's pardon of the 'good thief' crucified beside him, and there are a significant number of pardons, dating from 1380 onwards, which state that the recipient is being pardoned in recognition of Good Friday, and for no other reason.[104] On rare occasions, later medieval monarchs took more direct action in granting mercy to one of their subjects if they happened to pass by an execution about to take place. In such instances it seems that they were seeking to uphold what was perceived to be 'ancient' custom which derived from the orthodox belief in the 'harrowing of Hell', when, after Christ's death and before His resurrection, He redeemed the souls in hell.[105]

Petitioning for pardon meant becoming versed in a supplicatory culture with its own strategies, language and administrative procedures. While written documents were at the heart of the process, old habits of physical performance and ritual still found an echo in the petitioner's language of 'crying mercy'. Face-to-face performances of supplication might have been rare in practice by the fourteenth century but they still appeared in outlaw ballads to provide escapist notions of the idealised justice that only the monarch could bestow. So too, the satire of the Wakefield master in the Towneley Corpus Christi play *The Killing of Abel* demonstrates the dramatic potential of proclamations of royal pardon in a scene where Cain mockingly proclaims a pardon for his servant. These texts go some way to demonstrating the extent to which the law of the realm was still regarded as personal to the king. As the supreme lawgiver, he played an active role at the head of the judicial system, and the king's subjects valued their right to appeal directly to him for judgement. It was a process that was successfully navigated by a diverse range of people in the fourteenth century, and it lasted, albeit in different forms, well into the modern period.

Selden Society 24 (London, 1909), p. 139; Hurnard, *The King's Pardon for Homicide*, p. 65. In 1303 John Botetorte wrote to William de Greenfield, chancellor, concerning the proclamation of a pardon of murder: SC 1/28/51.

103 A. Minnis, 'The Construction of Chaucer's Pardoner', in *Promissory Notes on the Treasury of Merits: Indulgences in the Late Middle Ages*, ed. R. N. Swanson (Turnhout, 2006), pp. 165–91.

104 See Lacey, *Royal Pardon*, p. 35.

105 Lacey, *Royal Pardon*, p. 71. Langland referred to this tradition in the 'Harrowing of Hell' scene in Piers Plowman (Passus XVIII of the B-text).

3

The Scribes of Petitions in Late Medieval England

Helen Killick

In contemporary society, e-petitioning faces criticism on the grounds of accessibility; as documents that are easy to set up and to sign, they are viewed as potentially encouraging the promotion of frivolous causes or of 'slacktivism', political activism that has very little chance of achieving real-life impact and is largely aimed at promoting a feeling of well-being in the supporter.[1] In the words of one journalist: 'Opening a link, clicking on a send button … can anyone possibly take this seriously as a way of engaging in debate on any subject that matters? It's effortless moral outrage, requiring neither understanding nor commitment on the part of the clickers.'[2] By contrast, for the medieval petitioner, we would assume that understanding and commitment were prerequisites; no-one would go to the trouble of having a petition drawn up and presented who did not have a real grievance or belief that a particular issue required redress. The basis for comparison between medieval and modern petitioning is clearly very slight, but serves to underline the importance of accessibility and the role of the mediator. In contrast to petitioning today, the medieval petitioner required the services of a trained scribe who would be able to structure their request according to the appropriate forms. This chapter addresses the question of identity of these scribes, their role in the petitionary process and the implications this has for our understanding of petitioning as a means of accessing medieval justice. It draws on examples from petitions addressed to the highest English secular authorities: the king, parliament and chancellor.

The status of petitions is somewhat ambiguous; as Dodd has observed, 'they fit comfortably neither into the category of records produced by the Crown nor into the designation of "local" documents written independently

[1] H. S. Christensen, 'Political Activities on the Internet: Slacktivism or Political Participation by Other Means?', *First Monday* 16 (2011) <http://firstmonday.org/ojs/index.php/fm/article/view/3336/2767> [accessed 12 January 2018].

[2] *The Guardian*, 'Are online petitions a valid form of protest?' (11 January 2015) <https://www.theguardian.com/commentisfree/2015/jan/11/debate-online-petitions-valid-form-protest-ched-evans-oldham> [accessed 12 January 2018].

of influence from the royal secretariat'.[3] Previously, several commentators have argued that the petitions surviving in The National Archives are not themselves the originals, but copies drawn up by the chancery clerks.[4] This is now generally agreed to be a false supposition; however, the identity of those scribes responsible for drafting petitions remains a matter of debate. There are a number of potential scenarios in which petitions were drawn up. In some cases, a petitioner may have been responsible for drafting their own request; although there is some evidence of this, Dodd has argued that, owing to the necessity for an understanding of the appropriate form and language, in the majority of cases a petitioner would have needed the services of a professional scribe.[5] If we assume that a professional scribe was employed, there remains the question of whether a petitioner would travel to London in order to have their complaint written up by clerks in and around Westminster, or whether they would turn to scribes in their local vicinity. As travel to London would have been impractical or prohibitively expensive for many people at this time, this question has important implications for the extent to which petitioning was an option available to a wide section of the medieval population.[6]

As petitions do not contain any direct indication of authorship, in addressing this question we must turn to other evidence. There are two main ways in which petitions present clues as to the identity of their scribe. Firstly, the hand of the petition may suggest the level of professional training the scribe possessed, and in some cases (as we will see below), a positive identification may be made through comparison of this hand with other sources. Secondly, we can examine the language and form of a petition in order to see whether it conforms to traditional petitionary diplomatic, suggesting that its scribe had benefited from professional training or, in the case of English-language petitions, whether the orthography and vocabulary suggest an association with a specific regional dialect. It must be emphasised that these indicators are not in themselves conclusive. There is considerable overlap between the categories of 'professional', 'metropolitan' and 'local', as many

[3] G. Dodd, 'The Rise of English, the Decline of French: Supplications to the English Crown, c. 1420–1450', *Speculum* 86 (2011), 117–50, at 119.

[4] *An Anthology of Chancery English*, ed. J. H. Fisher, M. Richardson, and J. L. Fisher (Knoxville, TN, 1984), p. 21; M. Avery, 'Proceedings in the Court of Chancery up to c. 1460' (unpublished MA dissertation, University of London, 1958), p. 136; M. Benskin, 'Local Archives and Middle English Dialects', *Journal of the Society of Archivists* 5 (1977), 500–14, at 508; M. Laing, 'Studies in the Dialect Material of Medieval Lincolnshire' (unpublished PhD thesis, University of Edinburgh, 1978), pp. 44–6.

[5] G. Dodd, *Justice and Grace: Private Petitioning and the English Parliament in the Late Middle Ages* (Oxford, 2007), pp. 302–6.

[6] Dodd presents evidence that many petitioners did travel to Westminster to present their petitions personally; however, he stresses that this was not a prerequisite for success: Dodd, *Justice and Grace*, pp. 309–12.

regional scribes may have either had training in Westminster or have been influenced by formularies; this influence may extend to orthography as well as hand, form and style. Dodd therefore argues that, while, in general, a certain level of 'professionalism' and knowledge of the petitionary form were prerequisites for the scribes who drafted petitions, 'any number of different types of "men of letters" or "men of law" might have met those criteria, from the numerous scriveners, notaries, and lawyers operating in the localities, to an equally abundant pool of men of similar professions based in London, to the clerks and scribes who were directly employed within the government itself'.[7]

This study adopts the broad definition of the term 'petition' previously outlined by Dodd as referring to 'written entreaties presented in a formal manner to a higher authority',[8] and consequently draws on material from several types of document now surviving in various series in TNA: parliamentary petitions (SC 8, Ancient Petitions and C 49, Chancery: Parliamentary and Council Proceedings); chancery bills (C 1, Court of Chancery: Early Proceedings); chamberlain's bills (E 28, Exchequer, Treasury of the Receipt: Council and Privy Seal Records) and, finally, the sub-series containing 'signed bills of warranty' (C 81, Warrants for the Great Seal). It is important to emphasise that there is likely to have been considerable variation in the way petitions were drawn up according to their type and the context of their presentation. For example, in contrast to those petitions presented in parliament, which could include detailed accounts of the petitioner's grievance and made use of rhetorical language, the chamberlain's bills, which were presented to the king in his chamber often by the petitioner in person, were brief documents often containing little information other than 'who was petitioning and what they wanted'.[9] Parliamentary petitions were also more elaborate documents than chancery bills, but the latter were more likely to draw on legal terminology and precedent.[10] It is therefore likely that different branches of petitioning required different levels of skill and knowledge, and consequently relied on the services of scribes from a variety of backgrounds.

We must also take into account changes to the petitionary form occurring over time. Parliamentary petitions became increasingly complex and elaborate documents over the course of the fourteenth century, particularly in relation to the desired outcome; whereas it had been common simply to outline the complaint and petition the king for a suitable remedy, by the fifteenth century

[7] Dodd, 'Rise of English', 120.

[8] Dodd, *Justice and Grace*, p. 1 n. 2.

[9] G. Dodd, 'Patronage, Petitions and Grace: The "Chamberlains' Bills" of Henry IV's Reign', in *The Reign of Henry IV: Rebellion and Survival 1403–13*, ed. G. Dodd and D. Biggs (York, 2008), pp. 105–35, at p. 113.

[10] G. Dodd, 'Writing Wrongs: The Drafting of Supplications to the Crown in Later Fourteenth-Century England', *Medium Ævum* 80 (2011), 217–46, at 231–2.

some petitions contained detailed schedules of what was desired from the crown, including requests for specific legal actions.[11] Consequently, Dodd argues that the level of skill required in petition-writing increased over time, meaning that it became more likely that petitioners would turn to the services of professionals rather than drafting their own requests.[12]

It is important to acknowledge that even those petitions of a similar type may have been drawn up in a variety of ways. In exploring the various scenarios for the drafting of petitions it may be useful to consider Merja Stenroos' typology of medieval letters, which she places in four categories according to the circumstances of their composition as follows:

a) composed and written down by the sender
b) dictated by the sender to a scribe
c) drafted by the sender, fair copy produced by a scribe
d) drafted and written down by a scribe on behalf of the sender.[13]

When applied to petitioning, these scenarios may be viewed as representing points on a spectrum of personal involvement, with a) denoting the 'authentic voice' of the petitioner and d) describing an impersonal legal document. This is obviously an over-simplification; as we shall see, overlap between these categories was possible, and personal involvement is likely to have varied considerably within each of these categories according to the relationship between the petitioner and the scribe and the specific circumstances of the case. Analysis of these issues contributes to a wider debate regarding authorial voice in petitioning; while we may accept that petitions do not represent 'the unmediated, authentic voices of the king's subjects', their origins as oral pleas presented in the royal courts (and tendency to continue to reflect the spoken language of pleading) suggest that the personal input of the petitioner remained of great importance.[14] The orality and performative character of these documents have been explored through an analysis of their language, suggesting that in certain cases the petitionary form could be employed in the expression of highly personalised complaints.[15] The change

[11] Dodd, *Justice and Grace*, p. 303.

[12] Dodd, *Justice and Grace*, p. 306.

[13] M. Stenroos, 'Fugitive Voices: Personal Involvement in Middle English Letters of Defence', in *'Ye whom the charms of grammar please': Studies in English Historical Linguistics in Honour of Leiv Egil Breivik*, ed. K. E. Haugland, K. McCafferty and K. A. Rusten (Oxford, 2014), pp. 355–80, at pp. 358–9.

[14] W. M. Ormrod, 'The Language of Complaint: Multilingualism and Petitioning in Later Medieval England', in *Language and Culture in Medieval Britain: The French of England, c. 1100–1500*, ed. J. Wogan-Browne with C. Collette, M. Kowaleski, L. Mooney, A. Putter and D. Trotter (York, 2009), pp. 31–43, quotation p. 32.

[15] W. M. Ormrod, 'Murmur, Clamour and Noise: Voicing Complaint and Remedy in Petitions to the English Crown, c. 1300–c. 1460', in *Medieval Petitions: Grace and*

in the language of petitioning from French to English in the fifteenth century is likely to have increased the ability of the form to express the personal voice of the petitioner.[16] For the most part, evidence regarding the circumstances of drafting of a petition is simply non-existent; yet, in some cases the hand and language of a petition can be used to illuminate individual cases and provide clues as to overall trends. It is the aim of this chapter to provide an overview of the evidence available in examining this issue, and some ideas for potential further study.

Hand

The scribes of petitions did not sign their work, meaning that in the majority of cases we have no clue as to their identity beyond the appearance of the hand itself.[17] In this, it is clear that there is wide variation; some petitions are written in a more formal secretary hand, like that used in the government offices, whereas some are messier, more cursive, or similar to that we might see in literary documents. To date, there has been no comprehensive palaeographical overview of petitionary hands. In a preliminary survey of selected parliamentary and chancery petitions, Lister M. Matheson found 'a predominance of formally written but mixed hands ... combining in varying proportions anglicana and secretary features, and of anglicana hands, some of very current nature; secretary hands are in a clear minority, though there seem to be more among the Parliamentary petitions than among the Chancery ones'.[18] As anglicana was the hand favoured by clerks of the chancery, and secretary script emerged in the offices of the privy seal and signet in the second half of the fourteenth century, we might therefore conclude that many petitions were indeed the work of royal clerks and were drawn up within Westminster.[19] However, neither of these hands was the preserve of the central government offices, and Matheson's overall conclusion suggests a

Grievance, ed. W. M. Ormrod, G. Dodd and A. Musson (York, 2009), pp. 135–55; G. Dodd, 'Thomas Paunfield, the "heye Court of rightwisenesse" and the Language of Petitioning in the Fifteenth Century', in *Medieval Petitions*, ed. Ormrod et al., pp. 222–41.

16 G. Dodd in this volume.

17 Two possible exceptions exist in a chancery bill of c. 1450 (TNA, C 1/18/164) that contains the signature 'Northley' (see Avery, 'Proceedings in the Court of Chancery up to c. 1460', p. 136) and the 1321 Gascon petition signed by Gaillard du Sages, squire (see Guilhem Pépin, 'Petitions from Gascony: Testimonies of a Special Relationship', in *Medieval Petitions*, ed. Ormrod et al., pp. 120–34, at pp. 125–6. This document is discussed further below).

18 L. M. Matheson, 'Review of *An Anthology of Chancery English*, ed. John H. Fisher, Malcolm Richardson, and Jane L. Fisher (Knoxville, 1984)', *Speculum* 61 (1986), 646–50, at 649.

19 C. Johnson and H. Jenkinson, *English Court Hand A.D. 1066 to 1500* (Oxford, 1915),

wide variety in the background of petitionary scribes: 'The evidence suggests that the scribes of private petitions could be the petitioners themselves, professional scriveners (probably specializing in such documents), or moonlighting lower-level government clerks from different departments, as Thomas Hoccleve is known to have been, while Commons petitions probably drew more readily upon the resources of government clerks.'[20]

As there were important distinctions in the way common and private petitions were drawn up and received, we might expect them to be written by different types of scribe. A common petition, in theory, represented the interests of the wider community and was backed by the Commons in parliament; it is therefore plausible that they were written up by the chancery clerks who were employed in keeping the parliament roll.[21] However, a recent edition of common petitions finds evidence of chancery hands in their production for the first half of the fourteenth century only; thereafter, their hands bear more resemblance to the secretary script employed in the privy seal and signet offices and in other bureaucratic contexts.[22] This may in part be due to the fact that, from the late fourteenth century onwards, there was an increasing tendency for those private petitions that were considered to be in the public interest to be 'avowed' by the Commons and presented in parliament; from this period onwards, it is therefore likely that a significant number of common petitions were indeed drawn up outside Westminster.[23]

In some cases the hand of a petition allows us to identify it as the work of a known scribe. It is important to acknowledge the limitations of this approach; scribal attribution is not an exact science, and has been the subject of debate.[24] Nevertheless, when used in conjunction with other evidence, it can used to present a convincing case. Known identifications of scribes of multiple petitions to date are listed in the Appendix (Table I). A pioneering example here is the identification by Linne Mooney of the petition of the Mercers' Company against Nicholas Brembre in 1388 as the work of Adam Pinkhurst, scribe of the earliest copies of Chaucer's *Canterbury Tales*.[25] Recently, Mooney and Estelle

pp. xv–xxi; M. B. Parkes, *English Cursive Book Hands 1250–1500* (Oxford, 1969), pp. xiv–xx; P. Chaplais, *English Royal Documents* (Oxford, 1971), pp. 50–3.

[20] Matheson, 'Review', p. 649. As we shall see below, Matheson's intuitions regarding Hoccleve were proved to be correct.

[21] *Early Common Petitions in the English Parliament, c. 1290–c. 1420*, ed. W. M. Ormrod, H. Killick and P. Bradford (Cambridge, 2017), pp. 1–5.

[22] *Early Common Petitions*, ed. Ormrod et al., pp. 14–16.

[23] Dodd, *Justice and Grace*, pp. 143–55. An example of this process will be discussed in more detail below.

[24] See A. J. Fletcher, 'What did Adam Pynkhurst (not) write? A Reply to Dr Horobin', *The Review of English Studies* n.s. 61 (2010), 690–710; L. Warner, 'Scribes, Misattributed: Hoccleve and Pinkhurst', *Studies in the Age of Chaucer* 37 (2015), 55–100.

[25] L. R. Mooney, 'Chaucer's Scribe', *Speculum* 81 (2006), 97–138. While previous scholarship has dated this petition and those from the other guilds to 1387–8, recent work suggests a more specific dating to January or February 1388: R. Ellis, '*Verba vana*:

Stubbs have argued that Pinkhurst's hand appears in one other of the guilds' petitions presented on the same subject, that of the Leathersellers and White Tawyers.[26] Pinkhurst has also been identified by Simon Horobin as the scribe of a petition on behalf of Chaucer requesting the appointment of a deputy for his office of controller of the wool custom.[27] The Middle English poet and clerk of the privy seal Thomas Hoccleve has also been revealed to have authored several petitions.[28] The identification of Pinkhurst and Hoccleve in these documents formed the basis for a search for other petitions in their hands and in the hands of other known scribes operating in and around Westminster during this period.[29] This search has uncovered several more petitions written by Hoccleve and several in the hand of Richard Osbarn, clerk of the chamber of the London Guildhall between 1400 and c. 1437.

The reason that we are able to identify these three individuals as active in petition-writing is due to the existence of identifiable samples of their hands in both literary manuscripts and other documentary sources.[30] They are perhaps too 'high-profile' to be especially representative of petitionary scribes in general, yet their identification supports the existence of a network of trained scribes operating in Westminster and the City of London who could be drawn upon for a wide variety of commissions, whether official or literary in nature. The petitions written by all three of these men throw new light on the nature of the relationship between petitioner and scribe, suggesting that in many cases a petitioner would use the services of an individual who was personally acquainted with them in some capacity. There is evidence that Pinkhurst had a long-term connection with the Mercers' Company, beginning in 1385, from his involvement in property transactions with members of the

Empty Words in Ricardian London' (unpublished PhD thesis, London, 2012), pp. 104–6.

26 L. R. Mooney and E. Stubbs, *Scribes and the City: London Guildhall Clerks and the Dissemination of Middle English Literature, 1375–1425* (York, 2013), pp. 78–80. Robert Ellis has analysed the textual relationship between the guilds' petitions, but finds no evidence of a direct relationship between this petition and that of the Mercers' Company (Ellis, '*Verba Vana*', pp. 110–37).

27 S. Horobin, 'Adam Pinkhurst, Geoffrey Chaucer, and the Hengwrt Manuscript of the Canterbury Tales', *The Chaucer Review* 44 (2010), 351–67, at 354–5.

28 H. Killick, 'Thomas Hoccleve as Poet and Clerk' (unpublished PhD thesis, University of York, 2011), pp. 87–9.

29 This formed one of the research strands followed in the project 'The Writing of Petitions in Later Medieval England', funded by the Andrew W. Mellon Foundation (2011–13). I wish to thank the project team and in particular Professor Linne Mooney and Dr Holly James-Maddocks for their expert assistance in identifying these scribes.

30 For an overview of Hoccleve's work as a scribe of literary manuscripts, see Killick, 'Thomas Hoccleve', pp. 17–25. For the scribal careers of Osbarn and Pinkhurst, see Mooney and Stubbs, *Scribes and the City*, pp. 17–37, 66–85.

company and the appearance of his hand in the company account books.[31] His relationship with Chaucer is argued to have been more than that of a mere copyist of his works, but instead of someone who worked under Chaucer's close direction, and to whom he addressed the poem 'Chaucers Wordes unto Adam, His Owne Scriveyn'.[32]

The identification of Thomas Hoccleve as a scribe of petitions lends weight to the argument that, at least in some cases, they were drawn up centrally by one of the clerks of the government offices (in this case, the privy seal). This should not be conflated with the idea put forward by John H. Fisher and others that the surviving corpus of petitions are not the 'original' documents, but copies made by government clerks as an official record.[33] There are several ways in which the petitions in Hoccleve's hand suggest that petition-writing was an extra-curricular activity, rather than part of his daily duties at the privy seal. Firstly, they are relatively few in number; although further searches in TNA may well uncover more examples of Hoccleve's hand in the petitions, it seems unlikely that the current total of twelve will rise significantly.[34] Secondly, the hand employed by Hoccleve in several of the petitions differs in certain characteristics from that used in the privy seal records, suggesting that he viewed petition-writing as a different kind of task to the writing of official documents on behalf of the government administration. While still ostensibly a secretary hand, it has a slightly less formal appearance, and displays several traits in common with the hand employed by Hoccleve in the autograph manuscripts of his Middle English poetry (notably, in the case of the petitions on behalf of John Russell and John Muriden, a round 'w' rather than the bipartite form normally used in his privy seal work).[35] Finally, as with Pinkhurst, in several cases we can discern evidence that Hoccleve may have had a personal connection with the petitioner. In 1415 he drafted a petition on behalf of his under-clerk at that time, John Welde, requesting three oak trees from the forest of Warborough, South Oxfordshire.[36] It is unclear in this case why Welde, a government clerk, did not write his own request; perhaps he considered that Hoccleve, as the senior of the two men, had a greater ability to draft a successful petition, or

[31] Mooney, 'Chaucer's Scribe', pp. 106–12.

[32] Mooney, 'Chaucer's Scribe', pp. 105.

[33] See note 4 above.

[34] This may be compared to over 1,000 privy seal warrants and bills identified in Hoccleve's hand: see L. R. Mooney, 'Some New Light on Thomas Hoccleve', *Studies in the Age of Chaucer* 29 (2007), 293–340; Killick, 'Thomas Hoccleve', Appendix I.

[35] For a description of Hoccleve's book hand, see *Thomas Hoccleve: A Facsimile of the Autograph Verse Manuscripts*, ed. J. A. Burrow and A. I. Doyle (Oxford, 2002), p. xxxiv. For his documentary hand, see Mooney, 'Some New Light', p. 319.

[36] A. L. Brown, 'The Privy Seal Clerks in the Early Fifteenth Century', in *The Study of Medieval Records: Essays in Honour of Kathleen Major*, ed. D. A. Bullough and R. L. Storey (Oxford, 1971), p. 262.

perhaps this document was written during the period when Welde was one of the privy seal clerks who accompanied the king to Calais.[37] Towards the end of his life in 1424 Hoccleve is also found to have written a petition on his own behalf, a request addressed to the king's council for the corrody of the priory of Southwick, Hampshire.

Although Hoccleve viewed the drafting of petitions as separate to his day job as a clerk of the privy seal, there are indications that on occasion he was not above using his position to expedite the cause of the petitioner. This is indicated by the fact that in two cases he is found to have written both the original petition and the resulting privy seal warrant for the chancery authorising the request to be granted. The first of these cases occurs early in Hoccleve's career, in 1391, when he drafted both the request of William Menuesse concerning a dispute over the church living of Aldington, Kent, and the ensuing warrant for the chancery ordering further investigation and a resolution. The second case concerns Hoccleve's own petition for the Southwick corrody. The circumstances of this petition's presentation and response demonstrate the ability of a government clerk to short-cut the administrative process to suit his own interests. It was presented to the council on 4 July 1424 in the presence of Humphrey of Gloucester and other senior council members, and appears to have been immediately granted; both the privy seal warrant in Hoccleve's hand and the record of the grant in the close rolls are also dated 4 July, indicating that Hoccleve was able to write the authorising warrant immediately after presenting his petition.[38] The discovery that Hoccleve occasionally wrote petitions is not in itself particularly surprising. Privy seal clerks of this period were unwaged; even if they were fortunate enough to be granted an annuity from the king this was often irregularly paid, and they were forced to supplement their income from occasional gifts, revenue from church offices and rewards for carrying out writing tasks for specific individuals.[39] Petition-writing, particularly for wealthy clients, was potentially a lucrative business; we know that Hoccleve was paid two marks by the earl marshal, John Mowbray, in 1423 for writing a petition to the council on his behalf.[40]

With this in mind it seems probable that evidence may be found of other clerks of the privy seal who also took advantage of this opportunity. Investigation of this theory presents the problem, however, of identifying the hands of individual privy seal clerks; for most of Hoccleve's contemporaries

[37] A. L. Brown, 'The Privy Seal in the Early Fifteenth Century' (unpublished DPhil thesis, Oxford, 1955), p. 290.

[38] See J. A. Burrow, *Thomas Hoccleve* (Aldershot, 1994), p. 29. The privy seal warrant is TNA, C 81/682/1201a.

[39] T. F. Tout, *Chapters in the Administrative History of England*, 6 vols (Manchester, 1920–33), vol. V, p. 114; Burrow, *Thomas Hoccleve*, pp. 8–9.

[40] Burrow, *Thomas Hoccleve*, p. 17. The petition itself does not appear to have survived.

this is not possible, as we have no verifiable examples of their hand in other sources against which to compare.[41] There is potential for a study of this kind using privy seal writs from the mid-1430s onwards, as around this time it became common practice for privy seal clerks to sign their documents; this is the basis for Dodd's study of linguistic choices made by individual clerks during the period in which English was first introduced into the office.[42] Despite the presence of these signatures, the similarity of the scribal hands employed in the office and the fact that the clerks altered their hands depending on whether the document was in Latin, French or English makes identification of individual clerks a difficult task. However, it is possible to identify a distinctive 'office style': a neat, cursive secretary hand characterised by a pronounced right-sloping aspect, long ascenders and descenders and a heavy downward stroke in the letters 'f' and 's'.[43] Analysis of petitions surviving from this period reveals a number of documents featuring a similar hand, suggesting that Thomas Hoccleve was not the only privy seal clerk to have employed his skills in the task of petition-writing.[44]

A further example of a connection between the scribe of a petition and its subject matter is the identification of the hand of Richard Osbarn, clerk of the chamber of the London Guildhall in the first half of the fifteenth century, in a common petition of 1425 complaining that those accused of the crimes of treason, felony and Lollardy are being imprisoned for long periods of time without trial.[45] Osbarn's hand is recognisable in this document from his identification by Linne Mooney and Estelle Stubbs as 'the HM 114 scribe', notable for his role in copying several important manuscripts of Middle English literature of the early fifteenth century.[46] The motives behind this

[41] The two exceptions here are keeper of the privy seal John Prophete, who kept a journal of council proceedings (now in TNA, E 28/3; see J. F. Baldwin, *The King's Council in England during the Middle Ages* (Oxford, 1913), pp. 389–91; 489–504) and Robert Frye, whose personal correspondence survives in TNA, E 28/29 (see Brown, 'Privy Seal', vol. II, Appendix of Documents, pp. 353–70). To date, neither has been identified as having written petitions.

[42] G. Dodd, 'Trilingualism in the Medieval English Bureaucracy: The Use – and Disuse – of Languages in the Fifteenth-Century Privy Seal Office', *Journal of British Studies* 51 (2012), 253–83, at 264–6. There is some ambiguity as to whether these signatures represent the name of the clerk who drafted the document or the clerk who was responsible for checking it: see H. C. Maxwell-Lyte, *Historical Notes on the Use of the Great Seal of England* (London, 1926), p. 34; Tout, *Administrative History*, vol. V, p. 114.

[43] Examples of this hand can be seen in writs signed by the privy seal clerk Henry Benet in TNA, C 81/720 (1439).

[44] See, for example: TNA, SC 8/25/1203; SC 8/25/1222; SC 8/26/1275; SC 8/27/1301; SC 8/28/1357; SC 8/28/1363; SC 8/28/1363; SC 8/324/E660; SC 8/251/12528.

[45] H. Killick, 'Treason, Felony and Lollardy: A Common Petition in the Hand of Richard Osbarn, Clerk of the Chamber of the Guildhall, 1400–c.1437', *Historical Research* 89 (2016), 227–45.

[46] Mooney and Stubbs, *Scribes and the City*, pp. 17–28; A. I. Doyle, 'The Manuscripts',

petition are ambiguous; it is unclear whether the petitioners' sympathies lay primarily with the prisoners themselves or with the crown. As a common petition, it is also difficult to identify the individuals behind it or whether it originated from within parliament or was one of those private causes that had obtained parliamentary backing. Osbarn's identification as the scribe of the document serves to throw new light on these questions. Evidence of a wider concern at this time regarding false accusations and imprisonment without trial within the City of London suggests that the petition may have originated with a group of prominent London citizens with whom Osbarn would have been professionally, if not personally, acquainted; there is evidence of similar arrangements being employed in the drafting of common petitions emanating from London craft and mercantile guilds.[47] In addition, Osbarn's role in copying (and possibly translating) the *Epistola Luciferi*, a Lollard text, suggests that he had a particular interest in the petition's subject matter, and perhaps explains why the petition is notably lacking in any explicit condemnation of the crime of Lollardy.[48]

The preceding analysis has demonstrated some of the ways in which palaeographical identification of scribal hands can contribute to our understanding of the petitionary process. This approach has its limitations, in that the number of individuals whose hands are easily identifiable is relatively low. The identifications made to date of Pinkhurst, Hoccleve and Osbarn are reliant on the fact that these scribes are recognisable from their activity within London scribal networks. They are not necessarily typical of petition-writers in general, and their status as the copyists (or authors) of literary texts suggests that they may have taken more of an active role in the composition of the petition itself. This is especially true of Hoccleve, much of whose literary composition can be characterised as 'petitionary verse', taking the form of a complaint of straitened circumstances addressed to a noble patron in order to request financial aid. This has led a number of commentators to argue that his poetry was influenced by the forms and language of the petition; this being the case, we would expect him to have had a high degree of creative input when drafting these documents themselves.[49]

in *Middle English Alliterative Poetry and its Literary Background*, ed. D. Lawton (Cambridge, 1982), pp. 88–100, 142–147 (esp. pp. 94, 144, n. 22–23); R. Hanna, 'The Scribe of Huntington Library MS. HM 114', *Studies in Bibliography* 42 (1989), 120–33; R. Hanna, 'The Manuscripts and Transmission of Chaucer's Troilus', in *The Idea of Medieval Literature: New Essays on Chaucer and Medieval Culture in Honour of Donald R. Howard*, ed. J. M. Dean and C. K. Zacher (Newark, 1992), pp. 173–88.

[47] Killick, 'Treason, Felony and Lollardy', pp. 238–9; M. Davies, 'Lobbying Parliament: The London Livery Companies in the Fifteenth Century', *Parliamentary History* 23 (2004), 136–48.

[48] Killick, 'Treason, Felony and Lollardy', 241–2.

[49] N. Perkins, *Hoccleve's Regiment of Princes: Counsel and Constraint* (Cambridge, 2001), p. 38; Burrow, *Thomas Hoccleve*, p. 6; Killick, 'Thomas Hoccleve', pp. 91–3, 118–19.

Language

A more comprehensive idea of how and where the majority of petitions were drafted may be obtained through a study of their language. One of the ways in which scholars have attempted to throw more light on the geographical origins of petitions has been to examine the earliest petitions composed in English, in order to determine whether they display distinctive linguistic and stylistic features which indicate that they were drawn up by regional scribes.[50] With a very few earlier exceptions, English petitions begin to appear in the 1420s, and by the late 1430s they begin to outnumber those written in French; there is thus a substantial corpus of documents on which to base such a study.[51] As noted above, their provenance has been subject to misinterpretation; numerous examples of these documents are included in Fisher, Richardson and Fisher's *Anthology of Chancery English* despite the lack of conclusive evidence that they were indeed the products of chancery clerks.[52] While there is now general agreement that petitions were not written up within the chancery itself, their linguistic status remains a subject of debate, with some emphasising their regional character and others the adherence of their language to a nascent 'standard English'.

The most rigorous linguistic analysis of petitions to date has been conducted by the editors of the *Linguistic Atlas of Late Mediaeval English* (hereafter *LALME*). This monumental work, first published in 1986 and recently updated and made available online, is a survey of the surviving sources displaying linguistic variation in late medieval English. The editors examined material dating from approximately 1350 to 1461 that could be associated by context with a specific region. They analysed these sources according to a predetermined set of linguistic criteria, and on this basis assigned each a linguistic profile number representing a specific regional dialect. The original printed version of *LALME* listed around 200 petitions in its index of sources, but concluded that only a few of these displayed evidence of dialectal variation; the majority are

50 T. S. Haskett, 'The Composers of English Chancery Bills', in *The Life of the Law*, ed. P. B. H. Birks (London, 1993), pp. 9–23; M. Laing, 'Studies in the Dialect Material of Medieval Lincolnshire', pp. 44–6; M. Benskin, M. Laing, V. Karaiskos and K. Williamson, *An Electronic Version of A Linguistic Atlas of Late Mediaeval English* (Edinburgh, 2013), vol. I, General Introduction: <http://www.lel.ed.ac.uk/ihd/elalme/intros/atlas_gen_intro.html> [accessed 23 January 2018].

51 Dodd, 'Rise of English', 118; 122–3. The exceptions are the petition of John Drayton and Margery King dated 1343–4 (SC 8/192/9580) and the 1388 petition of the Mercers' Company (see above).

52 Fisher et al., *Anthology of Chancery English*; for criticism of this work see M. Benskin, 'Chancery Standard', in *New Perspectives on English Historical Linguistics: Selected Papers from 12 ICEHL, Glasgow, 21–26 August 2002, 2: Lexis and Transmission*, ed. C. Kay, C. Hough and I. Wotherspoon (Glasgow, 2004), pp. 1–39.

described as 'standard language' or 'of no dialectal interest'.[53] In the updated electronic version, which was completed in 2013 (*eLALME*), the editors have added to this number, bringing the total number of petitions included in their survey up to 361.[54] Almost one-fifth of these are assigned elements of regional dialect or described as possessing 'some local forms', but only ten petitions out of the total are deemed to be sufficiently linguistically interesting to warrant full analysis and allocation of a linguistic profile number.[55] It is perhaps telling that one of these is the complaint of Thomas Paunfield; this document is so unusual in character (in terms of its length, its use of the first person and the emotive quality of its rhetoric) that Dodd has argued that it should not strictly be viewed as a petition at all, but rather a personal testimony.[56]

The editors of *LALME* discuss in depth the problems faced in assigning a document to a particular region on the basis of its linguistic features: 'Men travelled, and so did their language … it is always possible that the language of a document does not belong to the place with which, on all other counts, the document itself is firmly associated.'[57] The key issue here is the emergence of a written standard, originating in London in the early fourteenth century, which began to influence regional forms of written English.[58] Owing to this development, many documents fall into the category of hybrid texts that are difficult to localise to any one region. The editors of *LALME* note that documents produced in areas closer to London are more likely to be deemed 'standard' or 'of no dialectal interest' than those produced, for example, in the north of England, as in these regions the line between standard English and local dialect is more difficult to draw. This is illustrated in Table II, which displays the total number of petitions included in *eLALME* broken down

53 A. McIntosh, M. L. Samuels, and M. Benskin, *Linguistic Atlas of Late Mediaeval English*, 4 vols (Aberdeen, 1984), vol. I, pp. 284–6.

54 Benskin et al., *eLALME*, vol. I, General Introduction: <http://www.lel.ed.ac.uk/ihd/elalme/intros/atlas_gen_intro.html> [accessed 23 January 2018]. Figures have been compiled from *eLALME*'s Index of Sources.

55 These are: LP 282, Cambridgeshire (TNA, SC 8/23/1143 A and B); LP 298, Norfolk (TNA, C 49/48/6); LP 325, Leicestershire (TNA, C 1/15/137); LP 5071, Devon (C 1/31/34–36); LP 5550, Hampshire (SC 8/28/1352); LP 311, Staffordshire (C 1/6/318 and 321). Two petitions were formerly assigned linguistic profiles but have been excluded from the revised edition: C 1/12/201 (formerly LP 435) and C 1/9/378 (formerly LP 434).

56 Dodd, 'Thomas Paunfield', 222–41. Matthew Giancarlo presents a linguistic analysis of this document in his, *Parliament and Literature in Late Medieval England* (Cambridge, 2007), pp. 224–8.

57 Benskin et al., *eLALME*, vol. I, General Introduction: <http://www.lel.ed.ac.uk/ihd/elalme/intros/atlas_gen_intro.html> [accessed 23 January 2018].

58 The emergence of a national written standard in the later medieval period is a subject that has attracted a high degree of controversy; for a recent discussion see T. W. Machan, 'Snakes, Ladders, and Standard Language', in *Imagining Medieval English: Language Structures and Theories, 500–1500*, ed. T. W. Machan (Cambridge, 2016), pp. 54–77.

according to region and according to the number from that region categorised as 'non-standard' English.[59] This demonstrates that, in general, the greater the distance of a petition's origin from London, the greater the likelihood of its language displaying distinctively regional forms. This analysis suggests, therefore, that although the evidence presented by *eLALME* in relation to the language of petitions finds a low degree of linguistic variation, this should not necessarily be taken as conclusive evidence of their metropolitan origins.

Furthermore, subsequent attempts to analyse the language of these documents in order to discern their regional origins have revealed different results. Most notable of these is the study of English chancery bills dating from between 1432 and 1443 conducted by Timothy Haskett.[60] Haskett claims this study to be based on examination of approximately 500 dateable bills in the file C 1/9; this is an over-estimation, as this file contains only 488 documents; not all of these are in English, and some of them are not bills but related legal documents such as answers, interrogatories and depositions.[61] Nevertheless, a reassessment of the contents of this file estimates the number of English bills to be in excess of 300, only eighty-eight of which are included in *eLALME*, and in contrast to the editors of that work Haskett's analysis finds considerable evidence of regional variation.[62] His methodology differs from that of *eLALME* in that it takes into account style and idiom; he argues that this can reveal as much about the origins of a document as its orthography and morphology. In this respect, he finds greatest variation in those bills from Cornwall, Devon and Somerset, which are particularly elaborate and florid in style.[63] On this basis of this study, Haskett rejects the suggestion made by Fisher and other scholars that the bills are copies drawn up by the chancery clerks, instead claiming that they were drawn up in the localities before being brought to the chancery. He argues that the authors of these documents were 'country lawyers', who, although fluent in the forms and phrases of administrative writing, adapted these to the language and syntax of their own particular region. The range of work carried out by these lawyers was very broad, encompassing much 'extra-legal' writing, and they would have represented the only point of contact with the legal system for the majority of people.[64] It is important to emphasise here that when Haskett refers to 'country lawyers' he means any legal professional operating outside the chancery; this could include scribes operating within London. However,

[59] Wales and Ireland have been excluded from this analysis because *eLALME* contains very few petitions from these countries.

[60] Haskett, 'The Composers of English Chancery Bills', pp. 9–23.

[61] Dodd, 'Rise of English', 123 states that this file contains 150 bills, of which 129 are in English; the discrepancy is due to the fact that this study considers only bills clearly dated from between 1437 and 1443.

[62] These estimates will be discussed in further detail below in relation to Table III.

[63] Haskett, 'The Composers of English Chancery Bills', p. 13.

[64] Haskett, 'The Composers of English Chancery Bills', pp. 21–3.

his analysis firmly supports the view that most petitioners to the chancellor could call on the services of scribes working within their local community. Kitrina Bevan, in her study of fifteenth-century clerks and scriveners in the south-west of England, finds evidence that provincial scriveners were not only responsible for drafting petitions but in some cases acted as intermediaries who personally presented these requests in parliament.[65]

The evidence presented by these analyses, while far from conclusive in determining the link between the regional origin of a petition and its language, does at least reveal that these documents are not uniform in character and exhibit a degree of linguistic variation. This makes the idea that they were drawn up centrally by a relatively small group of metropolitan scribes seem implausible. In addition, there is evidence to suggest that the number of English petitions included in *eLALME* remains only a fraction of the total, and therefore may not be a representative sample. Table III (p. 87) displays a reassessment of the number of total English petitions surviving from before 1461 in the relevant TNA series. It should be emphasised that, with the exception of the number given for English petitions in the series SC 8, which is based on a list compiled by the Public Record Office in 1935, these figures are estimates; they have been compiled using TNA's online catalogue, samples taken from the original files and evidence drawn from previous studies.[66] The end of the reign of Henry VI was chosen as a cut-off point as only material written prior to this date was included in *eLALME*; with this in mind we should take into account the fact that there are problems with dating some of these documents, particularly in the case of the chancery bills. Table III displays the number of English petitions analysed in *eLALME* according to TNA series. The majority of these are chancery bills, in the series C 1, and parliamentary petitions, in the series SC 8; extant petitions in other series have been largely overlooked. Overall, the new figures estimate the total number of English petitions surviving from before 1461 to be far in excess of the number assessed by the editors of *eLALME*.

The major new contribution here is formed by the petitions surviving in the series C 81, which have not yet been subject to close scholarly attention.

[65] K. Bevan, 'Clerks and Scriveners: Legal Literacy and Access to Justice in Late Medieval England' (unpublished PhD thesis, University of Exeter, 2013), pp. 230–3.

[66] English-language petitions in the series TNA, SC 8 (parliamentary petitions) are listed in OBS 1/1399. Estimates for other series have been compiled as follows: C 1 (chancery bills) contains 38 files within the date range; files 1–8 were checked in full and samples were taken from files 9–29 and 38–46; E 28 (chamberlain's bills) contains 54 files within the date range; numbers for files 35–62 were taken from Dodd, 'Rise of English', 125 and Appendix, samples were taken from files 63–88; numbers for C 49 (parliamentary petitions) were estimated based on searches in TNA online catalogue; C 81 (signed bills and other direct warrants) contains 92 files within the date range; files 1394–1426 and 1478–85 were checked in full and files 1427–77 were estimated based on samples.

Petitions surviving in this series have generally been referred to as 'signed bills': requests to the king or chancellor that have been converted into warrants to move the great seal by means of a minuting clause.[67] They were typically formulated in two sections: a heading and brief introductory paragraph in English, and a more extensive Latin section in the form of a warrant (sometimes appended as a separate document). In effect, the petitioner drafted their own warrant for approval by the king, which he would indicate by means of his sign manual (hence the term 'signed bills'). This may be compared to similar developments in the form of parliamentary petitions, which over the course of the fourteenth century had begun to include an increasing amount of detail regarding the outcome desired from the request, resulting in the fifteenth century in the practice whereby a petitioner would simply submit a document in the form of a pre-prepared warrant or letters patent in order to have it signed off by one of the government clerks.[68] Dodd has suggested that documents of this type indicate a growing necessity for the scribe of a petition to be familiar with the form and language of government instruments.[69] Indeed, many examples of this genre have more in common in appearance with official documents produced by one of the government offices than they do with earlier petitions.[70] In addition to a greater familiarity with the diplomatic of warrants, this type of petition required the scribe to be fluent in Latin; there is therefore perhaps a greater expectation that requests of this kind were drawn up centrally by professional clerks associated with the government administration. As this type of petition might contain only one or two lines of English text, the possibility for determining their origins through linguistic analysis is limited; it is therefore unsurprising that they have been overlooked by the editors of *eLALME*.

Examination of these files, however, reveals that not all of the petitions in this series are in fact 'signed bills', but that a significant proportion are formulated as traditional requests. A striking example is the petition to the king from Edward Ellesmere, who was treasurer of the chamber in the household of Queen Margaret of Anjou in 1452, regarding a dispute over holdings in Goring, Oxfordshire.[71] This document is written entirely in English, in a somewhat erratic and unprofessional-looking hand, and contains no record of the crown's response; indeed, it contains very little detail regarding the desired outcome beyond a request for the king's 'gracious remedie'. The

67 Maxwell-Lyte, *Historical Notes on the Use of the Great Seal*, pp. 152–6. These documents survive in TNA C 81/1394–1531.

68 Dodd, *Justice and Grace*, p. 305.

69 Dodd, *Justice and Grace*, p. 305.

70 See, for example, the petition of John Fawkes, clerk of parliament, dated 1447 (TNA, C 81/1480/6678).

71 TNA, C 81/1480/6704 (temp. Henry VI); A. R. Myers, *Crown, Household and Parliament in Fifteenth-Century England* (London, 1985), p. 213.

number of traditional petitions in this series lessens over time; they form the bulk of material in those files dated prior to 1441, but are slightly outnumbered by signed bills after this date.[72] Nevertheless, it is estimated that they are still very numerous in the period 1441 to 1461. Preliminary analysis of the text of these documents finds evidence of linguistic variation suggesting they were drafted by a regional scribe.[73]

As English-language petitions did not appear in significant numbers until the 1430s the question remains as to the extent to which we can apply the conclusions reached by such an analysis to earlier periods, when the overwhelming majority of these documents were written in Anglo-Norman French. As French was largely confined to the spheres of law and government in later medieval England, it may be assumed that the necessity to draft petitions in this language meant a greater need for the services of a professional scribe. Having said this, the extent of French literacy in England during this period remains a subject of debate; some have argued that there was a considerable degree of overlap between the two languages, with, in many cases, the line between French and English in a single document being difficult to draw.[74] Richard Ingham has presented evidence to suggest that French retained the status of a vernacular up until the late fourteenth century, after which it was passed on only as an imperfectly learned second language.[75] Assuming on this basis that French-language petitions dating from after this period are more likely to exhibit linguistic variation, Serge Lusignan conducted a linguistic analysis of seventy chancery bills written in French dating from between 1380 and 1403.[76] He found evidence of significant variation, but was unable to map these variations according to the petitioner's regional background. Nevertheless, he argues, on the basis of comparison with examples of privy seal letters, which by contrast contain few errors and

72 Of 51 requests in English dating from pre-1441, 39 are formulated as traditional petitions and 12 as signed bills.

73 A sample analysis was carried out using *eLALME*'s online 'fitting tool', which enables the construction of a linguistic profile on the basis of variant forms of common words: <http://archive.ling.ed.ac.uk/ihd/elalme_scripts/mapping/fitting.html> [accessed 18 January 2018]. Several petitions from the TNA series C 81 were found to contain spelling variants associated with a particular regional dialect, notably C 81/1426/9 (1440), localised to the Welsh borders, and C 81/1424/29 (1439), localised to the north-west of England.

74 W. Rothwell, 'English and French in England after 1362', *English Studies* 82 (2001), 555.

75 R. Ingham, 'The Transmission of Later Anglo-Norman: Some Syntactic Evidence', in *The Anglo-Norman Language and its Contexts*, ed. R. Ingham (York, 2010), pp. 227–51.

76 S. Lusignan, 'Communication in the Later Plantagenet Empire: Latin and Anglo-Norman as Regal Languages', in *The Plantagenet Empire, 1259–1453: Proceedings of the 2014 Harlaxton Symposium*, ed. P. Crooks, D. Green and W. M. Ormrod (Donington, 2016), pp. 273–89, at pp. 282–3.

exhibit a form of French closer to the continental variety, that this variation signifies that the petitions were drawn up in a variety of locations.[77]

Lusignan's results may be compared with those of Guilhem Pépin, whose study of petitions from Gascony to the English king reveals evidence that they were drawn up locally before being sent to Westminster.[78] The scribes of these documents ranged from the professional to the amateur; whereas some demonstrate a high level of competency and consistency in French, leading Pépin to surmise that they were written by clerks in the Anglo-Gascon administration who frequently travelled between Gascony and England, others contain more evidence of the local context of their production. The most unusual of these is the 1321 request of the people of Hastingues in the department of Landes, which is one of the only examples of a petition signed by its scribe, the squire Gaillard du Sages. The fact that, in this case, the people of a community turned not to a professional clerk or notary to draw up their grievance but instead to a literate man-at-arms leads Pépin to claim that 'anybody in Gascony was allowed to write a petition as long as he was able to write and to use French, or at least Latin'.[79]

Conclusion

The preceding analysis has demonstrated some of the ways in which we can attempt to identify the scribes of petitions. Overall, palaeographical and linguistic analysis of these documents suggests that their authors came from a variety of locations and professional backgrounds, and that we should therefore be wary of attempting to build up a picture of the 'typical' petitionary scribe. Identification of the hands of certain prominent individuals, such as Adam Pinkhurst, Thomas Hoccleve and Richard Osbarn, as the authors of petitions suggests the existence of a network of scribes within London who were known to carry out this kind of work and could be called upon if necessary. Yet evidence of the personal connections between these men and some of their clients perhaps indicates that, for them, petition-writing was more of an occasional task, undertaken for those with whom they were already acquainted, than a substantial part of their daily professional lives. The case of Hoccleve illustrates that government clerks did sometimes write petitions in order to supplement their income, but suggests that this did not constitute a large part of their scribal activities.

The extent to which Pinkhurst, Hoccleve and Osbarn can be seen as representative of petition-writers in general is debatable, as their identification is based at least in part on their work as the authors or copyists of literary

[77] Lusignan, 'Communication in the Later Plantagenet Empire', p. 283.
[78] Pépin, 'Petitions from Gascony', pp. 125–30.
[79] Pépin, 'Petitions from Gascony', pp. 125–6.

manuscripts. However, it is perhaps significant that they are found to have drafted parliamentary petitions, as these documents had become increasingly elaborate over the course of the fourteenth century, culminating in the adoption of an elaborate 'courtly' style that Dodd links to the influence of literary culture.[80] We might surmise, therefore, that petition-writing during this period required not only a command of the relevant forms and language but a high level of creative input.

Linguistic analysis of both English and French petitions has so far yielded mixed results, but varying degrees of dialectal variation suggest overall that, although some petitioners took advantage of the specialist skills of the clerks employed by the central government administration, the majority employed professional scribes in their own region. This provides further evidence that petitioning was a legal strategy accessible (at least in theory) to a wide range of people. Dodd's assessment of the social makeup of petitioners to parliament suggests that, although the majority came from relatively affluent backgrounds (predominantly from among landowners, merchants and the clergy), there were also significant numbers from members of the lower social classes.[81] A reassessment of the relevant TNA series suggests that the number of surviving English-language petitions from the first half of the fifteenth century is much greater than previously thought, and that more comprehensive linguistic analysis is necessary if we are to throw any further light on their origins. An analysis of this nature would have the potential to make a substantial contribution to our understanding of both the petitionary process and the linguistic culture of late medieval England.

[80] G. Dodd, 'Kingship, Parliament and the Court: The Emergence of "High Style" in Petitions to the English Crown, 1350–1405', *English Historical Review* 129 (2014), 515–48.

[81] Dodd, *Justice and Grace*, pp. 205–20.

Appendix

Table I. Identification of scribes active in multiple petitions

Scribe	TNA ref.	Petitioner(s)	Date	Subject	Attribution
Adam Pinkhurst	C 81/1394/87	Geoffrey Chaucer	1385	Request for appointment of a deputy for the office of controller of the wool custom	Horobin, 'Adam Pinkhurst, Geoffrey Chaucer, and the Hengwrt Manuscript of the Canterbury Tales', pp. 354–5
	SC 8/20/997	Mercers' Company of London	1388	Accusations against Nicholas Brembre	Mooney, 'Chaucer's Scribe', 97–138
	SC 8/21/1001B	Leathersellers and White Tawyers of London	1388	Accusations against Nicholas Brembre	Mooney and Stubbs, *Scribes and the City*, pp. 78–80
Thomas Hoccleve	C 81/525/7264	William Menuesse	1391	Concerning the church living of Aldington	Killick, 'Thomas Hoccleve as Poet and Clerk', pp. 87, 231
	SC 8/248/12400	John Russell, executor of the will of Margaret de Wingfield	1397–8	Request for confirmation of a grant made by Queen Anne	'Writing of Petitions' project (see n. 29 above)
	E 28/24/6	Henry Fowelere, sergeant of the king's larder	1399–1400	Request for a grant from the petty custom in the port of London	Killick, 'Thomas Hoccleve as poet and clerk', p. 231

Scribe	TNA ref.	Petitioner(s)	Date	Subject	Attribution
Hoccleve (cont.)	SC 8/250/12467	John Bole; Thomas Chode; John Trynche	1401	Request for annulment of outlawry	'Writing of Petitions' project
	SC 8/102/5069	Commons in Parliament	1402	Request that Robert de Markele should receive wages and fees granted by letters patent of Richard II	Ormrod, Killick and Bradford (eds.) *Early Common Petitions*, pp. 15 n. 5, 44–5
	E 28/25/26	Richard Aberhale	1404–5	Request for twenty-four oak trees from the forest of Haywode	Killick, 'Thomas Hoccleve as poet and clerk', p. 231
	E 28/25/28	William Bentle	1404–5	Request for one of two damaged ships in the port of Kingston	Killick, 'Thomas Hoccleve as poet and clerk', p. 231
	C 81/654/7128	John Muriden	1411–12	Regarding lands in Hundeston, Sook and Thorne Coffyn, Somerset	Killick, 'Thomas Hoccleve as poet and clerk', pp. 47, 89; 231
	SC 8/250/12477	William de Foreste of Brittany	1412	Request for letters of safe-conduct	'Writing of Petitions' project
	E 28/30/17	John Welde	1415	Request for trees from the forest of Warborough	Killick, 'Thomas Hoccleve as poet and clerk', pp. 88, 231
	E 28/45 (4 July)	Thomas Hoccleve	1424	Request for a living from the Priory of Southwick, Hampshire	'Writing of Petitions' project

Scribe	TNA ref.	Petitioner(s)	Date	Subject	Attribution
Hoccleve (cont.)	SC 8/250/12471	Roger Lassels	1425	Request for the advowson of the church of Kirkby Knowle	'Writing of Petitions' project
Richard Osbarn	E 28/36 (Dec)	Robert Spencer	1421	Request for licence to mine for gold and silver	'Writing of Petitions' project
	SC 8/94/4662	Richard Bradbury	1422	Concerning a suit against the Meverell family regarding lands in Derbyshire (damaged)	'Writing of Petitions' project
	SC 8/24/1197	Commons	1425	Regarding the holding of prisoners in the Tower without trial	'Writing of Petitions' project and see Killick, 'Treason, Felony and Lollardy', 228
	SC 8/125/6244	Merchants, owners, masters and mariners of England going to Guyenne	1427	Request for the appointment of a new Constable of Bordeaux following the death of Thomas Barneby	'Writing of Petitions' project
	E 28/50 (8 Mar.)	Sir Nicholas Horton	1428	Request for confirmation of letters granting the custody of Oye Castle, Picardy	'Writing of Petitions' project

Table II. Regional distribution of petitions included in *eLALME* (excluding Wales and Ireland)

Region	Counties	No. of petitions	No. designated 'non-standard' language	% of total
London		20	2	10
South East	Berkshire, Buckinghamshire, East Sussex, Hampshire, the Isle of Wight, Kent, Oxfordshire, Surrey and West Sussex	53	6	11
East of England	Bedfordshire, Cambridgeshire, Essex, Hertfordshire, Huntingdonshire, Norfolk and Suffolk	81	15	19
Yorkshire	South Yorkshire, West Yorkshire, East Riding of Yorkshire, North Yorkshire	21	4	19
South West	Gloucestershire, Wiltshire, Somerset, Dorset, Devon, Cornwall	65	13	20
East Midlands	Derbyshire, Leicestershire, Lincolnshire, Northamptonshire, Nottinghamshire and Rutland	61	22	36
West Midlands	Herefordshire, Shropshire, Staffordshire, Warwickshire	33	13	39
North	Cheshire, Cumberland, Westmorland, Greater Manchester, Lancashire, Northumberland, County Durham	10	5	50

Table III. Re-estimates of surviving English petitions dating from before 1461

TNA series	**SC 8**	**C 1**	**E 28**	**C 49**	**C 81 petitions**	**C 81 signed bills**	**Total**
eLALME	128	219	7	2	1		357
Estimate of extant total	484	Approx. 7600	Approx. 980	Approx. 300	Approx. 1300	Approx. 1600	Approx. 12,300

4

Patterns of Supplication and Litigation Strategies: Petitioning the Crown in the Fourteenth Century

Anthony Musson

Petitioning the crown as an individual involved seeking to gain the attention of the king either through an oral supplication recorded by the parliamentary clerks or via a document containing the request for grace submitted to the clerks in the petitioner's absence. Unless the petition was 'fast-tracked' and read out to the king and his council during a parliamentary session, it was delegated to a committee of 'auditors and triers' comprising members of the nobility, senior churchmen and legal experts. Some were responded to immediately, others were diverted to officials in particular branches of government (including the exchequer, chancery and the courts of king's bench and common pleas). While it appears from the instructions and comments endorsed on surviving petitions that it was a somewhat administrative means of achieving justice, it was not a purely bureaucratic process. Applications were read out to the panel, who, upon hearing it, discussed the merits and made their decision accordingly or sought advice from other departments.[1]

The supplicant made his or her submission trusting that a favourable response would be achieved. Much depended, however, upon the way the petition was framed and the language used in formulating it. In order to present the subject matter of the complaint and concomitant request for remedy in a suitably persuasive manner, the petitioner needed to employ not only an overarching narrative but also convincing legal arguments and a range of rhetorical devices. Petitions were thus inevitably 'artful constructs designed to get something done'.[2] This is an area in which 'a good deal of work remains to be done', as Mark Ormrod acknowledged, notably 'on

[1] G. Dodd, *Justice and Grace: Private Petitioning and the English Parliament in the Late Middle Ages* (Oxford, 2007), pp. 91–106; W. M. Ormrod, 'Voicing Complaint and Remedy to the English Crown, c. 1300–1460', in *Medieval Petitions: Grace and Grievance*, ed. W. M. Ormrod, G. Dodd and A. Musson (York, 2009), pp. 138–43, 145. There was also a strong undercurrent of orality in the communication of the action on the petition.

[2] W. M. Ormrod, 'Introduction: Medieval Petitions in Context', in *Medieval Petitions*, ed. Ormrod et al., p. 11.

the way in which words, phrase and forms were chosen by the writers of petitions to create effect and impact'.[3] Answering the call, this paper assesses changing patterns of supplication and corresponding litigation strategies adopted by medieval petitioners, exploring especially their discourses and linguistic approaches. In order to analyse and contextualise this multipurpose form, I will draw upon petitions presented to the king by a variety of supplicants, though with special focus on manorial tenants and litigants in the court of Chivalry. In particular, I will examine the mentalities and logistics involved, the advantages in terms of procedure and the concerns of litigants (the matters at stake and the corresponding legal issues raised), as well as the tactics and manoeuvres employed in pursuit of strategic aims.

In doing so this paper considers not only the challenges posed by the complex jurisdictional avenues available but also the obstacles and obstructions faced by those considering litigation. Moreover, it will demonstrate how an evaluation of the culture of supplication enables historians to gain insight into what was happening both within and outside the courts. Petitioning itself appears to have been both a shield and a sword, and a double-edged one at that. On the one hand, petitioning the crown offered an opportunity for the peaceful settlement of a dispute, thereby avoiding the rigour and expense of going to court. On the other hand, it provided a means whereby litigation could be initiated, or at least threatened, though it also enabled a quarrel to continue both inside and outside the court room, often through raising procedural complaints or requests. Clarifying the situation for the crown, albeit from their own *ex parte* point of view, supplication brought the hope of extra-judicial assistance and the possibility of remedying injustice.

Legal Agenda

In the first analysis, the visual distinctiveness of certain petitions, their length and the complexity of their requests (sometimes covering several points or distinct complaints) is a noticeable trait that strongly implies careful co-ordination on the part of the supplicant(s) and an underlying agenda. In most cases it also suggests that legal advice had been obtained and the petition professionally framed and worded accordingly to achieve redress from the oppressive behaviour of the wrong-doer(s).[4] Although the identity of their advisor is not known, the tenants of the manor of Sowerby and of Penrith in Cumberland, for example, jointly petitioned the king and council in

[3] Ormrod, 'Voicing Complaint', p. 145.

[4] For further discussion of 'multiple-clause' petitions see G. Dodd, M. Phillips and H. Killick, 'Multiple-Clause Petitions to the English Parliament in the Later Middle Ages: Instruments of Pragmatism or Persuasion?', *Journal of Medieval History* 40 (2014), 176–94.

1308–9 on a number of matters affecting their landholding. First, they claimed their respective manors were ancient demesne. They then asserted that things had changed with the reversion of the lands to the crown and the advent of a new bailiff.[5] Allegedly the tenants were being prevented from enjoying their customary rights (which they specify in detail for each manor) with regard to the woodland. They maintained that in the past they had been allowed to make essoins and have delays when attached for trespass against their lord (the king of Scotland) and that they had been accustomed to pay entry fines only for their ancient lands and not for the various approved lands beyond the manor for which entry fines were now being demanded.[6] The petition has an added political dimension in its claims against the Scottish king, but as both sets of tenants obtained inquiries into the veracity of their claims (as requested) the strategy adopted clearly paid off.[7]

Input from 'men of law' can also be inferred from the language and detail of the petitions. Some supplicants cited Magna Carta or highlighted specific legislation. William de Boys, for example, demanded delivery of the issues and rents that were due him from the manors not held of the king that he had inherited from his brother. In doing so he based his right on Magna Carta and the statute of Marlborough.[8] Seeking remedy for the situation he faced, Gerard de Braybrook drew attention to the fact that the king had ordained in parliament that no one should leave court without redress for cases where there was no existing remedy in chancery.[9] Joan, the widow of Ralph Basset of Drayton, claimed that the commissions of special oyer and terminer issued to Hugh Meynill against her and her servants contravened 'the statutes providing that an oyer and terminer should only be granted in cases of serious trespass and before justices of king's bench or common pleas'.[10] Similarly, Isabel, the widow of Richard de Cleterne, pointed out that in Edward III's reign charters of pardon were too commonly given regardless of the recent legislation.[11]

These petitioners do not give the precise chapter and verse, yet they were not just making vague allusions to legislation or making up citations. The essence of William de Boys' complaint is indeed featured in the statute of Marlborough of 1267 (at chapter 16),[12] while Braybrook's claim was founded on the famous chapter 24 concerning writs *in consimili casu* in the second statute

[5] Until recently they had been in the hands of the Scottish king.
[6] TNA, SC 8/2/65.
[7] The endorsement has the names of John de Swineburne and Hugh de Louther at the top, who may be those appointed to investigate.
[8] SC 8/35/1736.
[9] SC 8/36/1765.
[10] SC 8/32/1551.
[11] SC 8/39/1937; 1 Edward III, st. 2, c. 14, *SR*, vol. I, p. 256.
[12] 52 Henry III, *SR*, vol. I, pp. 23–4.

of Westminster (1285).[13] Joan Basset's petition of 1346 concerning commissions of oyer and terminer, despite not mentioning a specific statute, rightly reflects chapter 3 of the statute of Northampton (1328), which itself confirmed chapter 29 of the statute of Westminster (1285).[14] Similarly, Isabel Cleterne's petition certainly refers back to chapter 2 of the statute of Northampton and to chapter 13 of the statute of 1330.[15]

Petitioners (or their advisors) may have considered direct quotation from Magna Carta or another statute was a way of underlining the authority of their argument and thus the legitimacy of the claim. A petition from Robert de Thorpe of Suffolk, for instance, desiring 'such remedy as the law of the land and the provisions of the Great Charter', referred accordingly to several distinct 'poyntz' of the Charter during the course of his lengthy petition.[16] Robert Thorpe was son and heir of John Thorpe (d. 1324), who had held the manor of Combs in Suffolk directly from the king for an annual fee farm, which had escheated to the king as a result of a forfeiture in the distant past. The petitioner was claiming reimbursement of the issues erroneously taken by the escheator and remedy for the sheriff's wrongful distraint for payment of relief. In support of his case, Thorpe quotes directly from chapter 31 of Magna Carta (1225), 'we will hold it in the same manner that the baron held it', for which, unusually, the text breaks from the Anglo-Norman French of the petition into Latin 'Nos eodem modo eam tenebimus quo baro eam tenuit etc'.[17] By making precise reference to the original Latin text, Thorpe was emphasising both his specific claim and his understanding of the authority of the Charter. Since unfortunately he had mistakenly ('through ignorance') already performed homage to the king, the strength of his argument through invocation of that particular clause may have been undermined. Hedging his bets slightly in legal terms, therefore, he then cited the clause at the very end of the Charter: 'Also we have granted to them for us and our heirs, that neither we nor our heirs shall seek anything by which the liberties in contained in this charter may be infringed or broken; and if anything shall be sought after by any person contrary to this it shall not prevail and held for nothing.' The strategy succeeded to the extent that the certifications and inquests he had attached to the petition were scrutinised in chancery and the complaint itself was eventually ordered to heard by the king's council. In the meantime, though, as Robert Thorpe died in April 1330, it took Sir John de Clavering, who held the wardship of Thorpe's heir, to bring the case to the attention of the king in parliament. He did so in July of that year, whereupon

13 13 Edward I, *SR*, vol. I, p. 83–4.

14 2 Edward III, 13 Edward I, *SR*, vol. I, pp. 85, 258.

15 2 Edward III, 4 Edward III, *SR*, vol. I, pp. 257, 264.

16 SC 8/166/8297: 'tiel remedie qu la ley de la terre et les poyntz de la graunde Chartre'.

17 SC 8/8/355 (a duplicate of the previous one).

the matter was examined by the chancellor, treasurer, the justices of the two benches, barons of the exchequer and other wise men of the council, who duly acknowledged 'that it is specified in the great charter that the king will not have wardship by reason of escheat if a man held in chief of someone other than him, that it is the case that the aforesaid Robert held the same moiety at the fee-farm from the king ... and thereby the king ought not to have the wardship of the manors ... by reason of the minority of the heir of the said Robert'.[18]

Precise citations such as this appear to betray the influence of lawyers or at least personal reference to a statute book. Indeed, volumes of statutes were owned not just by men of law but a whole range of 'consumers' of legal literature, among whom were public officials, lay landowners, merchants, estate stewards, ecclesiastical institutions and urban corporations.[19] As Robert Thorpe's father played a key role in local justice in East Anglia during Edward II's reign the petitioner may well have had access to a copy of the Great Charter in any law books he possessed or been able to secure legal advice on the matter.[20] Equally, he would have had access to the sheriff's office, where copies of the Great Charter and other legislation were deposited.[21] It would therefore be unsurprising to find Thorpe's verbatim citation, though that in itself does not diminish the authoritativeness of the claim or the air of confidence he wished to project by its use.

Citation of statutory authority for the claim was not the only element used to persuade the king that a supplicant's case was worthy of attention: construction of a discourse that invoked antiquity and appealed directly to royal responsibility for the welfare of his subjects seems to have been particularly effective. As in the petition from the tenants of Sowerby and Penrith, the status of the petitioners can equally imply recourse to legal assistance,

[18] SC 8/266/13299 [1330?]; *PROME*, parliament of November 1330, C 65/2, mm. 7–5, item 19.

[19] D. C. Skemer, 'Sir William Breton's Book: Production of *Statuta Angliae* in the Late Thirteenth Century', in *English Manuscript Studies, 1100–1700*, ed. P. Beal and J. Griffiths, vol. VI (London, 1998), pp. 27–8, Skemer provides the contents and organisational scheme for Breton's statute collection at pp. 38–42; A. Musson, *Medieval Law in Context: The Growth of Legal Consciousness from Magna Carta to the Peasants' Revolt* (Manchester, 2001), pp. 122–3.

[20] A. Musson, *Public Order and Law Enforcement: The Local Administration of Criminal Justice, 1294–1350* (Woodbridge, 1996), pp. 37, 104, 133; Henry Summerson, 'Thorpe, John, first Lord Thorpe (c. 1270–1324)', *Oxford Dictionary of National Biography* (Oxford, 2004); online edn, January 2008, <http://0-www.oxforddnb.com.lib.exeter.ac.uk/view/article/27377> [accessed 12 July 2016]. Robert himself was employed by the king on various diplomatic missions abroad during this period and may have had access to specialised legal advice.

[21] J. R. Maddicott, 'The County Community and the Making of Public Opinion in Fourteenth-Century England', *Transactions of the Royal Historical Society* 5th series 18 (1987), 36–7.

and the framing of complaints from peasants is particularly intriguing in its employment of a discourse of ancient rights. Common perception of the downward extension of Magna Carta's provisions in this respect can be found in numerous petitions emanating from villagers invoking their real or imagined status as tenants of manors of the king's ancient demesne.[22] Tenants on manors that were or had once been royal land were accorded a range of special privileges, including protection from increases in rents and services owed, access to the royal courts and personal freedom.[23] For example, the ancient demesne tenants of South Tawton (Devon), who early in Edward II's reign sought confirmation of their customs and usages, were able to cite with appropriate detail that they were enrolled (*en roule*) as a result of a plea decided before oyer and terminer justices Ralph de Hengham and his companions during Edward I's reign. This action had been brought when the manor was in the hands of Richard de Pultemor on account of 'autres coustoums' demanded of them.[24] The second limb of their petition highlighted further problems they had allegedly encountered, complaining of the unreasonable behaviour of royal bailiffs in detaining livestock and wrongful distraints carried out by various lords that were interfering with their customary practices. Employing legal terminology to convey the bailiffs' actions (*par force e destresce*),[25] they were clearly advised on the construction of their petition. Justification for bringing their complaint (akin to the tenants of Bocking (Essex), who were under the jurisdiction of the prior's court leet) came from the fact that the lords were claiming royal privilege and other liberties (*plede regal e autre franchises*).[26]

The tenants of the ancient demesne manor of Fawsley (Northants) similarly did not cite Magna Carta by name, but emphasised their impoverishment (*sont en poveris*) through the severity of the demands made on them contrary to the practices established in the time of their forebears. Adding to the picture of injustice, they complained of suffering ejection from their common pasture by the lord of the manor, Simon de Daventry.[27] Claims of dispossession made

22 B. P. Wolffe, *The Royal Demesne in English History: The Crown Estate in the Governance of the Realm from the Conquest to 1509* (London, 1971), pp. 24–30.

23 R. S. Hoyt, 'The Nature and Origins of Ancient Demesne', *English Historical Review* 65 (1950), 145–74; M. K. McIntosh, 'The Privileged Villeins of the English Ancient Demesne', *Viator* 7 (1976), 295–328; C. Dyer, 'Memories of Freedom: Attitudes towards Serfdom in England, 1200–1350', in *Serfdom and Slavery: Studies in Legal Bondage*, ed. M. L. Bush (Harlow, 1996), pp. 277–95.

24 The writ they obtained mentions 'alias consuetudines et alias servicia'.

25 Translated as: 'by their power and right of distress' (a recognised common law remedy).

26 SC 8/142/7093.

27 SC 8/169/8406. As in the previous case, the arguments clearly struck the correct note with the king's council as a remedy was forthcoming: *Calendar of Chancery Warrants, 1244–1326* (London, 1927), p. 420.

by other ancient demesne tenants seem to draw implicitly on Magna Carta chapter 29, championing their free status. Using the language of disseisin, 'poor tenants' variously maintain they had been ousted from their land[28] and their inheritance[29] or had their houses knocked down and their lands seized so that their heirs could not enjoy them.[30]

Although the petitions were brought at different periods they tend to use similar language and arguments. As justification for their position they usually underline the antiquity of their customs and usages. Some cite Domesday Book,[31] while one group specifically cites King Harold, thus claiming their authority dated back prior to the Conquest.[32] Others simply state that they and their ancestors had enjoyed their lands 'saunz destourbance' from time immemorial.[33] This could be taken in legal terms to mean they were invoking the limit of legal memory (1189), a fictional time by which matters of ownership, possession and usage were (and still are) theoretically judged. Alternatively, they were perhaps using the term more metaphorically as simply constituting tradition or usage over a very long time.[34]

The appeal to ancient customs lies at the heart of Magna Carta (especially chapter 9), but the peasants also strongly believed that the actions against them were 'contrary to their laws' and prevented them from availing themselves of 'droit'. Certain tenants also clearly believed that their personal liberty (as well as their lands and possessions) was at stake: the tenants of Merton (Surrey), for example, requested protection for their bodies and chattels.[35] Such petitions provide an insight into perceptions of liberty and the grounds upon which claims of unjust treatment were founded. The perceptions of rights and privileges entertained by these disparate groups on a localised basis chimes with the belief of the townspeople and peasants of St Albans, who in a dispute in 1327 (and later during the Peasants' Revolt of

[28] For example: SC 8/201/10005 [1327?] (Old Windsor, New Windsor and Sunninghill, Berkshire).

[29] For example: SC 8/61/3007 [1348?] (Merton, Kent).

[30] SC 8/63/3133 [1334–5] (Ogbourne St George, Wiltshire).

[31] For example: SC 8/63/3142; SC 8/167/8334 (Manton); SC 8/61/3007.

[32] SC 8/61/3007 (Merton). In 1280 and 1364 the tenants of Crondall and Hessebourne in Hampshire claimed that their manors had been in the hands of 'the ancestors of the Lord King', which although fairly vaguely worded in fact represented an extraordinary feat of communal memory going back as far as the ninth or tenth centuries (and was accepted by Edward III in spite of the entry in Domesday Book which said it had always belonged to the Church): see R. Faith, 'The "Great Rumour" of 1377 and Peasant Ideology', in *The English Rising of 1381*, ed. R. H. Hilton and T. H. Aston (Cambridge, 1984), pp. 56–7.

[33] SC 8/201/10005: 'eyent en use du temps sont memorie ne cour'.

[34] P. Brand, '"Time out of Mind": The Knowledge and Use of the Eleventh- and Twelfth-Century Past in Thirteenth-Century England', *Anglo-Norman Studies XVI* (Woodbridge, 1994), 37–54.

[35] SC 8/61/3007.

1381) pointed the abbot of St Alban's to various 'charters of liberties' that they believed guaranteed their freedoms.[36]

The petitions from ancient demesne tenants manifest concern for the misuse of jurisdictional authority, thereby challenging the legitimacy of that authority.[37] As such, they also constitute an ongoing dialectic between personal freedom and villeinage played out both in a manorial context and with reference to the royal courts. Frequently they comprise allegations of illegality in terms of the behaviour of lords towards their tenants, notably attempts to downgrade their status (and thus their tenure) with detrimental consequences. The men of Mickleover (Derbys), for example, were aggrieved at the actions of the abbot of Burton upon Trent. Allegedly, he had distrained them (seized property for rent or services owed) in order to force them to acknowledge themselves as villeins when they were ancient demesne tenants.[38] The tenants of Manton (Rutland) (ancient demesne of the crown) were equally distraught. They said that they held their land freely of the abbot of Cluny, but had now been reduced to servitude following the removal of eighty acres, which had occurred without a corresponding reduction in the amount of rent owed. They were extremely worried because they were unable to pursue an action in law as a consequence of their impoverishment and reduced status.[39] The free sokemen of the manor of Harmondsworth (Middx) similarly encountered harsh and unjust treatment from their ecclesiastical landlord: distraints against their customary levels were compounded by the harm suffered by their lord's refusal to accept their legal status and his contravention of the findings of an inquest on the matter.[40]

Recourse to litigation and to the mechanism of petitioning the crown to achieve their aims was clearly not alien to the lowest orders of society.[41] Customary tenants were likely to issue such challenges outside their normal environment because the lord's control over the manor court was such that they were unlikely to be able to overturn or undermine his property interests in that forum. While a response to the circumstances alleged in such petitions

[36] Faith, 'Great Rumour', pp. 63–5.

[37] For a wide-ranging exploration of this theme see: S. Reynolds, 'Secular Power and Authority in the Middle Ages', in *Power and Identity in the Middle Ages: Essays in Memory of Rees Davies*, ed. H. Price and J. Watts (Oxford, 2007), pp. 11–22.

[38] SC 1/48/86 [sometime in Edward I's reign].

[39] SC 8/266/13288 [c. 1327–40].

[40] SC 8/203/10143: 'en contre lour droit estat et la forme del inquest … a lour graunt damage'. Whether this means an inquiry into their estate or a jury assessing the correct levels of amercement is not clear.

[41] P. R. Schofield, 'Peasants and the Manor Court: Gossip and Litigation in a Suffolk Village at the Close of the Thirteenth Century', *Past and Present* 159 (1998), 3–42; P. Schofield, 'Peasants, Litigation and Agency in Medieval England: The Development of Law in Manorial Courts in the Late Thirteenth and Early Fourteenth Centuries', in *Thirteenth Century England XIV*, ed. J. Burton, P. Schofield and B. Weiler (Woodbridge, 2013), pp. 15–25.

is not always forthcoming from the crown, it is noticeable that in the first half of the fourteenth century, before the growing discontent and concerted peasant requests for clarification of their status during the 1370s, efforts were made to examine claims and provide remedy where appropriate. By the later fourteenth century the benefits of common law were increasingly sought over the localised custom of the manor, testing the authority and resolve of landlords and the weakening bonds of lordship.[42] The grievance of the 'poures gentes' of Melbourne and King's Newton (Derbys), tenants of the ancient demesne manor of Melbourne, for instance, cites previous petitions to parliament and the king's council and requests the proper implementation of writs from chancery to uphold their rights as demanded by the 'ley de terre'.[43]

The petitions also reveal how peasants were using the mechanisms and processes of royal government to question issues of taxation and status. Requests for inquiry or confirmation of liability to tallage on the royal ancient demesne were made by various groups of tenants.[44] The crown's poor tenants of Archenfield in Herefordshire were particularly aggrieved that they had mistakenly been taxed by the county assessors 'contrary to their laws',[45] while the tenants of Tunstead, in the honour of the castle of High Peak (Derbys), the king's ancient demesne, claimed it was down to a clerical error that they had been placed on the rent roll in the first place.[46]

This questioning of the status quo and familiarity with Magna Carta penetrated further, extending to those at the lowest levels of society and clearly unfree. Addressing the prior of Christchurch Canterbury (their manorial lord), the customary tenants of the manor of Bocking articulated their complaints against a new bailiff (John le Doo) with express reference to Magna Carta. They cited breach of customary practice and the unreasonableness of new demands, and framed assessment of their liability for amercement (adopting the language of chapter 14), as needing to be 'by their peers according to the extent of their trespass'. Aping its phraseology, Magna Carta was clearly couched as applicable to them in that they claimed (or it was claimed on their behalf) the steward's behaviour was 'against all reason and the Great Charter'.[47]

The articulation of these feelings in petitions to the crown (and to manorial lords), setting out the nature of their grievances extremely clearly (some in contemplation of, or as a result of, legal proceedings) illustrates the burgeoning legal consciousness of members of the peasantry, whose

[42] SC 8/251/12549 (as in the dispute between the warden and college of Ottery St Mary and its manorial tenants).

[43] SC 8/8/366 [1324–5]. See also *CCR, 1323–1327*, p. 225.

[44] For example: SC 8/132/6562: 'poures gentz' of Oakham, Langham and Egleton, Rutland.

[45] SC 8/167/8334 [1334].

[46] SC 8/339/15976 [1334–5].

[47] J. F. Nichols, 'An Early Fourteenth-Century Petition from the Tenants of Bocking to their Manorial Lord', *Economic History Review* 2 (1929–30), 300–7.

formal status in the eyes of the law (as villeins) or low economic standing (as husbandmen and labourers) normally militated against active participation in legal matters beyond the manor court.[48] Since many of the complaints voiced in the late thirteenth and early fourteenth centuries were symptoms of long-running disputes,[49] they not only underline the impact of perceptions of Magna Carta but also confirm that these issues were not purely a reflection of the altered economic situation after the Black Death.[50]

Pushing the Legal Boundaries

While petitions often had an eye on the formalities of litigation, the format of the petition enabled individuals to couch their grievance on their own terms, which if the complaint did not easily fit within a common law remedy meant pushing the conceptual legal boundaries. William de Cleydon's grievance is unusual in that it not only relates to several clauses of Magna Carta but also confuses or conflates provisions of the Great Charter with the Forest Charter. Providing his credentials as a freeman, Cleydon boldly states with authority ('come il est contenuz en la grant charter') that a free man can erect a mill in his own land as long as it is not to the nuisance of his neighbours. This provision does not actually occur either in the 1215 or 1225 versions of Magna Carta, but rather forms chapter 12 of the Forest Charter (both 1217 and 1225). However, Cleydon (or his legal advisor) appears to have glossed the precise nature of the provision in his favour, in that chapter 12 speaks of the mill lying in the (royal) forest ('quam habet in foresta'), not simply forming his own land ('en son soil proprie issint') in the vill of Sudbourne. Further, in complaining that the bailiffs of John Sturmyn, keeper of Orford Castle (Suffolk), had detained his corn from this mill to his damage and disinheritance, and that this wrong had been committed 'without judgment', Cleydon seems to be invoking both chapters 19 and 29. He underlined his justification by asking the king for the justices of king's or common benches to inquire concerning this trespass 'according to law and reason and the purport of the Great Charter'.[51]

48 Musson, *Medieval Law in Context*, pp. 86–9; W. M. Ormrod, *Political Life in Medieval England, 1300–1450* (Basingstoke, 1995), pp. 40–1.

49 See, for example, the complex urban and manorial lord–tenant disagreements in St Albans: R. Faith 'The Class Struggle in the Fourteenth Century', in *People's History and Social Theory*, ed. R. Samuel (London, 1981), pp. 50–80; and the dispute between the villeins of Ogbourne and the abbot of Bec: M. Morgan, *The English Lands of the Abbey of Bec* (Oxford, 1946).

50 For example: SC 8/63/3142 (Ottery St Mary). For the broader historical context see: R. H. Hilton, 'Peasant Movements before 1381', *Economic History Review* 2 (1949), 117–36; M. Bailey, *The Decline of Serfdom in Late Medieval England: Bondage to Freedom* (Woodbridge, 2014).

51 SC 8/39/1943 [1317?].

A sense of how litigants were pushing the boundaries can also be gleaned from the endorsements to petitions, written comments on the back (or occasionally on the face) of the piece of parchment, within which citations of legislation can occur. These endorsements are presumably responses from those specially appointed at the start of parliament for hearing private grievances, panels that included lords, higher clergy and senior lawyers. They can also contain feedback from others of the king's council, such as the chancellor or treasurer, who had been specifically asked to respond. Not all petitions received a response. Some endorsements are more laconic than informative; others take the form of bureaucratic or ministerial instructions or internal memoranda rather than comments directed to the petitioner, though doubtless the outcome was relayed somehow.[52] If there was no action the petitioner often returned at the next parliament with a duplicate or similarly worded petition and sometimes added the lack of answer to the complaint.[53]

Some of the responses suggest that the petitioners were not wholly aware of the current law, perhaps citing outdated statute books or just 'trying it on'. The instruction to Wybert de la Clowere, the nephew and executor of Nicholas de Cantin, an alien merchant, for example, was that he should obtain a writ of debt in chancery rather than try and sue in the exchequer because he was not able to plead for debt at the exchequer as it was against Magna Carta: in this case chapter 4 of the *Articuli super cartas*, which had added the proviso that no common pleas should be held in the exchequer.[54] Other merchants seeking a special privilege from the court of the steward to hear pleas of debts for loans (for which it was claimed they otherwise would have no means of recovery) were similarly informed that this was contrary to Magna Carta.[55] In this case it was chapter 3 of the *Articuli*, which represented an attempt to confine the court of the steward and marshal (or the itinerant 'court of the verge', as it was known) to its proper business of hearing the complaints of members of the household rather than pleas of land, debt, contract or trespass relating to all-comers.

Petitioners' continued perception of the Great Charter as a legal authority can be seen more broadly in the types of grievance submitted that appear as elaborations of aspects of chapter 29 (and other provisions). John Mandour, for example, maintained that he was properly appointed under canon law ('fist duement par la ley de seinte esglise collacion') to the archdeaconry

[52] Dodd, *Justice and Grace*, pp. 52–60; G. Dodd and S. Petit-Renaud, 'Grace and Favour: The Petition and its Mechanisms', in *Government and Political Life in England and France, c. 1300–c. 1500*, ed. C. Fletcher, J.-P. Genet and J. Watts (Cambridge, 2015), pp. 270–1.

[53] This (as will be seen below) in itself could form a grievance founded on Magna Carta: delay in obtaining justice.

[54] SC 8/329/E932 [c. 1295–1315].

[55] SC 8/329/E939.

of Durham, but the appointment was later revoked by the king and given to an alternative candidate, Cardinal Pilet, who was later confirmed in the position under letters patent. Mandour argued for reinstatement on the basis of the injustice of the king's actions: that he had been ousted on false allegations ('suggestions nient veritables') and that writs to collect the fruits of his benefice had been issued unlawfully ('grantez en countre droit') and without process against him either in the royal courts or in the Church courts. Without stating it explicitly, Mandour's justification further underlined that this behaviour fell within the scope of chapter 29 of Magna Carta by alleging that this was patently against the law ('en countre la ley notariement'). In a final salvo, he emphasised the lack of adherence to the relevant 'laws of the land' by stressing that it offended both canon law and common law ('a les leys de seynt esglise e de realme'),[56] a volley that ultimately hit the mark, as letters patent were duly issued in August 1387 for Maundour to replace Cardinal Pilet in the archdeaconry.[57]

In many instances the focus of petitions raising or shadowing chapter 29 concern contentious issues related to legal disputes, including cases of wrongful imprisonment or outlawry.[58] Others involve specific procedural or substantive points.[59] The petitioners highlight conflicts of jurisdiction,[60] including alleged disseisin of rights 'wrongfully and without judgment',[61] and more general difficulties affecting the conduct of litigation or concerning the administration of justice.[62] In doing so they highlight problems with access to justice, including the convenience of the forum and the fairness of proceedings, issues that the crown had a duty to remedy. Many of these complaints ride on perceptions of the costs and delays inherent in litigation, which were subjective reactions to circumstances rather than objective criticisms of the system. The burden of costs and the length of time before a hearing took place were not unsurprisingly a nuisance for merchants,[63] but they were not the only ones affected. Ancient demesne tenants of Milton Keynes (Bucks) sought a remedy from the king because they claimed that a decision in their suit against their manorial lord (who had been demanding performance of unaccustomed services) was being unnecessarily delayed procedurally in a

56 SC 8/21/1021.
57 *CPR, 1385–1389*, pp. 349, 431.
58 SC 8/33/1635; SC 8/36/1799; SC 8/36/1800.
59 See, for example: SC 8/34/1667 (record and process); SC 8/37/1826 (procedural delays in an assize); SC 8/37/1834 (problem suing in an ecclesiastical court).
60 For example: SC 8/34/1658.
61 SC 8/268/13385: 'deseysi e hosta de cel gors a tort e saunz jugement'.
62 SC 8/32/1560 (alleges bribes and favour of justices); SC 8/37/1825 (urges empanelling of a jury of 'good people' rather than suspect ones); SC 8/31/1503 (alleges bribery of assize justice, John Bousser, so he would not allow challenges or exceptions); SC 8/39/1915 (complains inquisition procured and false indictments made).
63 For example: SC 8/329/E939.

form of judicial tennis: the justices in the court of common pleas informed them that 'lor pleinte' should be seen by the chancellor in chancery, who in turn responded that it ought to be decided by the justices of the bench. The delay itself was having repercussions in that allegedly the petitioners had been attacked and threatened by their lord in an attempt to prevent them from proceeding in the plea.[64] Such intimidation, whether actual or feared, was clearly preventing or inhibiting access to the courts to the extent that there were other ancient demesne tenants who sought the king's protection during their suit to ensure that nobody involved suffered molestation, came to any physical harm or had their property damaged.[65] The topicality of this line of argument can be seen in the fact that the issue was also one taken up by the Commons in 1378–9, who requested that 'all your lieges and subjects might be able freely and peaceably and in sure and safe protection of the king to go and come to your courts, to sue their actions or defend themselves without disturbance or hindrance'.[66] The cost of litigation and delays was an emotive issue that could easily be employed, as it reflected expectations of the benchmark of royal justice and not surprisingly remained a live issue despite being raised in parliament and reiterated in various statutes.[67]

They also demonstrate the interplay of sessions held by the various customary and common law courts (operating both provincially and centrally) and the ecclesiastical courts. The petition submitted in 1385 by William de Ashton, parson of the church of Swanscombe in Kent, concerned a writ of prohibition granted to Ashton subsequent to a suit brought against him in the court of Arches by the prior and convent of St Mary Overy (Southwark), which, it was said, should properly have been tried in the king's courts.[68] Unusually, the petition challenges the validity or legality of the endorsement[69] on an earlier petition presented in parliament by the prior.[70] Ashton must

64 SC 8/201/10006.

65 SC 8/61/3007: 'qil vous plese graunter un proteccioun pour les dits poures tenauntz duraunt lour seute qu nul homme les face mal ne moleste damage de corps ne de chateux'. See also SC 8/64/3171 (tenants of Northam).

66 F. Thompson, *Magna Carta: Its Role in the Making of the English Constitution, 1300–1629* (Minneapolis, MN, 1948; repr. 1978), pp. 13–14.

67 For example: *PROME*, parliament of February 1334, item 7: 'Also, the said community prays: because the chancery is a place where it is fitting for a man to have recovery and begin to sue his right by writ, that he might have the said writs without paying anything other than the fee of the seal, as the Great Charter wills, "We shall sell to no-one, we shall deny to no-one or delay right or justice", because many men have been delayed of their right and some disinherited because the clerks of the chancery have refused them writs which on other occasions used to be granted without paying anything, and also the king has suffered great loss from this.'

68 SC 8/20/985.

69 'Quel endosement est overtement encountre la leye'.

70 SC 8/139/6927. It is not clear whether this is implying they could not make such an endorsement or that the subject matter of endorsement was contrary to law.

have been shown or served with the response to the prior's petition (or it was communicated to him orally) because he cited the wording of the endorsement as evidence in his claim. Ashton's petition further mentions that the endorsement to the prior's petition was obtained 'in the present parliament'. It seems that Ashton either was present at parliament already (perhaps knowing the prior was submitting a petition) or reacted swiftly enough upon the outcome of the prior's petition to be there with his own response. In any event he must have had recourse to legal advice, as his response is crafted into a detailed and incisive riposte. His request flows naturally from the generality that no writ of consultation should be granted that was not in accord with the law of the land to the specific request that any such writ purchased in chancery as a result of this endorsement should be repealed. He ends with a plea for justice: to be able to have the common course of the law 'in salvation of the royal jurisdiction of the king'.[71]

Evidential Problems

The facts forming the subject matter of the petitions had to be marshalled in the appropriate manner and although the assertions afforded only a *prima facie* case and did not need proving to the evidential standards of the common law, documentary evidence might be required at a later date for trial or verification purposes. The petitions remind us of the value that contemporaries placed upon record-keeping and inform us about the expectation (on the part of both supplicants and officials) that evidence could be found to support or refute claims in official government records.[72] Frequently, searches in the records of the appropriate department (usually exchequer or chancery) were instituted as a result of a petition.[73] In 1320, for instance, Thomas Lovain claimed that the Roll of the Marshalcy would show that his father, Matthew, held his manor by homage and nothing more and that he performed service in Wales and so should not have to pay the levy imposed upon him. In response, the treasurer and barons of the exchequer were instructed to examine not only the Roll of the Marshalcy but also Domesday Book and other remembrances of the exchequer.[74] Alice Fesant, heiress to lands in the lordship of the Hospital of St John, requested that the steward of the court of

[71] SC 8/20/985.

[72] M. T. Clanchy, *From Memory to Written Record: England, 1066–1307*, 3rd edn (Oxford, 2013); M. Prestwich, 'English Government Records, 1250–1330'; P. D. A. Harvey, 'English Estate Records, 1250–1330'; G. Martin, 'English Town Records, 1200–1350'; R. Swanson, '*Universis Christi Fidelibus*: The Church and its Records', all in *Pragmatic Literacy, East and West, 1200–1330*, ed. R. Britnell (Woodbridge, 1997), pp. 95–106, 107–18, 119–30, 147–64.

[73] For example: SC 8/16/783; SC 8/16/787.

[74] SC 8/16/777.

the Prior of St John be asked to search the 'old rolls' concerning land division in the area and 'the best evidence they have' on the matter.[75] Proof of a debt owed to one supplicant it was said could be found on a bill under the seal of William de Northwell and on the account of the keeper of the wardrobe.[76] The petitions also reveal that some people kept documents in their own private archives. When Stephen de Reedness argued in 1322 that he had been gifted 200 acres of moorland in the West Riding of Yorkshire by a family whose ancestors claimed they had been seised of the lands since the Conquest and had subsequently been disseised by Henry de Lacy, earl of Lincoln (but were now in the king's hands), he was informed that the muniments belonging to the earl were to be searched.[77] Gunnora de Bingham asked for delivery of a charter, which she maintained was in the custody of Ralph Wake.[78] John and Joan de Braiton said that they could prove their claim through 'ancient charters and feoffments'.[79] Monastic institutions, in particular, made reference to their records. The prior of Coventry, for example, requested that remedy be ordained 'according to the purport of their muniments'.[80] The abbot of Bardney (Lincs) sought a protection that included a clause concerning the holding of pleas in his absence because, he argued, while out of the country he would not have access to the muniments he would need to respond adequately to the writs currently brought against him.[81]

The problems posed by lack of written evidence (especially with regard to contracts or inheritance matters) were sometimes felt to be insuperable and so in turn became the subject of a request for redress (particularly if it meant that facts could not be proved at common law). In one case the petitioners had been disinherited because their cousin had died suddenly without making a will and others had concocted a false testament and had it proved.[82] In another, it was claimed that an indenture had been made, but the constable had since died and had not pledged that the indenture was indeed of his own making.[83] The destruction of records during the Peasants' Revolt was sometimes provided as a reason for lack of documentary proof. In one instance the petitioner maintained he had been maliciously indicted before Sir John Cavendish at Bury St Edmunds and later acquitted at Hennowe (Suffolk) before the same judge upon his examination of the record and process of the case. Following the chief justice's death at the hands of the East Anglian rebels the record and process of this case together with others went missing, as did

[75] SC 8/20/963.
[76] SC 8/35/1720.
[77] SC 8/16/794. For other examples see: SC 8/33/1646; SC 8/35/1713.
[78] SC 8/1/13.
[79] SC 8/35/1745.
[80] SC 8/39/1950.
[81] SC 8/31/1545.
[82] SC 8/36/1759.
[83] SC 8/16/781.

the plea rolls that were in his keeping.[84] The records belonging to Reginald de Eccles, one of the Norfolk Justices of the Peace, were stolen and burnt during the 1381 uprising (so his executors explained) and Reginald himself lost his life.[85] One petitioner claimed that his letters had been destroyed by Hugh Despenser, the younger,[86] another that any proofs he possessed had been burnt by one of Queen Eleanor's executors.[87] Whether deliberately or accidentally started, fires frequently accounted for the destruction of documents and archives.[88] Other examples show how it was felt that justice was hindered if vital letters patent were missing,[89] or where redress was considered to be impossible because the current abbot had stolen the charters.[90] Documents in the hands of an enemy or legal adversary (especially if during a minority) could result in losses of ownership or disinheritance.[91] The potential damage that could be done to an individual or institution whose seal had been stolen, in legal and economic terms (using forged charters and other instruments), was incalculable and inevitably provoked recourse to justice at the highest levels.[92]

Petitions that conveniently maintain that the documentary evidence was missing or destroyed or that the star witnesses were unavailable ring alarm bells for historians. They may be founded on unfortunate circumstances, but may also be spurious appeals to veracity. While it may be that petitioning was their only hope for a way out of the situation, it may equally be that in some cases it was all part of the subtle gamesmanship of the experienced litigant. On another level, written proofs could be lost, but they could also (almost miraculously) be found again. Humphrey Bassingbourne stated that charters of Henry II and Richard I attesting to his forestership of the royal forest in the counties of Northamptonshire, Huntingdonshire and Buckinghamshire had been lost during the barons' war in Henry III's reign. He then claimed that they had been returned to him by religious men in about 1298 and were included with his petition (duly transcribed underneath).[93] It is not apparent

84 SC 8/20/984. The supplicant succeeded in obtaining a pardon for all things contained in the indictment.

85 SC 8/21/1028: his heirs, executors and tenants were requesting that the officers of the exchequer be instructed to cease their distraints against them for return of the records.

86 SC 8/34/1684.

87 SC 8/34/1699.

88 See, for example: SC 8/38/1886 (nuns of Cheshunt, Hertfordshire).

89 SC 8/2/100.

90 SC 8/13/622. For another case where theft of a letter or charter was alleged see SC 8/35/1711.

91 SC 8/40/1956 (Thomas de Musgrave). For documents stolen or illegally detained see also SC 8/33/1737; SC 8/34/1664; SC 8/40/1994.

92 SC 8/37/1829. For the wider context of this petition see SC 8/37/1830 and SC 8/37/1831; *CPR, 1330–1334*, pp. 63, 89, 131, 142.

93 SC 8/31/1550.

from the sources whether they were genuinely found in the safe-keeping of these 'religious men' or had in fact been re-inscribed or even concocted by them.[94]

Petitioning the crown could equally assist in ironing out evidential difficulties encountered in litigation, especially where lawyers were quibbling over matters of precise wording and the linguistic detail. Henry Foulden and his wife, Margaret, submitted that they had been assured in the previous parliament that an assize they had mentioned in their petition would remain in force in spite of some discrepancies in the wording and the spelling ('de scripture ou mysnomer') of the justices' names, since the wording of the ordinance was not clear and had proved open to argument. They requested clarification and an unambiguous statement so that it could apply to the example in their case and so take effect.[95]

It was not only problems with written evidence that could hinder the outcome of litigation, but also the apparent lack of sufficient living witnesses who might provide vital oral testimony. Ralph de Borstall's petition, however, maintained that there were more than two witnesses and other 'bones gentz' alive and that the sheriff had falsely returned the inquest against him, adding for good measure that even though the record and process had been called into the court of king's bench for the issue to be reviewed the case was continually adjourned and he was likely to lose his suit, contrary to due process of the common law.[96] In cases where it was alleged that the petitioner had not been able to produce the relevant deeds and evidences and many of the jurors and the relevant justices had died (so that there was insufficient evidence on which to base a writ of certification), a petition was considered a vital means of kick-starting the recovery process.[97]

Litigation in the Court of Chivalry

Under the procedures of the court of Chivalry, which followed those of Roman civil law, suits were initiated by bill. So the supplications made to the king usually form the basis of the complaint, setting out the legal position of the petitioner, which was then effectively referred on to the constable and marshal.[98] There are also petitions submitted that contain supplementary

[94] Clanchy, *Memory*, pp. 150–1, 171–2.

[95] SC 8/24/1167. There is no endorsement so it is not known what the outcome was.

[96] SC 8/35/1709. Such a claim could not be entirely substantiated by the petitioner.

[97] SC 8/35/1741 [c. 1328]. The record and process were to be viewed in chancery and the case remitted to the justices of assize in the relevant county 'to do what should be done according to what the statute has ordained'.

[98] M. H. Keen, 'The Jurisdiction and Origins of the Constable's Court', in *War and Government in the Middle Ages: Essays in Honour of J. O. Prestwich*, ed. J. Gillingham and J. C. Holt (Woodbridge, 1984), pp. 159–69.

requests (once the case was already being considered by the court) of either a procedural or an administrative nature (concerning witnesses, documentary evidence or the commissioners involved in the case) or by way of appeal against the decisions made by the court. This is particularly interesting in the dispute between William Montagu, earl of Salisbury, and his brother Sir John, who was a household knight and later steward of the household, which was initiated in the court of Chivalry in the early 1380s and dragged on until it was finally settled in 1394. The case is not one concerning disputed coats of arms or allegations of treason, but an indenture (or 'certain evidences') and a 'statute merchant' or 'statute staple' (a form of bond) for £10,000, which had allegedly been detained and the covenants infringed by Sir John.[99]

The proceedings of the case have not survived, but the tactics employed by the parties in the course of the dispute emerge from their various petitions. The earl of Salisbury, some time around 1384 or early 1385,[100] petitioned the king for matters to proceed without delay. He was worried about the absence, death or illness of certain witnesses to the case, which he claimed would be in 'graunt prejudice' of his right ('droit') and the prolonging of the matter.[101] In another petition – suggesting that problems in securing the presence of witnesses had not been resolved – he further urged the king to give the commissioners powers to 'compel and constrain' the witnesses to attend so they could be examined accordingly. The earl of Salisbury also turned his attention to the evidence relating to the case and called into question the acceptability of a document drawn up by a papal notary public as evidence appropriate to the custom and usage of the court (in spite of the fact that the court operated under civil law procedures for which notarised documents were commonplace). He required certification of the matter from the constable and marshal (or their deputies).[102] The requests regarding witnesses and the powers of the commissioners can be understood in the context of arguing delays to justice, which the king's grace was supposed to remedy. It does seem strange, however, that such a question regarding evidence was being posed through the medium of supplication to the king, rather than within the course of court proceedings, unless the court was adjourned at the time or it was considered a question lying outside its normal jurisdiction. Instructions issued from the chancery confirmed, however, that the court of Chivalry hearings were to go ahead, not withstanding the delays or an appeal by Sir John against the validity of proceedings.[103]

The tactics employed by the earl seem to have rankled with his brother. The former asked Richard II personally that he 'remember' the former's original

99 Details of the case were set out in a memorandum of 1397: *CPR, 1396–1399*, p. 172.
100 The date is unclear, but perhaps a year or two after the opening of the case.
101 SC 8/224/11168.
102 SC 8/231/11550.
103 *CPR, 1381–1385*, pp. 587–8.

petition, 'une supplicacion' delivered to parliament two years previously (that brought his brother John to the court of Chivalry to answer the earl), which in the king's presence, as Richard had agreed, would be determined 'by the laws of the court of Chivalry'.[104] The petition summarised proceedings and requested a record of this summary under the great seal, such as would be sufficient for future use before a judge. Careful repetition of the forum and the jurisdiction under which the dispute should be determined may have founded the basis of a counter petition by John Montagu. Suggesting that due process was not being followed, he requested that his brother's petition submitted at the last parliament concerning the dispute between them in the court of Chivalry be refused on the grounds that it was 'against the law of the land' ('encontre la ley de la terre').[105] In the context of the dispute this goes for the jugular, so to speak, although it is not entirely clear from the petition itself whether he was casting doubt on whether the case warranted trial in the court of Chivalry or, more probably, querying what the earl was doing by seeking the king's personal testimony together with confirmation of 'the truth of the matter' under the authority of the great seal.

In any event, this tactic clearly did not work, as judgement was given against Sir John Montagu by the president of the court, the constable of England (the then duke of Gloucester). Sir John again countered with an appeal for a hearing ('a l'audience') by the king himself on the grounds that the judgement was rendered on the basis of 'bad information' ('malveis information') and that the judgment contained 'many errors'. He therefore urged as 'law, reason and equity demand' that the record and process of the case come before the king in full parliament. His appeal against judgement duly received the apparently encouraging response: 'The king wills that right and reason be done.' This assurance of due process, however, did not operate to the benefit of Sir John: Richard II personally intervened again and the sentence against him was upheld. Accordingly the appeal was declined and Sir John himself was pronounced as being 'malveys' and condemned to pay the earl's costs, which amounted to the very significant sum of 2,500 marks.[106]

The manoeuvres of the parties in this case – in particular the approach to the king outside of the mechanisms of the court and the attempt to bring his influence to bear on proceedings – are significant but perhaps understandable, given the high-profile personalities involved. They also raise the spectre of whether the king's initial involvement at the earl's request

[104] *CCR, 1385–1389*, pp. 367, 375.
[105] SC 8/125/6228.
[106] SC 8/125/6226; C 49/47, no. 21. Ironically Sir John evaded payment, though attempts were made to enforce it and the duke of Gloucester was reprimanded by Richard II in 1389 for neglecting his official duty in this regard.

technically contravened one of the clauses on 'good governance' set out in the parliament of October 1385, which advised:[107]

> Also, if any persons try to inform or encourage the king in person to interfere with any matter concerning the law or a party [at law], may it please him to commit and pass on any such informers with their information and suggestions to his said council, and not to give credence or audience to these informers, but to allow his said council to do whatever pertains to the law, to his honour and estate.

The questioning of the judicial process and even the judgement given in the court of Chivalry, however, was not restricted to this particular case. In 1385 Roger Doget complained about the investigation carried out by the constable and marshal's deputies, Matthew Gourney and John de Roches, in the dispute between him and Philip Gilbert. This case concerned the ransom of a prisoner taken during the Flanders campaign. Doget maintained that the 'definitive sentence' had been given against him unjustly 'against good faith and in annulment of law' and requested the correction of certain errors in it.[108] Similarly, in 1389 William Hastorp cast doubt on the proper constitution of the court and the conduct of one of its officials, asking that new first instance justices (usually a mixture of knights and men of law) be assigned to the suit between him and John Dyneham (the various knights were unable to attend owing to royal business elsewhere), and stating that he believed Master Roger Page, clerk and doctor of law, 'for divers and reasonable causes' (not specifically mentioned) to be suspect.[109]

To some extent this was all part and parcel of the litigation process. The better documented Scrope v. Grosvenor case yielded petitions to the king in which the parties made claims about their opponents and tactically tried to gain advantage in their suit.[110] Scrope stated that Grosvenor, who had appealed the decision of the court, had then refused to plead in his appeal, claiming that Scrope had obtained the commission by fraud and that it had subsequently been revoked by the king. Scrope, refuting this, requested that the king order the commissioners to get on and try the case to prevent further delays from his opponent.[111] Scrope then followed this up with another petition asking the king to order Grosvenor to appear or otherwise forfeit the case.[112] Similarly,

107 *PROME*, parliament of 1385. See also W. M. Ormrod, 'Government by Commission: The Continual Council of 1386 and English Royal Administration', *Peritia* 10 (1996), 303–21.

108 SC 8/224/11159; SC 8/224/11199.

109 SC 8/225/11243.

110 For a printed version of the proceedings see: *De Controversia in Curia Militari inter Ricardum Le Scrope et Robertum Grosvenor Milites*, ed. N. H. Nicolas, 2 vols (London, 1832).

111 SC 8/185/9219.

112 SC 8/185/9218. See also the subsequent commissioned issued: *CPR, 1388–1392*, p. 40.

in the less well documented Morley v. Montagu (the son of Sir John who succeeded his uncle as earl of Salisbury), the former even denied the court's jurisdiction over the point in issue, protesting that his opponent's argument ought not to be accepted by the law and custom of arms.[113]

Conclusion

The crown's encouragement of complaints from its subjects fostered a barrage of supplications from all classes of society. The construction of a number of these petitions strongly suggests that legal input was available, with supplicants either citing Magna Carta and other statutes explicitly or drawing on the language of their provisions. Analysis also demonstrates that certain discourses were employed, particularly by manorial tenants, centring on issues regarding deprivation of freedoms and privileges and unfair or unreasonable treatment by those wielding authority (whether in financial, physical or property-related terms). Interestingly, the arguments and phraseology are not only coherent and well structured but seem fairly coordinated when looked at with hindsight and as a whole, markedly so given the disparate groups petitioning and the diverse chronology. Significantly, too, complaints channelled perceptions of unjustness and experiences of illegality arising from the operation or improper application of the legal processes themselves. Sometimes it was the interplay between the different courts and their respective legal procedures that were alleged to have caused the supplicant personal difficulties.

It would be easy to take these wholly at face value, as a reflection of reality, but some circumspection is necessary. Focusing on the voicing of the complaint and especially the combination of legal terminology and rhetoric enables the historian to understand the authority and legitimation the petitioner was trying to achieve and thus the aims and strategies behind the petition (whether actual court action was intended or not). During the 1380s, in particular, there appears to have been a flurry of action invoking, but also tactically refuting, the jurisdiction of the court of Chivalry or complaining about the judges and their judgements. This must be viewed in relation both to parliamentary concern at the expanding scope of the court's jurisdiction and attempts to restrict it[114] and, in a wider context, the options and possibilities in terms of legal fora available to litigants. Indeed, some of the actions brought in the court of Chivalry were disguised as genuine chivalry cases, but

[113] Printed in 'Morley vs. Montagu (1399): A Case in the Court of Chivalry', ed. M. Keen and M. Warner, in *Camden Miscellany* 34, Camden Society, 5th series, 10 (Cambridge, 1993).

[114] *Early Common Petitions in the English Parliament, c. 1290–c. 1420*, ed. W. M. Ormrod, H. Killick and P. Bradford (Cambridge, 2017), pp. 267–8.

in essence represented an alternative for a suit about land (such as a claim of usurpation of hereditary arms in 1393–4) or as a counter to malicious appeals and indictments (as occurred in 1438). Such cases demonstrate not only the demand by litigants and the ingenuity of their lawyers but also the need to see its development holistically in the context of an evolving English legal system.[115] Petitioning clearly formed a key role in its operation, as it did in the work of the emergent 'court of conscience' headed by the chancellor.[116]

Finally, the advantages of petitioning must be set in the broader context of the symbolic resonance of the 'due process' provisions of Magna Carta. The petitions reveal that supplicants were sometimes inventive in their legal arguments or pushed the boundaries of the original meaning of the Great Charter. At other times they harnessed it, futilely, to their cause and betrayed their own misconceptions or misunderstanding of the law. This in turn makes it possible to gauge contemporaries' respective attitudes towards 'law' and 'justice' and the extent to which their tenets were embedded in the psyche or legal consciousness of fourteenth-century men and women.

115 For a more comprehensive discussion of the origins and operation of the court see: A. Musson and N. Ramsay, *Law and Arms: The Medieval English Court of Chivalry* (forthcoming).

116 T. Haskett, 'The Medieval English Court of Chancery', *Law and History Review* 14 (1996), 245–313; D. R. Klinck, *Conscience, Equity and the Court of Chancery in Early Modern England* (Farnham, 2010).

5

Petitions of Conflict: The Bishop of Durham and Forfeitures of War, 1317–1333

Matthew Phillips

This chapter presents two case studies involving Louis Beaumont, bishop of Durham (1317–33). The first case study explores the bishop's dispute with the king of Scotland over the bishop's rights to ferry men and goods across the River Tweed, while the second relates the bishop's dispute with Sir Walter Selby, a former northern rebel, over a manor held by the bishop as a forfeiture of war. The two case studies provide an illustration of the multi-functional dimension of medieval petitions in England and the layers of meaning that become evident when supplications are considered within the historical context of their original presentation to the crown. The bishop's petition relating to the River Tweed, which forms the basis of the first case study, is shown to represent a tacit agreement between supplicant and king, the true nature of which was intentionally kept opaque from a parliamentary assembly reluctant to condone a course of action already predetermined by the king. The case illustrates how legal strategy and political developments were closely intertwined, and how the bishop's legal strategy was built around an acute awareness of political developments in which the timing of his petition was of pivotal importance. The second case study, which explores a longstanding dispute between Walter Selby and two consecutive bishops of Durham over the manor of Felling (located near Gateshead and within the palatinate of Durham), provides another example of the multi-functional purpose that petitions could serve. For the bishop, the dispute over the manor of Felling served as a test case in a broader jurisdictional dispute with the crown over the palatine right to forfeitures of war. Although confirmed in 1327, this right had never been fully tested in the absence of any major properties being forfeited after the reign of Edward I.

The Bishop of Durham, the King of Scotland, and the River Tweed, 1333

The complaint brought forward by Louis Beaumont, bishop of Durham, in the parliament of January 1333 appears, at face value, to represent a fairly routine petition seeking restitution for lost revenue.[1] Bishop Beaumont claimed that his predecessors had once enjoyed the right to ferry men and goods across the River Tweed between Berwick and Tweedmouth – a franchise worth more than £20 per annum.[2] This 'passage par bat' ('passage by boat'), was now held by the Scottish king and, although Bishop Beaumont had appealed to both King Robert I and, after his death, the guardians of Scotland during the minority of King David II, he had been unable to recover his rights. In his petition Louis also complained about losses to his fishery caused by Scottish boats anchoring in the river for more than an hour at a time, and asked Edward III to ordain a remedy to avoid the 'desheritance de sa Eglise e de la Corone' ('disinheritance of his church and of the crown').

The petition is unusual in a number of respects. First, it was common practice in medieval petitions for a supplicant to highlight shared interests with the crown and emphasise how a favourable resolution to the issue at stake would be to the mutual advantage of both the petitioner and the king. However, this supplicatory strategy was less common in petitions from bishops, who tended to avoid explicitly linking their interests with those of the crown. In the case of Bishop Beaumont's petition, the emphasis placed on shared interests was certainly a rhetorical flourish, but this was not without foundation. As Beaumont highlighted, revenue lost from the temporalities of

[1] It has been suggested by Constance Fraser that Beaumont's petition was presented shortly before a letter from Edward III, dated 3 February 1331, asked David II of Scotland to restore West Upsettlington to the bishop of Durham. However, it is clear that the letter highlighted by Fraser represents a royal response to an earlier petition from the bishop, as neither West Upsettlington nor the Treaty of Edinburgh – both of which are referred to in the letter – are mentioned in the petition that forms our focus here. Furthermore, there is additional internal evidence suggesting that Beaumont's petition concerning his franchise on the River Tweed was presented in January 1333. Beaumont's reference to having made pleas to the 'gardeinz Deschoce' ('guardians' being plural) indicates that the petition had been presented after the death of the first guardian, Thomas Randolph, earl of Morray, who had held the guardianship for three years after the death of Robert Bruce until his own death in July 1332, when he was replaced by the earl of Mar. Between July 1332 and the death of Louis Beaumont on 24 September 1333, only one parliament dealt with petitionary business and that was held in January 1333: *Northern Petitions Illustrative of life in Berwick, Cumbria and Durham in the Fourteenth Century*, ed. C. M. Fraser (Gateshead, 1981), pp. 35–6; *CCR, 1330–1333*, p. 283. The parliament of December 1332 did not deal with petitionary business: see *PROME*, parliament of December 1332, introduction.

[2] TNA, SC 8/105/5211; *Northern Petitions*, ed. Fraser, pp. 34–6.

his bishopric was also revenue lost by the crown, for when the see of Durham was vacant the profits derived from the temporalities went to the king. In this regard, Beaumont's petition is somewhat anomalous amongst the surviving petitions that were presented by medieval bishops in England. As we shall see, the rhetoric served a specific purpose in this case for it allowed the bishop of Durham to highlight an alliance of interests against the Scottish king.

The petition is also significant for the nature of the royal response. In his petition, Louis Beaumont asked Edward III to provide an unspecified remedy, thereby calling upon the crown to decide the manner in which this legal issue relating to the River Tweed might be resolved.[3] This was not remarkable in itself, but the response that Beaumont received was both unusual and cryptic: 'Quant le Roi verra temp ordeniera de remedie en ceste partie mes aore ne poet il mie' ('When the times comes the king will ordain a remedy in this part, now he has not the power').[4] This was highly irregular. Endorsements found on private petitions usually fall into one of several categories:[5] first, a request might be granted, either outright or with conditions attached;[6] second, a request might require further investigation, through either the appointment of an inquest or an order to search through relevant records in chancery, or by asking the supplicant to supply additional information;[7] third, a petition might be expedited to one of the great governmental departments – either the chancery or the exchequer – or sent before the king's bench or the council for consideration;[8] fourth, petitions could also be redirected to common law if the crown felt that the request could be sufficiently dispatched via the usual course of justice;[9] and, finally, petitions could also be rejected outright, with or without explanation.[10] The king's response to Beaumont's petition does not commend itself to any of these categories. The endorsement represents the promise of remedial action in the future, but also contains an open admission of the king's present inability to provide the bishop with redress. Furthermore, the petition was recorded as 'coram rege et magno consilo', indicating that this apparent admission of the crown's impotency to deal with the bishop's request was pronounced within the public context of the great council. It shall be argued below that the royal response to the

[3] See G. Dodd, *Justice and Grace: Private Petitioning and the English Parliament in the Late Middle Ages* (Oxford, 2007), p. 227.

[4] SC 8/105/5211; *Northern Petitions*, ed. Fraser, pp. 34–6.

[5] For further discussion, see *Northern Petitions*, ed. Fraser, pp. 78–88.

[6] For example, the bishop of Carlisle was granted '20 oaks in the forest of Inglewood' for the reconstruction of houses: SC 8/99/4905.

[7] 'A writ of chancery should be made ordering the treasurer and barons of the exchequer to enquire what damages the bishop sustained on this occasion and to cause allowance to be made to him in his farm': SC 8/280/13965.

[8] SC 8/46/2268: 'Ad consilium'.

[9] SC 8/97/4840: 'sue at common law against the people of the Cinque Ports'.

[10] SC 8/195/9740: 'Nothing is to be done'.

bishop's petition was not, in fact, an admission of the legal impotence of the English crown, and the public reading of the bishop's petition may even have been orchestrated by Edward III. Furthermore, the context of the parliament of 1333 sheds light on the pre-emptive capacity in which Beaumont presented his petition, and the tacit agreement with the English crown that this document came to represent. First, however, we shall explore the options for legal resolution to the petition open to Louis Beaumont in 1333.

A legal resolution to Beaumont's petition relied on the Treaty of Edinburgh. Concluded with the Scots by Roger Mortimer and Queen Isabella on 27 March 1328 in the name of Edward III, the treaty agreed in principle that Englishmen who had lost lands in Scotland since the outbreak of war in 1296 and Scots who had lost their possessions in England should be barred from pursuing their inheritances.[11] However, while the treaty dispossessed secular lords it contained a clause safeguarding ecclesiastical property. As Sonja Cameron and Alasdair Ross have demonstrated, the wording of the clause 'no manner of prejudice shall be done to the right of the Holy Church' formed a legal basis for the restoration of Church lands and a number of reinheritance grants issued between 1328 and 1330 invoked this clause of the treaty.[12] Indeed, in response to a previous supplication from the bishop of Durham concerning matters of dispute relating to Scotland, a royal letter had been sent to the Scottish king asking him to uphold the terms of the Treaty of Edinburgh.

In 1331 Beaumont had petitioned against Patrick Dunbar, earl of March, who was preventing him from taking possession of West Upsettlington, a settlement located west of Norham on the north bank of the River Tweed. In response, Edward III dispatched a letter to David II that made explicit reference to the Treaty of Edinburgh, reminding the Scottish king and his guardians that under the terms of the treaty 'men of religion of both realms should not be prejudiced concerning their possessions occupied during the war'.[13] As this example demonstrates, the Treaty of Edinburgh provided a legal basis upon which the bishop of Durham might have hoped to appeal to the Scottish for the restoration of his franchise on the River Tweed. However, by December 1332 political developments in Scotland had created a situation whereby Edward III could contemplate disregarding the treaty.

Under the leadership of Louis Beaumont's brother, Henry Beaumont, an army of 'disinherited' lords who had lost their Scottish titles following the Treaty of Edinburgh rallied around the pretender to the Scottish throne, Edward Balliol, and invaded Scotland as part of a private enterprise to reclaim their rights. Following two victorious battles, Balliol was crowned king of Scotland at Scone on 24 September 1332 and, consequently, England's

[11] Also known as the Treaty of Northampton, see S. Cameron and A. Ross, 'The Treaty of Edinburgh and the Disinherited (1328–1332)', *History* 84 (1999), 237–56.

[12] Cameron and Ross, 'The Treaty of Edinburgh', 244.

[13] *CCR, 1330–1333*, p. 283.

diplomatic relations with Scotland were in need of revision.[14] Questions were put to the Commons in the parliament of December 1332, asking their advice on how the king should proceed. In an opportunistic move by Edward III to gain a stronger bargaining position vis-à-vis Scotland, Geoffrey le Scrope, chief justice of the king's bench, informed those assembled in his opening address that the Treaty of Edinburgh should now be disregarded. This proposed revocation was a calculated move designed to exploit the tumultuous events north of the border, which Scrope delivered on the basis that the treaty was illegitimate in the first place, having been made when the king was a minor 'without his own authority'.[15] The revocation of the Treaty of Edinburgh in December 1332, therefore, explains why no letter was sent to the Scottish king in response to Beaumont's petition in 1333. It also explains the unusual nature of the petition's endorsement, which declared that the king did not have the power to provide the bishop with remedy.

By placing Louis Beaumont's petition within the context of the parliament of 1333, we can see that the petition was not designed to initiate diplomatic pressure on the Scottish, as his petition of 1331 had done. Rather, it was designed to gain royal recognition of his claim to rights on the River Tweed in anticipation of a royal military campaign. Indeed, military action had been proposed to the Commons in the very same parliament that revoked the Treaty of Edinburgh.[16] The implicit request contained in Beaumont's petition, therefore, was that when Berwick came into the crown's possession through military conquest the bishop's right to the passage by boat between Berwick and Tweedmouth would be restored to him and not granted to any other lord or individual. Read in this context, the royal response to Beaumont's petition was intended to provide recognition of the bishop's rights. The petition formed a tacit agreement between the crown and the bishop. The king signalled his consent that, when the forthcoming campaign was concluded, the disputed franchise would be restored to the bishop of Durham.

The rather opaque character of the dealings between the bishop and the crown documented in this petition raises questions surrounding the need for such covert communications. This is perhaps explained by the prevailing attitude in parliament. In December 1332 those assembled in parliament had been asked to advise the king on the best course of action with regards to the recent developments in Scotland. The Commons had replied that the matter was too important to be decided in the absence of so many prelates and great men. The king was asked to prorogue the parliament until January.[17] When parliament reconvened an agreed course of action remained elusive, and

[14] For discussion of the Dupplin Moor campaign, see C. J. Rogers, *War Cruel and Sharp* (Woodbridge, 2000), pp. 25–47.

[15] *PROME*, parliament of December 1332, item 1.

[16] *PROME*, parliament of December 1332, item 1.

[17] *PROME*, parliament of December 1332, item 1.

proceedings concluded with a pronouncement by the chancellor that Edward would seek the advice of the pope and the king of France.[18] As Clifford J. Rogers has pointed out, since Philip VI of France remained a staunch ally of David II, and the pope was malleable to French pressure, the outcome of the discussion in parliament 'practically amounted to a recommendation that the king do nothing, but allow the Treaty of Northampton [Edinburgh] once again to define Anglo-Scottish relations'.[19] In this respect, there was a gulf between the aspirations of Edward III, who was 'eager for arms and honour', and the unsupportive response that he received from parliament.[20] Although Edward had appointed what was, in effect, a war committee on the last day of the assembly, those wishing to present a petition at the parliament had been told to do so by 24 January – two days before the king had appointed his war committee and thereby publicly revealing his intentions to pursue a course of war.[21] In this context, there was an obvious political reason for the bishop to present his petition in terms of a general plea for support rather than making an explicit reference to an anticipated military campaign that the broader political community had been reluctant to support.

There was also a pragmatic reason for the bishop of Durham to present his petition in more general terms. Had the bishop explicitly tied his petition to an anticipated series of events he would have run the risk of making his request conditional upon the successful prosecution of a military campaign that was still in its embryonic stages in January 1333. Indeed, Edward Balliol had written to Edward III following his coronation in September 1332, recognising him as overlord and offering to restore Berwick to the English crown in return for Edward's support.[22] It was quite possible that an alternative course of events might create the conditions in which Beaumont could receive remedy. As such, the bishop focused on generalities and relied upon the crown to identify the nuances of his timing. Finally, it is also possible that the bishop's petition was designed to serve a broader function that helped to justify military action against Scotland. A complaint regarding the failure of the Scottish government to provide justice would have held political value at a time when Edward III revoked the Treaty of Edinburgh and sought to foster support in parliament for a campaign to Scotland. In this context, the petition from the bishop of Durham in January 1333 may have played a role in providing justification for the king's subsequent campaign in light of

18 *PROME*, parliament of January 1333, item 7; TNA, C 65/2, m. 1.

19 Rogers, *War Cruel and Sharp*, pp. 56–7.

20 *Scalacronica: A Chronicle of England and Scotland from A.D. MLXVI to A.D. MCCCLXII*, ed. J. Stevenson (Edinburgh, 1836), p. 162, citation p. 58.

21 *PROME*, parliament of January 1333, introduction, items 1 and 7.

22 J. Sumption, *The Hundred Years War, Volume I: Trial by Battle* (London, 1990), pp. 126–7; Rogers, *War Cruel and Sharp*, pp. 51–3.

the apathy towards the prospect of conflict that had been demonstrated by parliament.

Although Beaumont did not live to see his franchise on the River Tweed restored to the bishopric of Durham, his petition appears to have opened the way for his successor, Richard Bury (1333–45), to secure the right to ferry men and goods across the River Tweed between Berwick and Tweedmouth on 15 June 1334.[23] Following Beaumont's petition in the parliament of January 1333, Edward III reached Tweedmouth on 9 May and there joined forces with Edward Balliol, who was besieging Berwick.[24] On 19 July 1333, in an attempt to relieve the town, a Scottish army led by the guardian Sir Archibald Douglas was decisively defeated at the Battle of Halidon Hill and Berwick surrendered the following day. The administration of the town remained subordinate to the English chancery until the York parliament of February 1334 which dealt with the redistribution of property in Berwick.[25] Meanwhile, Louis Beaumont died on 24 September 1333 and, when the property in Berwick was redistributed, the 'passage by boat' between Berwick and Tweedmouth remained in the crown's possession. Although Richard Bury had received the episcopal temporalities on 7 December he was forced to petition for the return of the franchise relating to the River Tweed.[26] In response to Bury's supplication, an inquest was ordered and the bishop's right was subsequently upheld, with the passage by boat and its profits restored.[27] The inquest traced the franchise back to Bishop Anthony Bek (1283–1311). Therefore, although the franchise did not automatically revert to Richard Bury in February 1334, Beaumont's petition appears to have at least served a holding action, and ensured that when the other properties in royal custody were redistributed the ferry crossing remained in the possession of the crown.

The Bishop of Durham, Walter Selby and Forfeitures of War, 1318–46

A longstanding legal dispute between Louis Beaumont and Walter Selby, a former rebel and 'adherent of the Scots', provides an important case study relating to a broader conflict between the bishops of Durham and the English crown over forfeitures of war.[28] This conflict has received attention elsewhere, and falls within a body of work exploring the jurisdictional relationship

23 *CPR, 1334–1338*, pp. 395–6.

24 For what follows see Rogers, *War Cruel and Sharp*, pp. 48–76.

25 R. Nicholson, 'The Siege of Berwick 1333', *Scottish History Review* 40 (1961), 143, 154.

26 *CPR, 1330–1334*, p. 487; SC 8/261/13028; for a translation see *Northern Petitions*, ed. Fraser, pp. 36–8.

27 An exemplification of the inquest was provided on 12 March 1337: *CPR, 1334–1338*, pp. 395–6.

28 *CPR, 1317–1321*, p. 289.

between the palatinate of Durham and the English crown.[29] However, the significance of the dispute between Louis Beaumont and Walter Selby within this broader context has been overlooked and the petitions presented throughout the course of the quarrel have not been explored in detail.[30] Notably, the case demonstrates how the bishop of Durham utilised his contest with Selby as a way of reasserting palatine rights against jurisdictional infringements by the crown. The case also demonstrates the limitations of petitioning, since Walter Selby found himself in the unenviable position of being caught in a legal deadlock between royal and palatinate jurisdiction.

In response to a royal writ dated 13 March 1329, Louis Beaumont presented a petition explaining his refusal to restore to Walter Selby the manor of Felling. Walter Selby had forfeited his lands in 1317–18 after rebelling against the king. Beaumont believed that the royal writ was contrary to the law since it had been issued on the premise of upholding an agreement made in 1321 between Selby and the English besiegers of Mitford Castle. This was an agreement to which Beaumont had not been party. Furthermore, since the manor of Felling had been confiscated 'long temps einz ceo qe le dit Wauter ocupa le dit chastel sur le rendre de quel le dit couenant se tailla' ('long before the said Walter occupied the said castle for the surrender of which the said agreement was made'), the bishop of Durham petitioned that the writ should not be used 'encontre ley et resoun' ('against law and reason') nor deprive him of 'le dreit de sa eglise' ('the right of his church').[31] As a result of Beaumont's petition, Selby was redirected to pursue his case within the courts of the palatinate of Durham, where he was repeatedly denied justice. Between 1329 and his death in 1346, Walter Selby petitioned the crown on numerous occasions asking the king to exert pressure on the bishop of Durham, but was ultimately unable to regain his manor, despite repeated royal writs ordering the bishop to provide him with remedy. The origins of this dispute can be traced back to 1317, when Walter Selby took part in a series of disturbances in the north, in which Louis Beaumont was personally affected, and subsequently forfeited his English properties.

On 1 September 1317, near Rushyford on the road between Darlington and Durham, Louis Beaumont was attacked while en route to his consecration

[29] G. T. Lapsley, *The County Palatinate of Durham: A Study in Constitutional History* (London, 1900), pp. 31–75; C. M. Fraser, 'Prerogative and the Bishops of Durham, 1267–1376', *English Historical Review* 74 (1959), 467–76; J. Scammell, 'The Origin and Limitations of the Liberty of Durham', *English Historical Review* 81 (1966), 449–73; C. D. Liddy, *The Bishopric of Durham in the Late Middle Ages: Lordship, Community and the Cult of St Cuthbert* (Woodbridge, 2008), pp. 1–24.

[30] A brief account of the events is provided in H. H. E. Craster, *A History of Northumberland, Volume IX: The Parochial Chapelries of Earsdon and Horton* (Newcastle-upon-Tyne, 1909), pp. 58–61.

[31] SC 8/43/2121. A full edition of the petition is provided in *Northern Petitions*, ed. Fraser, pp. 259–61.

and enthronement in Durham cathedral. Gilbert Middleton took Beaumont captive and the bishop-elect remained a prisoner until his ransom was paid in mid-October.[32] The assault on Beaumont was the first stage in a wider series of disturbances perpetrated by Middleton, the precise motivation for which remains a matter of dispute.[33] As it relates to our current line of inquiry, a prominent part in Middleton's rebellion was played by Walter Selby, who seized the peel of Horton following the capture of Louis Beaumont and managed to hold out for four months after Gilbert Middleton had surrendered on 21 January 1318. The complicity of Selby in Beaumont's captivity at the outset of his episcopate adds a personal element to the bishop's refusal to follow royal instructions and restore the confiscated property.[34] Selby managed to escape capture when Middleton's garrison at Horton surrendered in April, but by this time his lands in England had been confiscated.[35] Selby now put his services at the disposal of the Scots and was placed in charge of Mitford Castle, which had been lost by the English in April 1318. Selby held Mitford until autumn 1321, when he negotiated the castle's surrender with Robert Umframville, earl of Angus, Ralph fitz William and John Eure, who agreed to treat with Edward II for the return of Selby's lands in England.[36] Following the surrender, however, Selby was transported to London and imprisoned in the Tower of London, where he remained until he was awarded a general pardon by Edward III on 13 March 1327.[37] The regency government of Mortimer and Isabella decided that Selby's lands should be restored, with the exception of those that had been granted to others, for which Selby should sue at common law.[38] However, unsatisfied with these arrangements, and perhaps anticipating resistance from the bishop

[32] M. Prestwich, 'Gilbert de Middleton and the Attack on the Cardinals, 1317', in *Warriors and Churchmen in the High Middle Ages: Essays Presented to Karl Leyser*, ed. T. Reuter (London, 1992), p. 181.

[33] Maddicott argues that Gilbert Middleton was in collusion with Thomas of Lancaster and the Scots: J. R. Maddicott, *Thomas of Lancaster, 1307–1322: A Study in the Reign of Edward II* (Oxford, 1970), pp. 204–7. Prestwich argues against this reading, concluding that the rising was uncoordinated and lacking any clear programme: Prestwich, 'Gilbert de Middleton', p. 190. Selby's alliance with the Scots once the Middleton rebellion had failed, however, lends support to Maddicott's assessment.

[34] In a petition presented in c. 1332, Beaumont made reference to his period in captivity, see SC 8/239/11939.

[35] Craster, *History of Northumberland*, p. 59.

[36] The surrender probably took place shortly before 22 November 1322, the date on which the castle was ordered to be restored to the earl of Pembroke. See Craster, *History of Northumberland*, p. 60, n. 1; SC 8/74/3660.

[37] *CPR, 1327–1330*, p. 36.

[38] The decision barred Selby's automatic restoration to his manor of Seghill, which had been granted to Bertram Monboucher for the term of his life by Edward II: *CPR, 1317–1321*, p. 239; SC 8/175/8735.

of Durham with regards to his manor of Felling, Selby attempted to gain restitution by direct appeal to the king.

At the parliament held at Salisbury in October 1328 Selby presented to the king the indented agreement he had received ten years earlier for the surrender of Mitford Castle and, on the basis of this agreement, petitioned for his properties to be 'restored to him without disinheritance'.[39] On 13 March 1329 a royal writ was dispatched informing Louis Beaumont that the king and council had decided that Selby's indentured agreement should stand, and the bishop was ordered to restore Selby to his manor of Felling.[40] Beaumont refused to execute this command and explained in his petition that he had never been party to Selby's agreement in 1321. To accept the terms of the agreement now would deprive him of the 'right of his church'.[41] Indeed, the right of his church cannot have been far from his mind, given that the king had repeatedly refused to provide restitution for various other estates that had escheated to the crown in contravention of the bishop's rights as lord palatinate.

Before proceeding with the Felling case it is worth briefly placing this dispute within the broader legal context of jurisdictional conflict between the palatinate of Durham and the English crown over forfeitures of war. In particular, an infringement of longstanding grievance was visited upon the palatinate by Edward I. Following the confiscation of the episcopal temporalities in December 1305 during the episcopacy of Bishop Anthony Bek, Edward I granted out Hart and Hartness, the forfeited manors of Robert Bruce, to be held directly from the king rather than the bishop of Durham.[42] The king also granted Barnard Castle, which had been forfeited by John Balliol in 1296, to Guy Beauchamp, earl of Warwick (c. 1272–1315).[43] Thus, when the temporalities of the diocese were returned to Bek by Edward II on 4 September 1307, they were diminished by the loss of several estates within

39 The petition is not extant, but a close letter dated 13 March 1329 refers to one having been presented in parliament at Salisbury: *CCR, 1327–1330*, p. 441. Shortly after parliament had ended Selby was granted the reversion of Seghill manor after the death of Bertram Monboucher, an act that foreshadowed the decision to restore in full all of Selby's other lands in a writ dated 5 November 1328: *CPR, 1327–1330*, p. 332. However, Bertram Monboucher sought remedy after being ejected by the sheriff of Northumberland by the enterprising efforts of Selby: SC 8/61/3034; *Calendar of Documents Relating to Scotland preserved in Her Majesty's Public Record Office, London*, ed. Joseph Bain et al., 4 vols (Edinburgh, 1881–8), vol. III, p. 177; *CCR, 1327–1330*, p. 456.

40 The order was repeated on 29 April, alongside a writ to the sheriff of Northumberland: *CCR, 1327–1330*, pp. 441, 456.

41 SC 8/43/2121.

42 C. M. Fraser, *A History of Anthony Bek* (Oxford, 1957), pp. 183–200; M. Prestwich, *Edward I* (London, 1988), pp. 540–5; G. T. Lapsley, *The County Palatinate of Durham: A Study in Constitutional History* (London, 1900), pp. 42–5.

43 Lapsley, *County Palatinate*, p. 43; *PROME*, parliament of 1316, item 15.

the palatinate that had been claimed by the bishop of Durham as forfeitures of war.[44] Bek's successor, Richard Kellaw (1311–16), raised the issue in the parliament of January 1316, where the bishop's attorney presented his case in detail but made little progress.[45] Louis Beaumont, perhaps aided by his close ties to Queen Isabella, received the concession in the first parliament of Edward III that he 'should have his liberty of such forfeitures' but with the proviso that those who had received lands from the king's progenitors should not be removed without the opportunity to appeal against the decision.[46] Beaumont was quickly frustrated, however, by the crown's seizure of Hugh Despenser's forfeited manors of Turnham Hall and Sandhall within the palatinate. Upon petitioning for restitution, the bishop was told that the council had been advised to retain possession of the estate.[47] The crown was also able to resist appeals from successive bishops with regards to the Bruce and Balliol forfeitures. As Constance Fraser has highlighted, the 'masterly inactivity' of the crown when responding to the bishop of Durham was justified on the basis that, as royal officers ought not act within the palatinate, the king could not order his sheriff to ensure that his writs were obeyed.[48] As such, the crown used the bishop's own palatine rights against him and as an excuse to avoid providing the bishop with remedy. Beaumont's successor, Richard Bury, was unable to gain possession of the properties, and the issue remained unresolved in 1470, when it was broached by Laurence Booth (1457–76).[49] In this context of frustrated palatine ambitions, the legal dispute over the manor of Felling takes on new significance as an important skirmish within a broader conflict over the right of the bishop of Durham to the forfeitures of war within the palatinate. Indeed, the Felling dispute was especially pertinent to this broader conflict given that the crown had, in fact, acted in contravention of the claims of the palatinate when the manor of Felling was first confiscated under Edward II.

Initially, the manor of Felling had been seized by the bishop of Durham following Selby's rebellion in 1317, but once again palatine rights were set aside and by 24 May 1319 Edward II had laid claim to the estate as a royal escheat, subsequently granting it to Thomas Epplingden to be held directly from the king.[50] Beaumont asserted that he had seized the manor as the right of his church, but was unable to gain remedy. Felling escheated to the crown once more on 13 March 1322, when it was forfeited by Epplingden

[44] *CPR, 1307–1313*, p. 2.
[45] *PROME*, parliament of 1316, item 15; TNA, SC 9/20.
[46] *PROME*, parliament of January 1327; TNA, C 49/6/1.
[47] SC 8/44/2154.
[48] *Northern Petitions*, ed. Fraser, p. 262; cf. Lapsley, *County Palatinate*, p. 74.
[49] SC 8/44/2166; Lapsley, *County Palatinate*, p. 46, n. 3.
[50] SC 8/44/2158; *CPR, 1317–1321*, p. 335.

for his participation in the Battle of Boroughbridge,[51] and the manor was still in the king's hand at the time of an inquisition held on 9 June 1327.[52] However, between June 1327 and 13 March 1329 – the date on which a royal writ ordered Selby's restoration – the manor appears to have been successfully recovered by Beaumont.[53] The royal order commanding the bishop of Durham to provide Selby with restitution therefore afforded Beaumont a prime opportunity to reassert his right to forfeitures within the palatinate. The palatine right was clearly outlined in the opening section of his petition, which referred to the manor of Felling as 'son droit et le droit de sa eglise par la forfeture le dit Wauter' ('his [Beaumont's] right and the right of his church by the forfeiture of the said Walter').[54] Beaumont's petition, therefore, was not merely used to justify the bishop's refusal to restore Selby to his manor of Felling. Rather, this refusal takes on broader significance in the context of the jurisdictional conflict between the palatinate and the crown. The bishop's petition is important because it represents a reassertion of palatine rights to forfeitures of war.

In response to his petition, Louis Beaumont gained reassurance from the crown that, if Selby pursued his claim to the manor of Felling, the bishop would be given the opportunity to defend his case.[55] Effectively, this decision blocked Selby's chances of regaining his property. The impetus for further action was deferred onto Selby himself and, since the manor fell within the bishopric of Durham, he was forced to prosecute his case within the courts of the palatinate, where he was unlikely to receive a favourable hearing. In a petition submitted after the death of Beaumont on 24 September 1333, Selby claimed that he had brought many writs before the late bishop in an attempt to gain restitution, but no action had been taken by Beaumont because the manor had been granted to Thomas Surteyse.[56] Again, in 1336, Selby complained that the bishop's justices refused to proceed on a writ of *novel dissesin*, which he had obtained from the bishop 'according to the liberty of Durham'.[57] Selby's only remaining recourse, short of retaking the manor by force, was to petition the crown to exert pressure on the bishop to provide restitution. Yet, while the crown was perfectly willing to ignore palatine jurisdiction when the king stood to profit from forfeitures of war – as successive

51 *Northern Petitions*, ed. Fraser, p. 249; SC 8/44/2158; *CPR, 1317–1321*, p. 335.

52 *CIM, 1307–1349*, pp. 219–20.

53 *CPR, 1327–1330*, p. 441.

54 SC 8/44/2158; *Northern Petitions*, ed. Fraser, p. 249; SC 8/44/2158; *CPR, 1317–1321*, p. 260.

55 SC 8/43/2121.

56 SC 8/8/394. On 27 December 1331 Beaumont granted the manor of Felling to his kinsman Ameury de Trew, which was confirmed, along with Trew's subsequent grant of the manor to Thomas Surteyse, by Edward III on 27 January 1332: *CPR, 1330–1334*, p. 240.

57 *CCR, 1333–1337*, p. 98.

bishops were well aware – the king was apparently unprepared to infringe palatine jurisdiction on the behalf of a third party.

In response to Selby's petition against the bishop's grant of Felling to Thomas Surteyse, it was noted that a writ should be 'sent again' to the bishop of Durham ordering him to provide either restitution or a reason as to why restitution should not be provided.[58] However, Richard Bury pursued his predecessor's policy of non-compliance and Selby was still petitioning for restitution in 1336 when, to add further support to his case, he cited a copy of the previous royal writ that had been sent to the bishop.[59] The saga then continued with a letter close sent to Bury on 10 May 1341 instructing the bishop to direct his justices to proceed without delay in the case of *novel dissesin* brought by Selby in the courts of the palatinate, and containing the somewhat telling phrase 'so that the complaint be not repeated to the king'.[60] Yet, the complaint was repeated on at least two further occasions[61] and, when Selby died at the hands of the Scots in October 1346, his manor of Felling remained in the hands of Surteyse family.[62]

The failure of Walter de Selby to gain restitution of his manor should not be attributed to royal indifference. Although a traitor during the reign of Edward II, Selby was a loyal subject to Edward III. Moreover, he held important military commands and died in the north campaigning against the Scots.[63] It seems unlikely that the royal orders sent to the bishop of Durham supporting Selby's claims were intended as a mere gesture of goodwill to placate a reconciled traitor. However, the crown was clearly unwilling to force the issue and take any measure of direct action against the bishop of Durham. Such a course had been taken in 1319, when the sheriff of Northumberland had seized the manor of Felling from the bishop to enforce Edward II's claim to the manor as a royal escheat. However, while the crown was quite prepared to undermine palatine rights when royal interests were at stake, or when the king stood to directly profit, there was a clear reluctance to take such action on the behalf of a royal subject. Interestingly, the repeated refusal of both Louis Beaumont and Richard Bury to carry out the king's orders did not adversely affect their own chances of applying or gaining redress in other disputes. Both bishops presented petitions and gained royal responses while the Felling dispute remained unresolved, demonstrating

58 The crown had in fact worked against its own directives, and confirmed Beaumont's grant to Thomas Surteyse on 27 January 1332: *CPR, 1330–1334*, p. 240; SC 8/8/394; *Northern Petitions*, ed. Fraser, pp. 265–6.

59 SC 8/74/3660.

60 *CCR, 1341–1343*, p. 98.

61 *CCR, 1341–1343*, pp. 642, 692.

62 Lapsley, *County Palatinate*, p. 43; Prestwich, 'Gilbert de Middleton', p. 181; A. E. Middleton, *Sir Gilbert de Middleton, and the Part he took in the Rebellion in the North of England in 1317* (Newcastle, 1918), p. 97.

63 Middleton, *Gilbert de Middleton*, p. 97.

the somewhat automated administrative response of royal justice when responding to supplications.[64] The refusal to obey royal commands in relation to one dispute apparently did not hinder the ability to gain redress in other, unrelated cases.

Conclusion

The two case studies explored in this chapter reveal how, beneath the routine, formulaic and administrative tone of petitions, there exist hidden functions and layers of meaning that become evident only when a petition is considered within the historical context of its original presentation to the crown. The bishop's petition relating to the River Tweed demonstrates that the government of Edward III was prepared to respond to petitions that were presented in a pre-emptive capacity. Although the bishop's claim was not automatically upheld following the capture of Berwick, the royal response at least represents a willingness to acknowledge requests contingent upon future events. As such, this petition represents a tacit agreement between supplicant and king, the true nature of which appears to have been intentionally obscured from a parliamentary assembly reluctant to condone a course of action already predetermined by the king. The case also illustrates how legal strategy and political developments could be intertwined. The bishop of Durham's legal strategy was built around an acute awareness of political developments, in which the timing of his petition was of central importance. Sensing the opportunity provided by royal designs for a military campaign to Scotland, the timing of the bishop's petitions allowed Beaumont both to gain reassurances about the protection of his rights ahead of the planned campaign and also to cultivate the goodwill of the king by contributing to Edward III's case for military intervention in the first place.

The second case study provides another example of the multi-functional purpose that petitions could serve. The petition from Beaumont relating to the manor of Felling served the dual purpose of providing justification for the bishop's refusal to act upon a royal writ as well as working to reassert the bishop's right to forfeitures of war within the palatinate of Durham. Beaumont's petition was presented in a rare context whereby, instead of seeking some form of grant or remedial action from the crown, he simply set out his case to justify non-compliance with royal orders. Although the act of petitioning itself was ultimately demonstrative of a supplicant's subordination to the goodwill of the crown, Beaumont's petition emphasises

[64] SC 8/44/2166; SC 8/44/2167; SC 8/239/11939; SC 8/311/15542; SC 8/44/2155; SC 8/108/5381; SC 8/174/8685A; SC 8/3/105; SC 8/43/2147; SC 8/44/2152; SC 8/44/2157A; SC 8/261/13028.

how not all supplicants shared equal footing. As Selby discovered, even a supplication that received a favourable response from the crown was not always sufficient to result in remedial action that would lead to a satisfactory outcome. The result of Selby's repeated petitions was a series of writs issued to support Selby's litigation within the courts of the palatinate, but the king was unwilling to undermine palatinate jurisdiction in order to provide Selby with remedy. As G. T. Lapsley has highlighted, the absence of any major properties being forfeited after those that were dispensed of by Edward I meant that the question of the bishop's legal right to forfeitures within the palatinate, although confirmed in 1327, was never fully tested.[65] The case of Felling demonstrates that the crown was not prepared to force the issue and infringe the jurisdictional privileges of the bishop. On this occasion the bishop of Durham was able to rely upon palatine jurisdiction to ignore royal orders and block Walter Selby's restoration to the manor of Felling.

In terms of late medieval supplicatory culture in England, both case studies explored in this chapter serve to illustrate how one medieval bishop was prepared to think innovatively about petitions and the purposes to which they might be put. The fact that Beaumont did so highlights an important dimension to petitioning in medieval England. Aside from providing access to royal justice, petitions also offered supplicants access to legal remedy through an act of royal grace. Crucially, in some exceptional cases remedy through grace can be demonstrated to have equated to the arbitrary exercise of the royal will, and furthermore, this was made available for purchase.[66] This holds broader significance in the sense that many petitions may have been presented to the crown in the hope that the personal intervention of the king would lead to a favourable resolution. Clearly, this was the case with Beaumont's petition relating to the River Tweed, as it depended upon the king understanding the nuances that lay behind the timing of the petition. In the case of high-profile supplicants such as bishops, who were not only Church leaders and members of the political elite but in many cases royal councillors, diplomats or ministers in government as well, it would be understandable if *hope* for the personal intervention of the king became an *expectation*. Certainly, the repeated supplications of certain fourteenth-century bishops, such as William Bateman, Walter Stapeldon and Thomas Arundel, indicate a faith in the power of petitions and perseverance in using them in search of resolution from the crown.[67] Even if bishops were reluctant to ask explicitly for the king's grace and goodwill when composing their petitions,

[65] Lapsley, *County Palatinate*, p. 47.

[66] M. Phillips, 'Urban Conflict and Legal Strategy in Medieval England: The Case of Bishop's Lynn, 1346–1350', *Urban History* 42 (2015), 14–15.

[67] M. Phillips, 'Church, Crown and Complaint: Petitions from Bishops to the English Crown in the Fourteenth Century' (unpublished PhD thesis, University of Nottingham, 2013), p. 259.

the petitionary system promoted a supplicatory culture characterised by a reliance on petitions as a way of accessing royal justice, but also as a way of seeking remedy through the goodwill of the king.

While Beaumont's innovative approach to petitions can be placed within a supplicatory culture in late medieval England in this broad sense, fitting Beaumont's petitions into a clerical supplicatory culture is more problematic. I have argued elsewhere that such a clerical supplicatory culture indeed existed. Notably, whereas petitions from lay supplicants often mirrored the language of 'common profit' found in common petitions, petitions from bishops mirrored the supplicatory character of the clerical *gravamina*, where requests were often confrontational and presented solely for the interest of the church.[68] This is not to say that bishops were reluctant to resolve their legal difficulties by approaching the crown. Around 230 petitions were presented by bishops in the late thirteenth and fourteenth centuries seeking some form of legal remedy and, although not every bishop presented a petition to the crown, at least one incumbent for each of the twenty-one dioceses of England and Wales sought remedy from the king at some stage.[69] It does appear, however, that petitions from bishops encapsulated a set of values, manifest through the use of language and rhetoric, that sought to assert the institutional independence of the Church. While Beaumont's petition relating to the manor of Felling conforms to the characteristics of this supplicatory culture – and actually shares with the clerical *gravamina* a concern over jurisdictional conflict with the crown – the bishop's petition relating to the River Tweed does not. This latter petition uncharacteristically made special mention of the mutuality of interest between supplicant and crown commonly found in petitions from the laity. Part of the explanation for this may lie in the fact that Beaumont had been elevated to the see of Durham at a time of heavy and persistent Scottish incursions into northern England. In addition to supplying English armies with provisions, Beaumont was forced to buy off Scottish attackers on eight separate occasions between 1317 and 1327, at a total cost of somewhere in the region of £5,000.[70] Although Beaumont did not live long enough to see his rights on the River Tweed restored to the church of Durham, his actions reveal a concern to remunerate the bishopric's treasury following a prolonged period of irregular outgoings. Beaumont's petition was unusual in the sense that it was presented pre-emptively – that is, the bishop presented it in anticipation of future events on which the success of his petition was contingent – indicating a particular eagerness on the bishop's part to augment his treasury.

[68] Phillips, 'Church, Crown and Complaint', p. 255.

[69] Phillips, 'Church, Crown and Complaint', Appendix F.

[70] C. M. Fraser, 'Beaumont, Louis de (d. 1333)', in *Oxford Dictionary of National Biography* (Oxford, 2004); online edn, January 2008 <http://www.oxforddnb.com/view/article/1880?docPos=2> [accessed 8 July 2017].

6

A Tale of Two Abbots: Petitions for the Recovery of Churches in England by the Abbots of Jedburgh and Arbroath in 1328

Shelagh Sneddon

Among the articles of the peace treaty ratified by King Robert I of Scotland at Holyrood on 17 March 1328 and by King Edward III of England at Northampton on 4 May, a treaty by which England renounced all claims of overlordship or sovereignty over Scotland, is the following clause: 'And it is the intention of the said King of Scotland, and of the aforesaid messengers and proctors of the said King of England that, by the treaties that are now made, no manner of prejudice should be done to the right of Holy Church in the one realm or in the other.'[1] Holy Church was quick to take advantage of this. On the day before the signing of the treaty, 16 March, Robert I inspected a number of charters granted by his predecessors to Durham Priory, thus confirming its possession of its Scottish cell at Coldingham; in England, the close rolls show instructions given on 31 August 1328, and again on 28 October, for the restoration of lands and possessions seized during the war to a variety of religious houses in Scotland.[2] Two petitions asking for the return of such property, from the abbot and convent of Jedburgh and the abbot of Arbroath, survive in the SC 8 class at The National Archives, Kew, as numbers SC 8/16/756 and SC 8/16/757. We know from external evidence that they were presented to the Salisbury parliament of October 1328.[3] Both concern the return of churches: Jedburgh claimed Arthuret in Cumberland and the advowson of Abbotsley in Huntingdonshire; Arbroath asked for Haltwhistle in Northumberland. The

[1] *The Acts of Robert I, King of Scots 1306–1329*, ed. A. A. M. Duncan, Regesta Regum Scottorum, vol. V (Edinburgh, 1988), no. 341: 'Et est lentencion du dit roy Descoce et des avanditz messages and procurers le dit roy Dengleterre qe par les tretiz qe ore se fount nule manere de preiudice soit faite au droit de seint eglise en lun roiaume ne en lautre.'

[2] *Acts of Robert I*, ed. Duncan, no. 340; *CCR, 1327–1330*, pp. 314–15, 337. The beneficiaries include Durham, God's House, Berwick, the brethren of the Holy Trinity of the bridge of Berwick, and the abbeys of Melrose, Kelso, Jedburgh and Dundrennan.

[3] TNA, C 145/109/6 for Arbroath; SC 8/173/8644 for Jedburgh.

petitions received similar responses: inquisitions were to be held and justice was to be done; as a result, Haltwhistle was returned to Arbroath on 25 May 1329 and Arthuret to Jedburgh on 22 February 1330.[4] (The inquisition into the advowson of Abbotsley was delayed by the death of one of those appointed to hear it and it remained in the king's hand, although the parson was ordered to pay the abbot the pension due from the church.[5])

What immediately strikes the reader of these petitions is the very different strategies used by the supplicants. In this chapter I examine these strategies and what they say about the two houses and their occupants during the First Scottish War of Independence. I will touch on questions of national and spiritual identity and how these were affected by the wars, and in doing so will contribute to the research on Scottish and border identities in this period.

The constitutional crisis that led to the Wars of Independence arose suddenly, following a time of relative peace between Scotland and England. As Michael Brown argues, Alexander III 'regarded the English kings as his kinsmen, lords and friends. Personal contact between the two royal families was more frequent and cordial than at any other period ... Alexander and most of his chief vassals held lands in both realms without problems, and the king was comfortable in an aristocratic world which included the Plantagenet dominions and the kingdom of France.'[6] Nine out of the thirteen Scottish earldoms were held by magnates with lands on both sides of the border, and senior officials such as the justiciars of Scotia and Lothian and the chamberlain were often men with land in England.[7] Members of the Bruce, Balliol and Comyn families fought for Henry III at Lewes.[8] Cross-border landholding went beyond the great families. 'A number of families, and not just those of great substance in both kingdoms, would have been faced with a great dilemma if they had been forced to choose between the kingdoms,' Alan Young writes.[9] Within a few years they would be forced to make this choice.

For the community in the borders the links were even closer, the roots deeper. G. W. S. Barrow, examining the period from the eleventh to the thirteenth centuries, suggested continuities across the four northern counties

[4] Inquisition into Haltwhistle held at Newcastle-upon-Tyne, 7 March 1329: *CIM, 1307–1349*, no. 1038, resulting in *CPR, 1327–1330*, p. 394. Inquisition into Arthuret held at Carlisle 23 January 1328/9: *CIM, 1307–49*, no. 1035, resulting in *CPR, 1327–1330*, p. 496.

[5] SC 8/118/5879; *CCR, 1327–1330*, p. 337 (28 October 1328): order to parson to pay.

[6] M. Brown, *The Wars of Scotland 1214–1371*, The New Edinburgh History of Scotland vol. IV (Edinburgh, 2004), pp. 65, 66.

[7] A. Young, 'Noble Families and Political Factions in the Reign of Alexander III', in *Scotland in the Reign of Alexander III*, ed. N. H. Reid (Edinburgh, 1990), pp. 1–30, at pp. 16–17.

[8] Brown, *Wars of Scotland*, p. 65.

[9] Young, 'Noble Families', p. 21.

of England, lowland Scotland and, indeed, Wales in elements as diverse as place and personal names, styles of landholding and demands made by lords on their tenants.[10] Andy King has described a border society where 'until 1296, the Englishmen and Scotsmen of the borders comprised – in some respects – a single community'.[11] He documents a society where the language and culture were so similar that more than once armies were unable to tell friend from foe. Many of Scotland's monasteries – Jedburgh, Melrose, Kelso, Dryburgh – were located close to the border, on either side of which were men of similar background, speaking a similar dialect of northern English.

Monastic life only strengthened these links. As Michael Brown observes:

> As members of religious orders with houses across Latin Christendom, the monks and friars inevitably continued to operate in a wider ecclesiastical world which involved close links with England. The Scottish Dominicans and Franciscans were considered by their orders to belong to English provinces, while the custom of giving supervisory duties to the founding mother-houses of Benedictine and Cistercian abbeys meant that many Scottish religious communities were inspected by English monks. As offshoots or cells of English institutions, the priories of Coldingham and the Isle of May were even staffed by English monks recruited from Durham Cathedral and Reading Abbey respectively.[12]

In his introduction to the new edition of the Melrose chronicle, Dauvit Broun points to how one of the earliest scribes refers to Bede as 'the honour and glory of our people' and highlights descriptions of Scots as 'violent' and 'wicked' in entries for 1216, 1235 and 1258 – a use of language that 'would be unlikely if the monks of Melrose regarded themselves, too, as Scots'.[13] He does, however, note: '[A] process of "Scotticisation" that is first detected in the annal for 1215 ... in which both the south-east and Galloway are referred to as within "Scotland"', although 'it is not until material entered into the chronicle no earlier than 14 April 1286 that there are references to a monk of Melrose or anyone hailing from the south of the kingdom as a Scot.'[14]

[10] G. W. S. Barrow, 'Northern English Society in the Twelfth and Thirteenth Centuries', *Northern History* 4 (1969), 1–28, reprinted in G. W. S. Barrow, *Scotland and its Neighbours in the Middle Ages* (London, 1992).

[11] A. King, 'Best of Enemies: Were the Fourteenth-Century Anglo-Scottish Marches a "Frontier Society"?', in *England and Scotland in the Fourteenth Century: New Perspectives*, ed. A. King and M. Penman (Woodbridge, 2007), pp. 116–35, at p. 117.

[12] Brown, *Wars of Scotland*, p. 128.

[13] D. Broun, 'Melrose Abbey and its World', in *The Chronicle of Melrose Abbey: A Stratigraphic Edition*, ed. D. Broun and J. Harrison, vol. I (Woodbridge, 2007), pp. 1–12, at p. 10.

[14] Broun, 'Melrose Abbey', pp. 10–11.

Among the monks whose names he can discover are several from southern Scotland, such as Adam of Smailholm, Reginald of Roxburgh and William of Duns, as well as Adam of Lennox, from further north, and men from Yorkshire and Cumbria.[15] Emilia Jamroziak uses the same chronicle as evidence for the abbey's ties with the wider Cistercian community, but also mentions its close links with its mother house, Rievaulx, and with the wider Cistercian world of northern England. 'This remarkable continuity of cultural identity was possible,' she argues, 'because of continuing recruitment of monks from Yorkshire as well as a legacy of the large northern English linguistic and cultural zone encompassing both Northumbria and the Borders.'[16] Other border abbeys suggest that this sense of a community that differed from those north and south of it, but was not greatly affected by the border, was not limited to the Cistercians of Melrose. A 'John, called of York, monk of Kelso' is found on the witness list of a document of 1269; and Adam of Dryburgh, writing at Dryburgh in 1180, stated that he was 'in the land of the English, and in the kingdom of the Scots' – acknowledging both the political identity of Scotland and the cultural, English-speaking, border one.[17] Other inmates came from further afield. Jedburgh, for example, had problems with a canon called Ingeleram of Cologne, who was expelled for arson and theft in around 1297, but sent back to the abbey in 1309 by Edward II.[18]

During the thirteenth century, however, Scottish kings and clergy attempted to make the church more national, and to limit outside influences. Michael Brown writes:

> There are strong indications that these ties [of Scottish monasteries with English mother houses] provoked opposition from Scottish clergy. In the 1230s and again during the 1260s the Scottish Franciscans sought to establish themselves as a distinct province of the order … . In a similar vein, the bishops of St Andrews led attempts to detach the priories of Coldingham and the Isle of May from their English mother-houses, in the latter case successfully transferring the priory of the Isle of May to St Andrews cathedral. During the 1280s the pope conceded that non-Scots

15 Broun, 'Melrose Abbey', pp. 7–8.

16 E. Jamroziak, 'Cistercian Identities in Twelfth- and Thirteenth-Century Scotland: The Case of Melrose Abbey', in *New Perspectives on Medieval Scotland, 1093–1286*, ed. M. Hammond (Woodbridge, 2013), pp. 175–82, at p. 177.

17 *Liber Sanctae Mariae de Calchou: Registrum cartarum abbacie Tironensis de Kelso, 1113–1567*, ed. C. Innes, 2 vols, Bannatyne Club 82 (Edinburgh, 1846), no. 290: 'Johanne, dicto de Ebor', monacho de Kelch'; Adam of Dryburgh, *De Triparto Tabernaculo*, in *Patrologia Cursus Completus, Series Latina*, ed. J.-P. Migne, 221 vols (Paris 1844–64), vol. CXCVIII, cols 609–792, at col. 723.

18 *Calendar of Documents Relating to Scotland preserved in Her Majesty's Public Record Office, London*, ed. J. Bain et al., 4 vols (Edinburgh, 1881–8), vol. II, no. 969; *CCR, 1307–1313*, p. 236: he was to be well treated because he had 'suffered at the hands of the Scots'.

> should not be appointed to head religious houses in the province, further recognising and extending the rights of Scots to hold the chief offices of the Scottish church.[19]

Furthermore, 'these efforts to limit influences from outside the Scottish province had consistent, active support and leadership from the crown'.[20] Indeed, the papal inhibition to which he refers prohibited non-natives of Scotland not only from becoming heads of Scottish religious houses but even from taking the habit there.[21] The 'Scotticisation' seen by Broun in the Melrose chronicle can be seen as part of a wider trend within the Scottish church.

Despite this, at the time of the death of Alexander III cross-border links were still strong. The Wars of Independence cut across that. A century of peace on the border gave way to war, and any imprecise or shared identity was replaced by a binary Scots/English one. Armies and warfare brought destruction. Colm McNamee shows the devastating effects of Scottish raids in the years after Bannockburn on the north of England, especially in tenants abandoning their land.[22] These were not the only refugees, as petitions from this period show. The former burgesses of Roxburgh, who fled their burgh 'in peril of their lives' to Berwick, Bamburgh and Newcastle, for example, complained that the bailiffs of those places would not let them work, but treated them as foreigners.[23]

The border abbeys were especially vulnerable. In 1316 the bishop of St Andrews described Kelso as 'destroyed by common war and long depredation of goods, through plunder, fire and slaughter, and, it pains us to say, its monks and lay-brothers seek food and clothing, as beggars, in other religious houses of the realm of Scotland'.[24] R. B. Dobson stated that 'during the reign of Edward II the Durham monks were compelled to abandon Coldingham for the first of many times', and an entry on the close rolls for 20 September 1323 arranged for other houses to receive canons of Egglestone Abbey, 'as it has been so destroyed by the Scotch rebels that the canons cannot live together

[19] Brown, *Wars of Scotland*, p. 128.

[20] Brown, *Wars of Scotland*, p. 128.

[21] *Calendar of Entries in the Papal Registers relating to Great Britain and Ireland: Papal Letters, Vol. I, A.D. 1198–1304*, ed. W. H. Bliss (London, 1893), p. 497; discussed by M. Ash, 'The Church in the Reign of Alexander III', in *Scotland in the Reign of Alexander III*, pp. 31–52, at p. 35.

[22] C. McNamee, *The Wars of the Bruces: Scotland, England and Ireland 1306–1328* (East Linton, 1997), chap. 3, 'The Raiding of Northern England 1311–1322', pp. 72–122.

[23] SC 8/280/13999: 'Pour perile de lures vyes', perhaps as early as 1297, but more probably 1314–15.

[24] *Liber Sanctae Mariae de Calchou*, ed. Innes, no. 309: 'Per communem gwerram et diuturnam depradacionem bonorum spoliacione, incendio, strageque destructum, et quod dolentes referimus monachi et conversi ejusdem per alia loca religiosa regni Scocie victum mendicantes querunt et vestitum'.

there'.[25] Their position close to the border also meant that, as Keith Stringer writes, 'the important abbeys of Dryburgh, Holyrood, Jedburgh, Kelso and Melrose were effectively swallowed up into an English "pale" from 1296 to 1314'.[26] The confusion, violence and destruction of this period forms the backdrop to these petitions.

The first thing that stands out about SC 8/16/756 is that it is in Latin. Of the just over 1,500 Latin documents in the SC 8 series in The National Archives, the majority are copies of writs, charters and other ancillary documents, formerly attached to petitions in the files. Others are, strictly speaking, letters that contain requests, rather than petitions. Of the small number – under 450 – of actual petitions, most date from before 1300. Looking at those supplicants who petitioned in Latin after that date, two factors seem to emerge. The first is that of Latin as an international *lingua franca*: a petition from an English merchant to the king of France from 1307 × 1314 is in Latin,[27] as is a petition of c. 1337 from the community of the realm to the pope.[28] The other factor is still more pertinent: Latin was the language of the clergy. The abbot of Abingdon petitioned in Latin in 1318[29] and the prior of Sele in 1306,[30] while the clergy of the province of Canterbury used Latin for their petition of c. 1377.[31]

For a petition from a religious community to the king of a foreign country, therefore, it would seem that Latin was the ideal language, something matched by the formality of this petition. It opens with an elaborate address to the king – dignified as 'illustrious' – and council. It is from the abbot and convent, discussed and agreed to in chapter, and the careful naming of the diocese adds to the solemn tone. Then there is the standard clause explaining the circumstances: they have been expelled from their churches of Arthuret and Abbotsley during the wars, and Edward II has inducted his own clerics into these churches. This is followed by the request: 'since peace has now, of God's gift, been brought about between the aforesaid realms' they ask the king and council to return the churches to them and to remove Edward II's presentees. The petition ends on the formal note on which it began, asking for the appropriate letters to be sent to the necessary persons.

The distinction between England and Scotland is made very clear in this petition. The abbot and convent address Edward III as their lord, but also as

[25] R. B. Dobson, 'The Last English Monks on Scottish Soil: The Severance of Coldingham Priory from the Monastery of Durham, 1461–78', *Scottish Historical Review* 46 (1967), 1–25, at 3; *CCR, 1323–1327*, p. 139.

[26] K. Stringer, 'Arbroath Abbey in Context, 1178–1320', in *The Declaration of Arbroath: History, Significance, Setting*, ed. G. Barrow (Edinburgh, 2003), pp. 116–41, at p. 131.

[27] SC 8/273/13633.

[28] SC 8/269/13427.

[29] SC 8/30/1465.

[30] SC 8/279/13939.

[31] SC 8/135/6717.

king of England. They speak of the 'wars and dissensions between the realms of England and Scotland', and the peace made 'between the aforesaid realms'. The word *regnum*, used in both these quotations, is a loaded one. At the start of the Great Cause to determine the Scottish succession it was established that Scotland was a realm and could not simply be split between the descendants of the heiresses, as an ordinary inheritance might be, but in his settlement of 1305 Edward I downgraded its status to that of land, *terra*, and the English continued to refer to it as such for the next twenty years. It was not until the treaty of Northampton/Edinburgh that the English conceded that Scotland was an independent realm and that the English king had no rights over it. The abbot and convent of Jedburgh parade this concession: 'the realms of England and Scotland', 'the aforesaid realms' – the absolute parity in status leaps out at the reader. Jedburgh's request for the return of the two churches is based firmly on the peace treaty, and their words 'so that nothing is to be done or attempted [which is] prejudicial to the churches or ecclesiastical persons on either side' strongly echo the relevant clause of the treaty: 'that … no manner of prejudice should be done to the right of Holy Church in the one realm or in the other'.

So why should Jedburgh petition in this way? Another petition, SC 8/173/8644, sheds some light on the matter.[32] It can be dated on internal evidence to c. 1323, and is from four men, William de Tyndale, Adam de Langcestre, Adam de Levyngton and Andrew de Chollerton, who describe themselves as 'canons of the house of Jedburgh'.[33] They state that they and their abbot 'because they were born in England',[34] were driven out of Scotland – again a 'land', 'la terre Descoce' – by 'Robert de Brus and his power … after the battle of Stirling' – by which they mean Bannockburn.[35] They have since remained in the king's faith, living off their abbey's possessions in England, listed as Arthuret, Abbotsley, the manor of Lee Hall in Tynedale and the land of Troughend in Redesdale. Four years previously the abbot died and the king seized these lands and churches into his hand. The churches have been donated under the influence of Hugh le Despenser, but the other lands remain in the king's hand: they request the return of both lands and churches, as they are fallen into great poverty. This petition met with a favourable response: a first endorsement, stating that it seemed to the council that the king should provide for these canons from their house's lands, was replaced by one ordering that the tenements be delivered to a William de Uston, who was to give the canons a sustenance of 20 marks from them.

[32] Edited in *Ancient Petitions Relating to Northumberland*, ed. C. M. Fraser, Surtees Society 176 (Durham, 1966), no. 25, pp. 30–1.

[33] SC 8/173/8644: 'chanouns de la Meson de Jedeworth'.

[34] SC 8/173/8644: 'par la reson qils furint neez en Engilterre'.

[35] SC 8/173/8644: 'Robert de Bruys et son pouer les enchaca hors de la terre Descoce apres la Batayl de Strivelyne'.

The abbot's name was William de Jarum (from Yarm near Middlesborough), and he was elected in 1296, after the previous abbot, John Morel, had resigned, or was perhaps expelled, as in 1299 he is found as a Scottish envoy to the court of Philip IV of France.[36] One possible scenario is that he too left with a body of canons, and that Jedburgh was repopulated by Edward I with English canons. This interpretation is favoured by C. M. Fraser, who suggests in the commentary to her edition of SC 8/173/8644 that the 'presence of English canons in a Scottish border abbey may be attributed to the policy of Edward I of infiltrating reliable elements into Scottish establishments'.[37]

However, the entry in the patent rolls granting Jedburgh permission to elect suggests that there were already English canons in the abbey: William de Jarum is one of three canons who came to Edward I to ask for this permission and when, later, Edward notified the bishop of Glasgow of his election, he is described as the prior of the convent, suggesting that he had been at Jedburgh for some time.[38] It seems likely that Jedburgh, located close to the border, on one of the major routes between the two countries, contained both Scots and Englishmen. Further support from this comes from the names of many of the English canons. While Adam of Levington may come from as far south as Suffolk (there is a Levington there, on the River Orwell), William of Yarm, William of Tynedale, Andrew of Chollerton, Adam of Lanchester and William of Corbridge (sent with Peter Gernoun to present the newly elected abbot to the king),[39] seem to have origins in the very north of England. This appears to reinforce the 'border community' described by King and others, where Jedburgh might be seen as a 'local' house by men on both sides of the border.

Further information about the flight of the canons can be found from another document, C 49/4/11, apparently a memorandum of another petition.[40] It begins:

> Be it remembered, that in the seventh year of the reign of our lord the present king Edward, whom God preserve, on the same day following the one on

[36] A. Beam, 'The Northern Rebels of 1296, Part II: Northumberland', *The Breaking of Britain: Cross Border Society and Scottish Independence, 1216–1314*, feature of the month, February 2013, <http://www.breakingofbritain.ac.uk/blogs/feature-of-the-month/february-2013> [accessed 3 January 2018]; Barrow, *The Kingdom of the Scots*, p. 227.

[37] Fraser, *Petitions Relating to Northumberland*, p. 31.

[38] The licence to elect is *CPR, 1292–1301*, p. 202, dated 14 September 1296. Printed in *Documents Illustrative of the History of Scotland (1286–1306)*, ed. J. Stevenson, 2 vols (Edinburgh, 1870), vol. II, p. 106. Notification to the bishop of Glasgow of election, and instruction to the earl of Surrey to restore temporalities to the new abbot: *CPR, 1292–1301*, p. 204, dated 24 September 1296. Printed in *Documents Illustrative of the History of Scotland*, ed. Stevenson, vol. II, pp. 106–7.

[39] *Calendar of Documents Relating to Scotland*, ed. Bain, vol. II, no. 836.

[40] It has clearly been cut off a longer series of documents. It is edited in *Calendar of Documents Relating to Scotland*, ed. Bain, vol. III, Appendix I, p. 313.

> which Roxburgh castle was lost [i.e. some months *before* Bannockburn] … the abbot of Jedburgh, because he wished to save his faith and his oath to our said lord the king, left his aforesaid house of Jedburgh, and came to England, and remained there in great hardship with eleven of his canons.[41]

It continues that the abbot died at Thornton-on-Humber and that the goods belonging to Jedburgh left by him to support his canons have been seized by the king with the procurement of Sir William de Clyf (rather than Hugh le Despenser), and Arthuret and a manor in Tynedale have been given away. The eleven canons could have sustenance from these things, and they possess a sentence from Rome against all those who disturb them in their possession. The document ends with a claim that they have done nothing against the king to merit their losing their goods or their church being disinherited.

Twelve was the ideal number for an Augustinian house – although this was not always adhered to – so the abbot and eleven canons may well have been the entire body, and must in any case have been a sizeable proportion of the monastery. When they fled in 1314, they must have left a much-depleted and quite possibly a completely empty house behind them.

The timing of the flight is presented slightly differently in the two accounts. C 49/4/11 states that the abbot left of his own accord because 'he wished to save his faith and his oath to our said lord the king' on the day after the taking of Roxburgh castle in February 1314: an honourable and dignified departure that had brought subsequent hardship. SC 8/173/8644, on the other hand, paints a picture of 'ethnic cleansing' by a vindictive Robert Bruce in the wake of his victory at Bannockburn. In either case, it is clear that the canons left in 1314, but it is not until 1317 that we find a protection granted to Abbot William, 'so long as he and his men remain in England and are of the king's faith and peace'.[42] He evidently had some lands to live off, as it is stipulated that 'nothing is to be taken of his corn etc.', but no details are given. From references in other documents it would seem that he and many of his canons were living at Thornton-on-Humber, where he died in January 1319,[43] but some seem to have been elsewhere. Thornton-on-Humber complained about the burden the canons were placing on them,[44] but so did the prior of Nostell in Yorkshire, in whose house John of Hexham, canon of Jedburgh – another

[41] TNA, C 49/4/11: 'Fait aremembrer, qe lan du regne nostre seignur le Roi Edward qore est qe Dieu gard, septisme, mesme le iour suwant qe le chastel de Rokesburgh fust perdu … Labbe de Jeddeworthe, pur coe quil voleit sauuer sa foy et son serment deuers nostre dit siegnur le Roi, voyda sa mesoun de Jeddeworthe auantdit, et vyent en Engleterre, e la demora a graunt meschefe ove unze de ses Chanoyns'.

[42] *CPR, 1317–1321*, p. 7, dated 27 July 1317.

[43] On 10 January 1319 the king ordered the abbot and convent of Thornton-on-Humber to deliver his goods to the bishop of Glasgow, notwithstanding any previous orders to keep them safely: *CCR, 1318–1323*, pp. 50–1.

[44] *Calendar of Documents Relating to Scotland*, ed. Bain, vol. III, no. 893.

north-country name – had been living for two years, and Guisborough priory also complained of maintaining several canons driven from their houses, including a Guy of Jedburgh, so it would seem that the canons had been split up.[45]

The death of Abbot William in 1319 would seem to date SC 8/173/8644 to c. 1323; but, despite the favourable answer to the petition, the only definite record that we have of practical measures is from March 1327, when Edward III committed Jedburgh's English lands, Lee Hall and Troughend, to William de Uston, with instructions to find twenty marks yearly from them for the four canons.[46] This is so similar to the response to SC 8/173/8644 that it suggests either that that petition is from 1327, and its 'iiii' a miscopying of 'viii', or that this order is the continuation of a provision that the canons were already receiving. In any case, it is surely significant that, in 1327, only eighteen months before the abbot and convent of Jedburgh would request the return of Arthuret and Abbotsley, Edward III was making provision for the renegades from the secular lands of the abbey. It is notable that these manors are not mentioned in SC 8/16/756.[47]

The canons had apparently tried to return to Jedburgh. On 19 June 1325 the pope made arrangements for the hearing of the case between Adam of Lanchester, canon of Jedburgh (whom we have seen as one of the small group of renegades above), and 'Robert called "Marshal", canon of the same', that, during the war between England and Scotland, Adam, with Abbot William and *five* other canons, 'betook themselves for safety to England; the abbot died, and Robert taking that office on himself shut the doors in the face of Adam and the canons on their return, and denounced him as apostate and excommunicate'.[48]

Interestingly, we have a much smaller number of canons fleeing to England here, although it is possible that these five were the survivors of the original eleven, or those who wished to return. But they clearly represented a threat to the new, pro-Scottish Jedburgh, whether this was a rump of the original abbey or a repopulation from some other house. If Jedburgh had to contend with a living and vocal band of opponents for Arthuret and Abbotsley, this may

45 SC 8/319/E391: 'E le vauntdite Prieur de un frere Johan de Hexceldesham, chanoigne de Gedeworth sez deux auntz par nostre seignur le roy ad este charge'. For Guy, see: *Calendar of Documents Relating to Scotland*, ed. Bain, vol. III no. 892 from TNA, C 47/22/4/48.

46 *CFR, 1327–1337*, p. 27. Andrew is named here as Ralph de Chollerton.

47 Although they may have petitioned for them separately.

48 *Calendar of Entries in the Papal Registers relating to Great Britain and Ireland: Papal Letters, Vol. II, A.D. 1305–1342*, ed. W. H. Bliss (London, 1895), p. 245. We do not know how the pope's appointees (the bishop of Glasgow and the abbots of Kelso and Melrose) decided, but perhaps the sentence from Rome mentioned in C 49/4/11 was the result of their deliberations.

explain why the current abbot and convent clung so tenaciously to the text of the peace treaty, and why their petition was so stiff and formal.

This is not the last petition from Jedburgh on this subject. As has been said, although the rector of Abbotsley was ordered to pay the abbot the pension due from the church on 28 October 1328, the inquisition into the advowson was delayed by the death of one of those appointed to hear it, and a second petition, SC 8/118/5879, was presented to complain about this. Significantly, this is from the abbot alone, referring to himself as 'the Abbot of Jedburgh in Scotland', and is in French, and although it again provides a near quotation of the treaty of Northampton/Edinburgh, this is referred to as being between 'our lord the king and my lord Robert de Bruys', who, significantly, is not awarded his royal title.[49] The stern approach of 1328 had been abandoned.[50]

The second petition, SC 8/16/757, asking for the return of the church of Haltwhistle, in Northumberland, comes from the abbot of the Tironensian house of Arbroath. Here, too, there is a story of changing fortunes and conflicted loyalties. This petition is much more conventionally written in French, the normal language of petitioning in this period, and in its structure it is a very typical petition of its day. It begins with a relatively informal address to the king and council, followed by an explanatory clause introduced by 'monstre' and a request introduced by 'prie'. Unlike the Jedburgh petition, it is from the abbot alone. Its tone is conciliatory, stressing links with England, and, unlike the Jedburgh petition, it uses the more neutral 'terre' for both England and Scotland.

The first link with England is the dedication of the abbey; and the petition begins with it: 'To our lord the king and his council the Abbot of Arbroath shows that, whereas the church of Arbroath is founded in honour of St Thomas of Canterbury.' Arbroath was founded in 1177 by King William the Lion, who dedicated it to St Thomas Becket, martyred seven years earlier. This is not the only document to stress this dedication. In a letter of 3 May 1329 Robert I, writing to ask Edward III to expedite this business, gives as one reason 'consideration for the veneration of St Thomas of Canterbury, in whose honour our ancestors, the kings of Scotland, founded that said monastery of Arbroath and, with a pious mind, endowed the same monastery with the aforesaid church of Haltwhistle'.[51] Both king and abbot clearly feel that Thomas of Canterbury should evoke a pious response in the English king.

[49] SC 8/118/5879: 'labbe de Jeddeworth Descoz'; 'nostre seignur le roy et monsire Robert de Bruys'.

[50] This petition would seem to date from between 1330, when Arthuret was returned, and 1333, when Jedburgh's possessions were again forfeited: *CPR, 1330–1334*, p. 457.

[51] TNA, C 81/162/2645: 'habita consideracione ad veneracionem sancti Thome Cantuariensis in cuius honore antecessores nostri reges Scocie dictum monasterium de Abirbrothoc fundaverant ipsumque monasterium predictam ecclesiam de Hautwisill dotaverant pia mente'.

And there was every reason to suppose that it would. Michael Penman has drawn attention to Robert I's own particular devotion to St Thomas, while also noting Edward III's annual visits to Canterbury and use of the saint in propaganda against Scotland and France.[52] An appeal to a favourite saint would thus seem to be a natural way to secure King Edward's benevolence; but there was more to it than that. Thomas Becket, martyred on the orders of the English king, could also be a symbol of resistance to English royal authority. Penman notes that 'the contemporary verse which records the king's ... Bannockburn speech (preserved in a fifteenth-century chronicle manuscript) invokes Andrew and Thomas in the same breath'.[53] Penman notes how 'the "Irish Remonstrance" of 1317, issued by Irish supporters of the Bruce invasion of 1315–18, invoked Becket's cause against the English crown as if "for justice and the defence of the church"', and concludes that:

> [T]he Scots were ... surely similar to the French in invoking Becket in the course of tensions with England's crown. Yet, at the same time, such was the English crown's veneration of Thomas ... that Scottish devotion and journeys to Becket and his tomb may equally have been deployed as a means of ingratiation with the Plantagenet house.[54]

So Thomas of Canterbury has two aspects: on the one hand a saint whose cult links Scotland and England, King Robert and King Edward, and on the other a reminder to the Plantagenet kings of their past sins, and especially of their need to respect the rights of the Church. He was thus the ideal saint for the return of Haltwhistle.

The petition then gets down to business. Arbroath's possession of the church of Haltwhistle is mentioned, and there follows the curious story of the abbot's predecessor, who, during the war, fled Scotland for Durham, where he lived off the esplees of Haltwhistle 'until the day he died in the faith of our lord the king of England'. Edward II, acting under evil counsel, then intruded another cleric into the church; the petition then finishes with a plea for the church's return. In this way a two-fold argument for the restitution of Haltwhistle is built up, a belt-and-braces approach made clear in the request clause:

> [T]he said abbot prays that his church of Arbroath might be restored to the aforesaid church of Haltwhistle, according to the form of the peace treaty which has been confirmed between the two kings, and as his immediate predecessor died in the king's faith, and at no time since did any man of Scotland have anything in that church that he could forfeit.

[52] M. Penman, 'The Bruce Dynasty, Becket and Scottish Pilgrimage to Canterbury, c. 1178–c. 1404', *Journal of Medieval History* 32 (2006), 346–70, at 360–1.
[53] Penman, 'Bruce Dynasty', 358.
[54] Penman, 'Bruce Dynasty', 359, 352.

The return of Haltwhistle is requested under the terms of the peace treaty, but, if that alone would not suffice, it was held by a man who lived always in the faith of the king of England, so there was no reason for the king to have seized it and to have presented to it. In keeping with the tone of the petition, these actions are explained as the result of 'evil counsellors'. Many petitioners in the early years of Edward III sought to have Edward II's decisions overturned on the grounds that he acted under the influence of evil counsellors. It is noteworthy that the Jedburgh petition makes no excuse of this kind: it merely states that 'it pleased the lord king, the father of the present lord king' to expel them from their churches.

In fact, the abbot of Arbroath presented, implicity or explicitly, three reasons why the church should be returned: 1) it was required by the peace treaty; 2) the previous abbot, who held it, died in the faith of the king of England, so there was no reason for Edward II to have seized it, which he did, in any case, under malign influence; and 3) it would honour the English saint, Thomas of Canterbury, to whom Arbroath abbey is dedicated.

So who was this former abbot who fled to England and lived off Haltwhistle? We can trace the story from documents in the *Liber Vetus* of Arbroath Abbey. His name, apparently, was John of Arbroath or John of Angus,[55] and he is attested as abbot from 1303.[56] Like William of Yarm, he seems to have been elected as a man acceptable to the English regime, although, unlike him, there is nothing to suggest that he was actually English. We have a number of letters about him from his successor, Bernard, who, far from sharing his antipathy to the Scottish regime, was Robert I's chancellor. From these we learn that John was absolved of his office at All Saints 1309 – shortly after Arbroath came back into Scottish hands.[57] He seems to have left the abbey and to have gone to Berwick. A letter from the first half of 1310 recommends him and his business to the chancellor of England, stating that he has been at Berwick for some time, suffering from want of sustenance, 'because of our lord the king's enemies being in his aforesaid house'.[58] He appears to have been provided with the living of Haltwhistle as a solution to his problems. On 27 July 1310 he acquired a letter of protection from Edward II in which he is styled 'John, abbot of Aberbrothok, parson of the church of Hautwysele'.[59]

[55] For 'John of Arbroath' (Johannes de Aberbrothoc): *Liber S. Thome de Aberbrothoc, registrorum Abbacie de Aberbrothoc*, ed. P. Chalmers, 2 vols, Bannatyne Club 86 (Edinburgh, 1848–56), no. 324. For 'John of Angus' (Johannes de Angus): *Liber S. Thome de Aberbrothoc*, ed. Chalmers, no. 331.

[56] *Liber S. Thome de Aberbrothoc*, ed. Chalmers, no. 322, dated 26 December 1303.

[57] The Scots regained control of Arbroath around 1308–9: Penman, 'Bruce Dynasty', 355. For John's leaving at All Saints 1309: *Liber S. Thome de Aberbrothoc*, ed. Chalmers, no. 332.

[58] TNA, SC 1/35/55: 'per inimicos domini nostri regis apud domum suam predictam existentes'. Not dated, but it must be after John left Arbroath, and before 6 July 1310, when John Langton, bishop of Chichester, ceased to be chancellor.

[59] *CPR, 1307–1313*, p. 266.

Initially, steps seem to have been taken in Scotland to limit his resources. On 3 December 1310 King Robert ordered Arbroath to cease payment of pensions 'to any persons not profitable to the said house, and especially those living outside the realm'.[60] This would seem to refer, perhaps among others, to the former abbot, John, and to be a move to prevent the goods of the house coming into enemy hands. In practice, since Haltwhistle was outside King Robert's control, it probably had little effect.

In 1312 a different tactic was tried. In a letter of 2 February the abbot and convent asked the bishop of St Andrews to make a provision for John and 'one companion from our community'[61] in the church of Haltwhistle, 'provided, however, that he is obedient to his abbot and order as is fitting, and the property of the said church remains with us and our monastery in full right'.[62] This was clearly an acquiescence in established fact, but it may well also have appeared to the abbot and convent as an opportunity. Haltwhistle was vulnerable to being taken into the English king's hand as the property of 'Scottish rebels', and to have someone there who was still a member of their house, even if only in name, would keep their claim alive.[63] We should note that Bernard was careful to stress the need for John's obedience, and that Arbroath abbey retained full rights in Haltwhistle.

But the situation collapsed quickly. Just over six months later, on 20 August 1312, Bernard issued another letter, informing all who read it that the 'procuratorium' granted to John in Haltwhistle was again revoked.[64] From a letter sent the next day to Abbot Adam of Kilwinning (another Tironensian house), it would appear that John had been captured in England by one Peter de Stratheren, and was being held to ransom.[65] Bernard and his convent pronounced themselves

60 *Acts of Robert I*, ed. Duncan, no. 14: 'Quare vobis in fide et fidelitate quibus nobis tenemini tenore presencium inhibemus ne aliquas pensionum soluciones de cetero faciatis quibuscunque personis dicti domui non proficientibus et precipue se habentibus extra regnum nisi per quas nos cum nostro consilio aperte viderimus quod veraciter dicte domus commodum fieri poterit in effectu.'

61 *Liber S. Thome de Aberbrothoc*, ed. Chalmers, no. 324: 'uni socio de nostro collegio'.

62 *Liber S. Thome de Aberbrothoc*, ed. Chalmers, no. 324: 'ita tamen quod abbati suo et ordini sicut decet sit obediens, et proprietas dicte ecclesie penes nos et monasterium nostrum remaneat pleno iure'.

63 Indeed, Haltwhistle had been taken from Arbroath in 1304, by the bishop of Durham, and they had petitioned for its restitution: C 47/22/9/40. In the same year the Augustinian house of Lanercost petitioned for the church: C 47/22/9/39.

64 *Liber S. Thome de Aberbrothoc*, ed. Chalmers, no. 332.

65 *Liber S. Thome de Aberbrothoc*, ed. Chalmers, no. 333: 'Quia nuper intelleximus quod frater Johannes, dudum abbas monasterii de Aberbrothoc et modo simplex monachus, de guerra captus fuit in Anglia per Petrum de Stratheren seu per quosdam de familia ipsius, et detentus est tanquam captivus penes ipsos pro redempcione facienda.' Stringer ('Arbroath Abbey in Context', pp. 131–2) understands Bernard to be describing John as a 'mere monk of war', but I think that the later repetition of 'pro tali simplici monacho' suggests rather that he is making it

ready to pay the ransom, if the king and council authorised it 'for such a simple monk', and asked Adam to stand surety and to take delivery of Brother John, pending his return to Arbroath. Bernard clearly did not want John to attempt to use the revenues of Haltwhistle to ransom himself.

It would seem that John returned to Haltwhistle, however. Two documents in the *Registrum Palatinum Dunelmense* from late 1313 clearly situate him there. In the first, dated 14 November 1313, Bishop Richard Kellaw ordered his sequestrator to relax the sequestration placed on 'the religious man, the lord ... abbot of Arbroath, the rector of the church of Haltwhistle, in our diocese' on account of debts due to the king of England, which he had now paid; this notwithstanding any visitation dues (*procurationes*) or other debts still owed by him, which were to be claimed in the appropriate legal fashion.[66] Visitation dues were in fact due from Haltwhistle for a papal nuncio, Arnold, cardinal-priest of St Prisca, and the second document is a letter of acquittance, acknowledging receipt of 22s 6d from 'the religious man, lord John, abbot of Arbroath, the rector of the church of Haltwhistle' as his church's contribution to this *procuratio*.[67] From these letters it can be seen that, in English documents at least, John's claims to the abbacy were in no way a dead letter.

From these letters we gain a new perspective on our petition as the continuation of an established policy of Arbroath towards Haltwhistle: to acquiesce in the holding of the living by the former abbot, while continuing to stress that he was a monk of their house and to claim ultimate rights in the church. This effectively solved two problems. As there were few Tironensians in England, there would be no obvious refuge for John there, and there was always the danger of his becoming a scandal to the order. If he was living off Haltwhistle he was not in some house of alien monks, nor was he bringing the order into disrepute. And, at the same time, with Haltwhistle in loyal English hands, there was no reason for Edward II to seize it.

Such a petition might not perhaps seem like the work of Robert I's chancellor. But the writer is not Abbot Bernard – he was appointed bishop of Sodor in 1328, and on 19 March in that year, shortly before this petition was written, an Abbot Geoffrey granted a charter at Arbroath.[68] Might his relative newness and insecurity in office, and his knowledge that he was succeeding a man intimately associated with the Bruce regime, explain its conciliatory tone?[69]

clear that John, while still a monk of Arbroath, no longer has any claims to the abbacy; the words 'de guerra' explain the circumstances of his capture.

66 *Registrum Palatinum Dunelmense, 1311–1316*, ed. T. D. Hardy, 4 vols, Rolls Series 62 (Durham, 1873–8), vol. I, pp. 467–8: 'Religiosus vir, dominus ... abbas de Abbrebrothok', rector ecclesiae de Hautwsill', nostrae dioecesis'.

67 *Registrum Palatinum Dunelmense*, ed. Hardy, vol. I, pp. 479–80: 'Religioso viro, domino Iohanne abate de Abberbrothok', rectore ecclesiae de Hautwisel'.

68 *Liber S. Thome de Aberbrothoc*, ed. Chalmers, no. 361.

69 Abbot Geoffrey was one of those who accepted Edward Baliol after Dupplin Moor

These two petitions show similarities, and differences, in the fates of these abbeys and the English churches in their possession in the Wars of Independence. But how typical were they? Only eleven miles from Jedburgh, the Tironensian house of Kelso seems to have had a very similar history. Its abbot, Richard, was 'on Balliol's side in 1292', according to Barrow, and, like John Morel, seems to have continued his allegiance to the Scots.[70] A letter patent of 7 August 1299 granted permission to elect a new abbot, in response to a request from the chapter complaining of 'the long and voluntary absence of brother Richard, lately ... abbot', whom Edward I called 'a rebel against our faith and friendship, and one who provides aid and counsel to our enemies'.[71] Like Jedburgh, the monks apparently decided that an Englishman would be most acceptable. An entry on the patent roll dated 20 October 1299 reveals that Thomas of Durham ('de Dunolmia'), the monk who brought the request to Edward, had been elected.[72] Thomas also seems to have been prior of Kelso's daughter house of Lesmahagow, and his allegiance to Edward I clearly caused problems. Writing in 1315, Bishop Robert Wishart of Glasgow pointedly called him 'Thomas of Durham the Englishman'[73] and stated that 'the said English prior was not only a despoiler of the goods of Lesmahagow priory, but also of the monastery of Kelso when, through usurpation, he bore the name of abbot there'.[74] Thomas was succeeded around 1307 by an Abbot Walran, whose allegiance we do not know,[75] but, from around 1317, the abbot of Kelso was one William of Ancrum, who had been chamberlain under Abbot Richard.[76] William was clearly a Scottish loyalist – had he spent the

in 1332: R. Nicholson, *Edward III and the Scots: The Formative Years of a Military Career, 1327–1335* (Oxford, 1965), p. 93.

70 G. W. S. Barrow, *The Kingdom of the Scots: Government, Church and Society from the Eleventh to the Fourteenth Century* (Edinburgh, 2003), p. 227.

71 *Documents Illustrative of the History of Scotland*, ed. Stevenson, pp. 392–3: 'cum ecclesia vestra de Kelsou per diutinam et spontaneam absentiam fratris Ricardi nuper abbatis vestri, fidei nostrae et amicitiae rebellis, nostrisque inimicis auxilium et consilium praebentis, pastoris sit solatio destituta', printed from TNA, C 66/119, m. 16.

72 *CPR, 1292–1301*, pp. 442, 448. Printed in *Documents Illustrative of the History of Scotland*, ed. Stevenson, vol. II, pp. 398–9.

73 *Liber Sanctae Mariae de Calchou*, ed. Innes, no. 188: 'Thomas de Durram anglicus'.

74 *Liber Sanctae Mariae de Calchou*, ed. Innes, no. 188: 'Dictus prior anglicus erat non solummodo bonorum prioratus de Lesmahago sed et monasterii de Kelchou dum per usurpacionem nomen ibidem gessit abbatis dilapidator'.

75 *Liber Sanctae Mariae de Calchou*, ed. Innes, nos 42, 43.

76 A fourteenth-century Kelso rental describes how Richard transmuted the service of the tenants of Bowden (Roxburghshire) into money: 'per assedacionem fratris Willelmi de Alincroma, tunc camerarario [sic] sui': *Liber Sanctae Mariae de Calchou*, ed. Innes, vol. II, p. 462. See also A. Smith, 'Re-establishing Scottish Independence in 1314: The Example of Kelso Abbey', *The Breaking of Britain: Cross Border Society and Scottish Independence, 1216–1314*, feature of the month, March 2011, <http://www.

intervening period in Kelso, keeping his head down, or had he been expelled and returned?

National identity was not the only factor in deciding whether a monk stayed or left. We also have a petition from c. 1305–6 from an exiled monk of Kelso, asking to be allowed to return.[77] He gave his name only as Peter – 'Peres, moyne de Kelzou en Escoce' – and proffered nothing of his reasons for leaving. Edward I had placed him in the Benedictine priory of Norwich 'during the war in Scotland' as the Close Roll entry responding to this petition states, which suggests that he may be an Englishman or of English sympathies, but this was not at all to his liking; the monks 'are not of his religion, nor do they use such service as he ought to use'.[78] He begged the king 'that he of his grace might allow him to return to his own house, or live elsewhere among people of his religion of grey monks, to save his soul and his profession'.[79] Edward wrote to Kelso telling them that Peter had his permission to return.[80] Clearly loyalty could be felt for one's religious order, as well as for one's nation. This petition may shed some light on why John of Arbroath chose to live off Haltwhistle, rather than join a community in England.

In the Premonstratensian house of Dryburgh, too, the canons John de Dyttinsale and Hugh de Dalnewik were apparently 'expelled by the Scots from the house on account of their English nationality'.[81] Like the renegade canons of Jedburgh, they were granted the English possessions of their house to live off, in this case the tenements, rents and fisheries of Dryburgh in Berwick and in the River Tweed.

If more northerly abbeys such as Arbroath might not be expected to have the same mix of Scottish and English monks as those in the Borders, Abbot John's tale is by no means unique there. Thomas of Balmerino, abbot of Scone, seems to have been deposed around 1303 and replaced by Henry Man; in 1306 he appeared as a prisoner in England. Apparently he succeeded in recovering his abbacy around 1312, only to be replaced once again by Man.[82] The Cluniac priory on the Isle of May was a daughter house of Reading

breakingofbritain.ac.uk/blogs/feature-of-the-month/march-2011-re-establishing-scottish-independence> [accessed 3 January 2018].

77 SC 8/119/5936.

78 SC 8/119/5936: 'les moynes de Norwyz qe ne sunt de sa religion ne tel servise usunt cum il deyt user'.

79 SC 8/119/5936: 'qe il de sa grace le volie returner a sa meson demeyne ou aliurs entre genz de sa religion de gris moynes pur sa alme e sa profession saver'.

80 *CCR, 1302–1307*, p. 427, dated 16 February 1306. It is interesting that this order had to be given because the abbot and convent 'fear to admit him into their house without the king's licence'.

81 *CPR, 1313–1317*, p. 557, dated 21 October 1316.

82 See *The Heads of Religious Houses in Scotland from the Twelfth to the Sixteenth Centuries*, ed. E. Watt and N. Shead (Edinburgh, 2001), pp. 198–202.

Abbey, founded on an island given to the abbey by David I,[83] and as such it might have been expected to have suffered in the Wars of Independence. In fact, Reading Abbey, in severe financial difficulties, seems to have sold the priory to the bishop of St Andrews early in 1288, and it was transferred to the Augustinian priory attached to St Andrew's cathedral.[84] Reading, under a new abbot who deplored his predecessor's actions, took steps to recover the Isle of May and its mainland property at Pittenweem, petitioning both King John Balliol's parliament of February 1293 and Edward I.[85] He appears to have been successful in recovering the priory, for a writ of Edward from 1305, restoring the priory to Reading yet again, describes how it was 'delivered to the abbot ... after the realm of Scotland came to his hands by the rebellion of John de Balliolo ... and which the abbot held peacefully as a cell ... until William le Waleys and his accomplices, lately insurgents against the king in those parts, ejected the abbot and his men'.[86] Here we have another case of expulsion of English monks, and the beneficiaries seem to have been the Augustinian canons of St Andrews. But apparently they too were of mixed loyalties. A petition from Thomas de Houburn, canon of St Andrews, which Duncan dates to 'certainly not after mid-1302' states that he had been ousted from the Priory of Pittenweem by the Scots, and had been living 'at the king's alms and grace' since then.[87] Another document shows that he was given shelter at the abbey of Leicester.[88] Duncan describes him as 'an Englishman', although Howburn, as a place name, is found both in southern Scotland and northern England. Whatever his nationality, and although he was the beneficiary of Wallace's expulsion of the Reading Cluniacs, he seems to have been loyal to Edward I.

These two documents and their very different strategies of petitioning add to our knowledge of Scottish religious houses, the conflicted loyalties of their members and their difficulties and dilemmas in the Wars of Independence. But the peace of 1328 was not the end of the wars, or of their troubles. Any gain Arbroath and Jedburgh had from these petitions was short-lived. While the treaty of Northampton/Edinburgh made provision for the return of clerical lands, the lands of secular lords were not mentioned, deliberately, and in accordance with Bruce's wishes. The result was to leave in England a

83 A. A. M. Duncan, 'Documents Relating to the Priory of the Isle of May, c. 1140–1313', *Proceedings of the Society of Antiquaries of Scotland* 90 (1956–7), 52–80.

84 Duncan, 'Documents Relating to the Priory of the Isle of May', 63.

85 *Records of the Parliaments of Scotland to 1707*, 1293/2/5, 1293/2/7, <http://www.rps.ac.uk> [accessed 3 January 2018]; SC 8/275/13701, which Duncan, 'Documents Relating to the Priory of the Isle of May', 77–8, dates to 1296–7.

86 *CCR, 1302–1307*, p. 249, dated 24 March 1305, quoted in Duncan, 'Documents Relating to the Priory of the Isle of May', 64.

87 *Calendar of Documents Relating to Scotland*, ed. Bain, vol. II, no. 1964. Duncan, 'Documents Relating to the Priory of the Isle of May', 64.

88 *Calendar of Documents Relating to Scotland*, ed. Bain, vol. II, no. 1965.

body of people with claims to Scottish lands, which they were not prepared to drop, who were able to exploit the feeling of the young king and others that the peace was a shameful one that should never have been accepted. By 1332 Edward Balliol, son of the deposed king John Balliol, had invaded Scotland, won a victory at Dupplin Moor, and was receiving the king of England's support. The changing situation again put the monasteries' possession of their vulnerable English churches in jeopardy. When, on 24 June 1332, Edward III presented John de Gayneford to Arthuret, he claimed the right through the vacancy in the see of Carlisle.[89] Apparently Jedburgh objected, for the king nominated another candidate, John de Penreth, to the abbot and convent for presentation to the vicarage two weeks later.[90] But when, on 3 August 1333, the king presented John de Pokelyngton to the church, it was 'in the king's gift by reason of the forfeiture of the abbot of Jeddeworth on account of the war of Scotland'.[91] Abbotsley too was lost. On 12 April 1340 the king granted it to William de Felton, 'on account of the forfeiture of the abbot of Jeddeworth in Scotland', and gave him licence to alienate it in mortmain to the master and scholars of Balliol College, Oxford.[92] The fate of Haltwhistle is less clear, but eventually it too must have been forfeited.[93] Just as the Jedburgh petition, with its emphasis on the demands of a peace treaty between two sovereign realms and the rights of Holy Church, and the Arbroath petition, with its manipulation of its late pro-English abbot and its appeal to veneration for an English saint, achieved similar results, when it was in Edward's interests to uphold the terms of the treaty of Northampton/Edinburgh, so the Scottish abbeys' precarious hold on their English possessions did not survive the renewal of hostilities. In the end, it was political realities, not the careful wording of their petitions, that affected the abbots' recovery of their churches.

Appendix: Text and Translation of the Two Petitions

TNA, SC 8/16/756

D*omi*no suo, d*omi*no regi Angl*ie* illustri *et* co*n*silio suo, significant abbas *et* convent*us* monasterii de Jeddeworth', Glasguen*sis* dioc*esis*, q*uo*d ipsi sunt *et* ab antiquo fueru*n*t veri rectores eccl*es*ie de Artureth', Karl*eonensis* dioc*esis*,

[89] *CPR, 1330–1334*, p. 309.

[90] *CPR, 1330–1334*, p. 315, dated 8 July 1332. After the previous presentation to John de Gayneford was revoked, John de Penreth was finally presented on 16 August: *CPR, 1330–1334*, p. 316 (abortive presentation on 11 July), p. 322 (revocation of previous presentation of John de Gayneford) and p. 326 (final presentation).

[91] *CPR, 1330–1334*, p. 457.

[92] *CPR, 1338–1340*, p. 461.

[93] Robert de Dighton was still parson on 9 December 1332, when he acknowledged a debt to Queen Philippa: either Arbroath had felt compelled to retain him, or he had been reinstated: *CCR, 1330–1333*, p. 617.

eam in usus proprios habentes; sunt *etiam et* ab antiquo fuerunt veri patroni ecclesie de Alboteley, Lincolnensis diocesis. Sed propter guerras *et* discordias inter regna Anglie *et* Scocie, placuit domino regi, patri domini regis nunc, eos ab ecclesiis predictis expellere *et* alios clericos inducere *et* induci facere in easdem. Unde cum pax sit iam obtenta, Deo dante, inter regna predicta, ita quod nichil factum vel attemptatum sit ecclesiis vel ecclesiasticis personis utrobique preiudiciale, supplicant dicto domino suo, domino regi *et* eius consilio, quatenus velint eos ecclesiam suam predictam de Artureth', *et* ad presentacionem suam ad ecclesiam de Alboteley resumere, *et* clericos institutos in eisdem in eorum exheredacionem ammovere, *et* super hoc episcopis locorum *et* aliis ministris domini regis scribere *et* mandare.

Endorsement: Soient certeins gentz assignez denquere, en presence des clers qe ore sont persones de mesmes les eglises a ce apelez sil voillent estre, si les predecessors labbe de Jeddeworth' avant la guerre mue tindrent leglise de Arturet en propres oeps come suppose est *etc.*, *et* de queu temps *etc.*, et sil furent seisiz del avoeson de Abboteley avant la guerre *etc.* ou nemie, *et* de queu temps *etc.*, et si le roi presenta a les eglises par cause de la guerre ou par autre, et si par autre donqes par quele cause, *et* coment. *Et* lenqueste returne, soit fait droit. Irrotulatur.

To their lord, the illustrious lord king of England and to his council, the Abbot and convent of the monastery of Jedburgh, in the diocese of Glasgow, show that they are, and of old were, the true rectors of the church of Arthuret, in the diocese of Carlisle, holding it to their own uses; they are, and of old were, also the true patrons of the church of Abbotsley, in the diocese of Lincoln. But on account of the wars and dissensions between the realms of England and Scotland, it pleased the lord king, the father of the present lord king, to expel them from the aforesaid churches and to induct, and have inducted, other clerics into the same. Wherefore, since peace has now, of God's gift, been brought about between the aforesaid realms, so that nothing is to be done or attempted that is prejudicial to churches or to ecclesiastical persons on either side, they pray to their said lord, the lord king and his council, that they might be pleased to receive them back to their aforesaid church of Arturet, and to their presentation to the church of Abbotsley, and to remove the clerics instituted into the same to their disinheritance, and to write and give commands for this to the bishops of the places and to the lord king's other ministers.

Endorsement: Certain people are to be appointed to inquire, in the presence of the clerics who are currently the parsons of the same churches, to be summoned for this if they wish to be present, if the predecessors of the Abbot of Jedburgh, before the war was moved, held the church of Arthuret to their own use as is claimed etc., and from what time etc., and if they were seised of the advowson of Abbotsley before the war etc., or not, and from what time etc., and if the king presented to the churches because of the war or for some other cause, and if for another then for what cause, and how. And when the inquisition has been returned, justice is to be done.

TNA, SC 8/16/757

A n*ost*re seign*ur* le roi *et* son counseil monstre labbe de Aberbrothoc' qe, p*ar* la ou la esglise de Aberbrothoc' est founde al hon*ur* de Seynt Thomas de Canterburs, *et* a cel eglise est annex, *et* ad este de temps dont memor ne court, la eglise de Hautwesel en le evesche de Dorem en p*ro*pre oeps, et q*ua*nt la guerre sourdy entr*e* les deux t*er*res celui qe feust abbe de Aberbrthoc a ceux temps se myt hors de la t*er*re Descotz, tanq*e* a Dorem, *et* illoeq*e*s despendy les esplez del eglise de Hautwesel tanq*e* au jour qil morust a la fei n*ost*re seign*ur*, roi Dengleterre. *Et* apr*es* la mort de cely abbe, malveys p*ro*curors firent entendant au roi, pier n*ost*re seign*ur* le roi qore est, q*e* ycele eglise poait doner; et il le dona a un clerk qe unqor la tent, a g*ra*nt pr*e*judice *et* g*ra*nt damage del eglise de Aberbrothoc. Par qoi le dit abbe p*ri*e qe sa eglise de Aberbrothoc soit restituit de lavant dit eglise de Hautwesel, solonc la fourme du tretyz de la pees qest afferme entr*e* les deux rois, et desicome son p*ro*scheyn p*re*decessour moruyt a la fey le roi, *et* unqes puis nul ho*m*me Descotz rien en cele eglyse navoit q*e* forfer poait.

Endorsement: Petici*on*es de Scocia. Soient c*er*teines gentz assignees de enquere, en p*re*sence du clerk q*e* est ore p*ar*sone de la dite esglise a ceo appellez, sil voille estre, si le dit abbe ou ses p*re*decessours avant la guerre mue tiendrent la dite esglise en p*ro*pre oeps come est suppose *etc.*, *et* de queu temps *etc.*, *et* si le roi p*re*senta a mesm*e* lesglise p*ar* cause de la guerre ou p*ar* autre cause, *et* si p*ar* autre adonq*e* p*ar* quele *etc.* *Et* lenquest ret*ur*ne, soit fait droit. Irr*otulatur*.

To our lord the king and his council the Abbot of Arbroath shows that, whereas the church of Arbroath is founded in honour of St Thomas of Canterbury, and to that church is attached, and has been from time immemorial, the church of Haltwhistle in the bishopric of Durham to their own use, and when the war arose between the two lands, he who was Abbot of Arbroath at that time took himself out of the land of Scotland, to Durham, and there he spent the esplees of the church of Haltwhistle until the day he died in the faith of our lord the king of England. And after the death of that abbot, evil proctors gave the king, the father of our lord the present king, to understand that he could give that church; and he gave it to a clerk who still holds it, to the great prejudice and great harm of the church of Arbroath. For which reason the said abbot prays that his church of Arbroath might be restored to the aforesaid church of Haltwhistle, according to the form of the peace treaty which has been confirmed between the two kings, and as his immediate predecessor died in the king's faith, and at no time since did any man of Scotland have anything in that church that he could forfeit.

Endorsement: Certain people are to be appointed to inquire, in the presence of the cleric who is currently the parson of the said church, to be summoned for this if he wishes to be present, if the said Abbot or his predecessors, before the war was moved, held the said church to their own use as is claimed, and from what time etc., and if the king presented to the same church because of the war or for some other cause, and if for another then for what etc. And when the inquisition has been returned, justice is to be done.

7

'By Force and Arms': Lay Invasion, the Writ *de vi laica amovenda* and Tensions of State and Church in the Thirteenth and Fourteenth Centuries

Philippa M. Hoskin

In January 1296, by order of Oliver Sutton, bishop of Lincoln, Thomas Paynel and William, son of Robert of Whitwell, displayed in the church of Gosberton all the weapons and other objects that they had gathered together 'for the fortifying of their bodies or the construction of machines', and which they had used in a recent violent intrusion there.[1] Thomas and Robert had not been alone in this attack. It had also involved Sir Ranulph de Rye – a man who perhaps considered himself to be the church's patron, who the following year would have the penance he had been charged to perform following the incident remitted[2] – and his servant, Ralph Nodinay of Gosberton, who was excused the beating originally imposed upon him.[3] Thomas and Robert, however, did not have their penances remitted. The display of weaponry at Gosberton was followed by their walking barefoot to Lincoln cathedral, where again they would display the equipment they had used to violate the church's property and attack its personnel, before handing it over to the church. These events at Gosberton have, understandably, been described as an example of thirteenth-century anti-clericalism: hostility shown by lay people towards the Church and clerics.[4] Violent altercations between clergy and laity and legal complaints in both secular and ecclesiastical courts are points at which we can see dissatisfaction with the clergy surface. These could result from

[1] *The Rolls and Register of Bishop Oliver Sutton 1280–1299*, ed. R. M. T. Hill, 8 vols, Lincoln Record Society (1948–86), vol. V, p. 122; *Reg. Sutton*, ed. Hill, vol. IV, pp. 70–2, 78–9.
[2] *Reg. Sutton*, ed. Hill, vol. V, p. 201.
[3] *Reg. Sutton*, ed. Hill, vol. V, p. 132.
[4] D. M. Owen, *Church and Society in Medieval Lincolnshire* (Lincoln, 1971), pp. 138–42; A. Miller, 'Knights, Bishops and Deer Parks: Episcopal Identity, Emasculation and Clerical Space in Medieval England', in *Negotiating Clerical Identities: Priests, Monks, and Masculinities in the Middle Ages*, ed. J. Thibodeaux (Basingstoke, 2010), pp. 214–18; R. Hill, 'Public Penance: Some Problems of a Thirteenth-Century Bishop', *History* 36 (1951), 221–3.

disillusionment with the performance of a particular cleric's pastoral ministry, particularly in a period of papally sponsored ecclesiastical reform where higher standards of duty came to be expected, or might arise from economic disputes, for example over the payment of tithes, as the balance of what was considered fair and reasonable shifted in response to changes in the agricultural economy of the parish. The issues of tithes and ministry could also come together: negligent clergy – the absentees, the pluralists and the ill-educated – who did not provide resident replacement clergy were conceived of as breaking the bond of mutual obligation between clergy and laity because despite not providing the spiritual care that was their responsibility they still collected tithes, leading their parishioners to question the value they received from such arrangements.[5]

The invasion of church property – of the sacred space that was the consecrated church building – is, however, about much more than anti-clericalism. Cases where armed bands occupied churches tell us very little about local opposition to particular clergy or to clerical bodies and landowners. Rather, such incidents provide an opportunity to examine how disputes over Church property, particularly the advowson (the right to choose a parish incumbent), played out across the unstable boundaries that lay between the separate legal jurisdictions of Church and State, and to learn something about how jurisdictions were understood, tested, contested and sometimes exploited by the laity as well as by clerics. This paper considers incidents of violent seizure of church property during the thirteenth and fourteenth centuries through the perspective of the English common law writ, *de vi laica amovenda*, which was developed to assist the Church in dealing with such incidents. In doing so, it shows how the practical seizure of Church property was often also a symbolic assertion of lay rights over matters the Church claimed for its own, and an informed strategy to maximise the likelihood of winning disputes in a context where legal solutions were weak.

The Parish Church and the Laity

In considering such disputes, it is important to remember that who 'owned' the parish church – and therefore who could be said to invade it – was a

[5] R. N. Swanson, 'Problems of the Priesthood in Pre-Reformation England', *English Historical Review* 105 (1990), 845–69; see, for example, *Registrum Hamonis Hethe Diocesis Roffensis A.D. 1319–1352*, ed. C. Johnson, 2 vols (Oxford 1948), vol. I, p. 113; *Reg. Sutton*, ed. Hill, vol. I, pp. 54, 115, vol. IV, p. 82, vol. VI, p. 125. For a summary of the situation at law, drawing on a number of cases, see R. H. Helmholz, *The Oxford History of the Laws of England, Volume 1: The Canon Law and Ecclesiastical Jurisdiction from 597 to the 1640s* (Oxford, 2004), pp. 505–8 and Owen, *Church and Society*, pp. 136–40.

matter of perspective. In England, by the end of the twelfth century, the issue of ownership of parish church buildings and the land on which they were placed had been settled, largely in the Church's favour,[6] but this did not mean that the laity lost a sense of ownership in these buildings, or indeed lost interest in the identity of their clergy. Many churches' patrons – the individuals who had the right to nominate a new clergyman for a vacant church and send him for approval to the bishop – were descended from those who had established these individual churches, had owned the land on which it was built and who had contributed substantially to the fabric. Where patrons were monastic houses, rather than individuals, there was still a sense that the house had a corporate ownership of the church and that they had invested significantly in it.

In addition to these patrons, ordinary parishioners could also consider themselves to have a significant stake in local church property. The thirteenth century was a period during which responsibility for the management of the physical fabric of parish churches was shifting: some bishops maintained that the clergy had responsibility for the upkeep of the whole church, while others increasingly accepted a division whereby the clergy and laity split responsibility between themselves, with the nave, where the laity gathered for services and usually the largest part of the church, becoming the responsibility of the parishioners. Thus, lay investment in the fabric of parish churches was significant. In the late thirteenth and early fourteenth centuries the laity of the parish were collecting for the repair and maintenance of the church's fabric and making bequests towards its structure and its ornamentation.[7] In some cases even the upkeep of the chancel, the area of the church in which the clergy officiated, became a lay responsibility, with some lay patrons, rather than the incumbents, becoming responsible for the expense. Meanwhile, parish gilds made themselves responsible for the maintenance of parts of the church, or for internal decoration and beautifying – paying, for example, for wax to keep lights burning at particular altars. Parish gild membership gave members a sense of community and belonging that was rooted firmly in the physical fabric of the church.[8] Even those urban religious gilds with a larger

[6] S. Wood, *The Proprietary Church in the Medieval West* (Oxford, 2006), pp. 730–54; L. Barshack, 'The Communal Body, the Corporate Body and the Clerical Body: An Anthropological Reading of the Gregorian Reform', in *Sacred and Secular in Medieval and Early Modern Cultures*, ed. L. Besserman (Basingstoke, 2006), pp. 109–15.

[7] C. D. Cragoe, 'The Custom of the English Parish Church: Parish Church Maintenance in England before 1300', *Journal of Medieval History* 30 (2010), 11–17; and for an example of the clergy still taking responsibility for the fabric in the 1270s see F. W. Maitland, *Select Pleas in Manorial and other Seigniorial Courts, Volume 1: Reigns of Henry III and Edward I*, Selden Society 2 (London, 1889), p. 150.

[8] On the community of the parish, living and dead, together, see J. Bossy, 'The Mass as a Social Institution 1200–1700', *Past and Present* 100 (1983), 41–50. On gilds and parishioners and their approach to parish fabric see K. Farnhill, *Guilds and the Parish*

scope often selected a particular church in which to hold their services and to which they would contribute to the upkeep and ornamentation.[9]

The laity also had possession of the church in another way, through the burial of their dead. A patron's family might be interred within the church itself – even, indeed, within the chancel – while the parishioners' predecessors surrounded the church, being buried in the churchyard, which was in itself ecclesiastical property. As a result the laity felt a real and enduring sense of co-ownership of the physical building in which they gathered to worship, and it is thus unsurprising that, in spite of the Church's attempts to reserve the interior of the church, and the churchyard, for sacred functions, and despite diocesan statutes against this, the parishioners made use of it for secular as well as religious purposes, as market, meeting place, fortress and venue for liturgical drama.[10] The church's bells marked the passage of their days, calling them to service, recording deaths, directing their prayers during the day and rallying them in times of danger.[11] It was a place of security for the individual. Those who took sanctuary within it could claim forty days in which secular law could not touch them without coming under the ban of excommunication.[12] The parish church also had other connections with the law. It was the place in which local witnesses were called together to provide evidence about the vacancy of the benefice and to give their opinions about who held the right to present the clergy.[13] It was also the place in which those who violated the church or resisted its rulings were publicly named in sentences of excommunication, and from which such offenders were barred until ready to make amends by performing public penance, such as the one with which this paper opened. The physical building of the church was both the site for the acting out, and the resolution, of disputes.

Additionally, this sense of possession could stretch beyond the building to include a feeling of investment in the clergy who filled the church. The

Community in Late Medieval East Anglia (York, 2001), pp. 102–17, where he explores the activities of the gilds of Swaffham in relation to the fabric and ornaments of the church and points out that the work of individual gilds here was not mediated through churchwardens, as Kumin had suggested was the case in B. Kumin, *The Shaping of a Community: Rise and Reformation of the English Parish, c. 1400–1560* (London, 1996), pp. 101–2.

9 See, for example, P. Hoskin, 'The Accounts of the Medieval Paternoster Gild of York', *Northern History* 44 (2007), 7–33.

10 See J. G. Davies, *The Secular Use of Church Buildings* (New York, 1968), p. 95; R. Kieckhefer, *Theology in Stone: Church Architecture from Byzantium to Berkeley* (Oxford, 2004), p. 283.

11 J. H. Arnold and C. Goodson, 'Resounding Community: The History and Meaning of Medieval Church Bells', *Viator* 43 (2012), 112–18, 121–2; *Councils and Synods with other Documents Relating to the English Church II A.D. 1205–1313*, ed. F. M. Powicke and C. R. Cheney, 2 vols (Oxford 1964), vol. I, p. 175, vol. II, p. 1123.

12 See Helmholz, *The Oxford History of the Laws of England, Volume 1*, pp. 495–7.

13 Helmholz, *The Oxford History of the Laws of England, Volume 1*, p. 338.

patron could, by the thirteenth century, only nominate a new incumbent to a church, but this right still held real value. It gave them an important piece of patronage that could be used to maintain and extend their networks of influence, providing life-long maintenance for a family member or payment for professional administrative or legal services.[14] While ordinary parishioners had no direct role to play in the appointing of the parish incumbent, they might provide for chantry priests to perform extra, supplemental services, and still had opinions about what was and was not an adequate standard of parochial duty and could, and would, complain of their clergy's behaviour if it fell below what was expected.[15]

The parish church was, then, safeguarded and invested in by the whole parish community, and a great many people felt some sense of ownership over both the building and the way in which it was staffed. It was also, however, a space over which the Church as an institution claimed absolute authority, as well as an area that was, ultimately, sacred and from which the Church claimed the power to exclude the laity if necessary. The ground and fabric were ritually consecrated, set apart for the performance of prayers and the mass. The excommunicate could be barred from it as part of their separation from their community. To damage or misuse it – even to enter it in the interests of secular justice to forcibly remove a criminal – was, in canon law, to commit sacrilege. It was also a structure for much of which the laity increasingly took responsibility, with which their families had engaged over generations. To talk of its entry and fortification by the laity as an invasion was, then, to use the language of the Church. To the laity who seized, or who ordered the seizing of, a parish church, the building was, at least partly, theirs as well, so when they took occupation it asserted their rights as well as making a visible and disruptive statement. It is also important to recognise that armed lay invasions, or forcible occupations of churches, were not ultimately about the ownership or use of the space itself. Instead, the church building acted as a proxy for something intangible. This was something that could not be seized, invaded or occupied, but which powerful laymen valued highly and would fight for: the advowson, or the right to select the parish's next incumbent on the death or resignation of the previous one.

From the 1230s one weapon in the Church's armoury for dealing with lay seizure of church property was the writ *de vi laica amovenda*. An examination of the cases in which it was used demonstrate that lay claims over local ecclesiastical space can often be seen as reflections of much broader contests regarding the extent of power and authority of Church and State, areas about which there was still much uncertainty. These invasions, and the legal responses to them, show the ways in which the laity could exploit – or

[14] For an overview of the possibilities see E. Gemmill, *The Nobility and Ecclesiastical Patronage in Thirteenth-Century England* (Woodbridge, 2013), pp. 68–98.
[15] Swanson, 'Problems of the Priesthood in Pre-Reformation England', 847–9.

protest against the exploitation of – shifting and permeable legal boundaries that complicated the issues surrounding ecclesiastical property.

The Development of the Writ

The writ *de vi laica amovenda* concerned the possession of property and needs to be considered in relation to the parallel development of a far more common English writ, that of trespass. The writ of trespass developed out of the process of appeal in the thirteenth century as a way of bringing complaints of various wrongs (trespass in c. 1200 meaning the breaking of obligations) before the king's court. Its origins can be seen in the 1220s, when a writ to begin a complaint of trespass alleging breach of the king's peace appears, modelled on a writ used in the old criminal appeal, and by the 1250s regular payments for writs of trespass, under that name, appear in the fine rolls.[16] Following Edward I's inquiries into the behaviour of lower administrative and legal officials, and his reforms of the legal system in 1274, it became possible for complaints – including some trivial complaints of trespass – to be removed from local courts to the king's court on the grounds that the complainant feared local bias. This quickly became a significant administrative burden, filling the king's court with low-level cases, and, in response, three years later, the Statute of Gloucester set a number of legal limitations. Now only those trespass cases alleging the use of force could be brought before the king's justices. Thus the writ of trespass came to include both the allegation of breach of the king's peace together with the allegation of the use of force and arms (*vi et armis*).[17] By the end of the thirteenth century, then, the writ of trespass was about the breaking of the obligation to uphold the king's peace, specifically through the illicit, forceful, seizure of property.

De vi laica amovenda also developed in the second and third quarters of the thirteenth century and was also about property seizure. In simple terms, as its Latin name says, it was a writ requiring the sheriff to remove a lay force that had taken possession of property.[18] The similarities between it and the writ of

[16] *The Roll of the Shropshire Eyre of 1256*, ed. A. Harding, Selden Society 96 (London, 1981), pp. xxxii–xxxvi.

[17] R. C. Palmer, *English Law in the Age of the Black Death 1348–1381: A Transformation of Governance and Law* (Chapel Hill, NC, 1993), pp. 143–56.

[18] It could also be used against a clerical invasion, although it is not clear whether this was only when accompanied by a lay element. Rodes, in a very brief consideration of this writ, doubted whether a clerical force could have justified *de vi laica amovenda*'s use: R. E. Rodes, *Ecclesiastical Administration in Medieval England* (Notre Dame, IN, 1977), p. 196. But in 1292 Northfield church was said by the bishop of Worcester, when requesting the writ, to be invaded by a clerical and lay force, and for a monastic invasion leading to the request for the writ see below: TNA, SC 8/331/15593.

trespass led to some early confusion. On one occasion in the 1230s Henry III reprimanded a sheriff who had been sent, said the king, to a church to remove a lay force under the writ *de vi laica* not to seize the fruits of the church.[19] Such seizure of property could, however, have been a reasonable response to a failure to appear in court following a writ of trespass. Although references to some early copies of the writs survive in the close rolls, and there are one or two surviving original returned writs,[20] most of our evidence is in the form of the requests for the writ addressed by the higher clergy to the king.

In its early years, before the 1250s, *de vi laica* was occasionally used for lay as well as ecclesiastical property, for instance in cases of manorial intrusion.[21] Even from its first appearances, however, it was most frequently applied to cases involving ecclesiastical property. The writ was usually issued at a bishop's request and asked for the use of the secular arm (that is, for secular intervention through the office of the sheriff). It had become what Fitzherbert described it as in 1534: a writ for the removal of a lay force from churches and parsonage houses, but usually used for intrusions into churches.[22] Like the writ of trespass, it was about the infringement of a mutual obligation expressed through seizure of property. By 1300, requests for the writ, like the writ of trespass, express this standardly by alleging that the bishop's rights have been invaded by force and arms.[23]

[19] *CCR, 1234–1237*, p. 496.

[20] The writ was returnable (that is, the document to be sent back to royal government at its completion with a note of its success or otherwise on the dorse) or not at the request of the individual petitioning for it.

[21] In June 1253 it was used against the lay force inhabiting the manors formerly of William le Rus, in which the king had given his escheator full seisin: *CCR, 1251–1253*, pp. 379–80. The same writ may be intended in March 1243, when the sheriff of Herefordshire is instructed to remove the lay force ('omnem vim laicam quam invenerit resistentem amovendo') which is preventing William Gravenel entering into full seisin of land he now holds from his wife's marriage portion following the couple's divorce: *CCR, 1242–1247*, p. 89. While usually requested by bishops, there is one instance of request by a papal legate and it could, in the case of churches to which the king collated, be requested by the king himself: A. Fitzherbert, *The New Natura Brevium of the Most Reverend Judge Mr Anthony Fitzherbert*, 6th edn (London, 1755), pp. 121–2.

[22] Fitzherbert, *The New Natura Brevium*, p. 120.

[23] The phrase 'vi et armis' appears in the February 1293 request for the writ from the bishop of Lincoln for the church of Thame, by which point the writ had apparently attained standard form: *Reg. Sutton*, ed. Hill, vol. IV, p. 64 and see below. However, the standard form noted in a 1318 writ register uses 'vi armata': *Early Registers of Writs*, ed. E. de Haas and G. D. G. Hall, Selden Society 87 (London, 1970), p. 140 with its overtones of Roman civil law, a version which appears in some thirteenth-century requests for the writ – see, for example, W. Prynne, *The Third Tome of an Exact Chronological Vindication and Historical Demonstration* ... (London, 1668), p. 794.

The Uncertain Boundaries of Law

The nature of these infringed episcopal rights was not specified, but the circumstances of the writ demonstrate that it was used when ecclesiastical law, and the Church's right to exercise that law, were ignored. Such local breakdowns in the maintenance of obligations and the failure to respect the rights of other people or groups could sometimes come about as a result of broader civil disorder. In times of civil war the seizure of power by different secular factions often meant that the practical authority of the Church came into doubt; lay invasion might result from a realisation that there was no real hope that any court, secular or ecclesiastical, could offer solutions to local disputes and that taking that law into one's own hands was a viable – perhaps even a necessary – alternative. During the baronial wars of the 1260s, after the defeat of the king at the Battle of Lewes, there was a flurry of requests for the writ. These involved attacks on both those who had opposed the barons and baronial sympathisers. Some of these church invasions may, perhaps, have been the results of combatants taking refuge in sacred property, which subsequently led to armed forces attempting to extract those seeking asylum.[24] Church invasions in the 1260s, however, spread far beyond the counties most closely connected with engagements in battle to Cambridge, the Isle of Wight, Westmorland, Lancashire and Somerset. Some, at least, of these must have been the result of individuals taking advantage of situations where the exercise of authority was uncertain.[25] In 1268, following the Dictum of Kenilworth, which had cast doubt on the status of some lords and the spiritual authority of some bishops, there was a series of lay seizures of churches evidenced by requests for the writ.[26] In 1297 the example of royal seizure of the secular property of bishops and other clerics, along with the king's statement that the law should not be used against laymen assaulting clergy, seems to have encouraged people to take up arms to resolve local disputes with the Church and its clergy.[27] There was a steady run of lay

[24] In England in August 1265 the people of Evesham were ushered into the church for safety before the start of the battle there. In France in 1360 the people of Châtres (Département Eure et Loire) attempted, unsuccessfully, to oppose combined troops from England and Navarre by digging ditches around their church and retreating inside it: O. Laborderie, J. R. Maddicott and D. A. Carpenter, 'The Last Hours of Simon de Montfort: A New Account', *English Historical Review* 115 (2000), 378–412; S. K. Cohn Jr, *Lust for Liberty: The Politics of Social Revolt in Medieval Europe, 1200–1425* (Cambridge, MA, 2006), pp. 37–8.

[25] SC 8/331/15612; SC 8/331/15613; SC 8/331/15620; SC 8/331/15621; *CCR, 1261–1264*, pp. 389, 402.

[26] See the churches of Watlington (Norfolk), Therfield (Hertfordshire), Fotherby and Scalford (Lincolnshire), Houghton on the Hill (Leicestershire) and Trewell (Nottinghamshire): SC 8/331/15614; SC 8/331/15615, SC 8/331/15616.

[27] *The Chronicle of Bury St Edmunds 1212–1301*, ed. A. Gransden (Oxford, 1964), pp. 143–7.

invasions in this period which, despite the king's statement, also resulted in a number of requests for the issuing of the writ.[28] In 1327–9 there was another run of seizures reported, nine across the dioceses of Canterbury, Exeter, Lincoln and York.[29] The peaks in complaints, particularly in the 1260s and 1320s, match those noted in other sorts of uprisings against the Church attributed to legal uncertainty.[30]

Lay invasion could also arise in contexts where the nature and extent of secular jurisdiction was uncertain in the longer term. Border areas, such as Tynedale and the Welsh marches, were contested regions where the writ of the king did not run. In the late thirteenth century the Tynedale clergyman, Roger, rector of the church of Whitfield, had his church seized by a lay force led by the Whitfield family, and his realisation that jurisdiction in the area was uncertain meant that he did not request a writ to remove it but sought other forms of legal remedy.[31] In the Welsh marches in the early fourteenth century attempts were made to use the writ but, it seems, without success. At St Ishmael, Gloucester abbey's recently presented parson was driven out by a lay force instructed by Henry of Lancaster, who claimed the right of presentation to the church for himself and his family. Two requests for *de vi laica* resulted but neither could succeed since it was not clear that there was any sheriff with the authority to act. Henry's actions here make it clear that he understood both the advantages and disadvantages of this situation. He knew that his lay force was unlikely to be removed from the church, but equally he was aware that the parish was not securely under any particular diocesan court where a dispute about rights of presentation could be settled.[32] He therefore had little option but to resort to a physical seizure of the property.

Most often, however, those cases which resulted in requests for the writ were not due to the unavailability of legal remedies arising from the suspension of the courts during periods of civil war or to the failure of the secular or ecclesiastical law to operate at the boundaries of English territory, but were instead the result of the complexities of the interface between Church and State, where claims to possession and ownership of one aspect of the parish church were disputed.

[28] SC 8/197/9842; SC8/331/15586; SC8/331/15589; SC8/331/15600; SC8/331/15607; SC8/195/9708; *CCR, 1296–1302*, p. 203.

[29] SC 8/235/11724; SC 8/237/11833; SC 8/235/11713; SC 8/236/11756; SC 8/236/11769; SC 8/236/11771; SC 8/257/12814; SC 8/236/11770; *The Register of Adam de Orleton, Bishop of Hereford (A.D. 1317–1327)*, ed. A. T. Bannister, Cantilupe Society (Hereford, 1907), p. 127.

[30] S. K. Cohn, *Popular Protest in Late Medieval English Towns* (Cambridge, 2013), p. 229.

[31] P. M. Hoskin, 'Church, State and Law: Solutions to Lay Contumacy in the Anglo-Scottish Borders during the Later Thirteenth Century', *Historical Research* 84 (2011), 559–71; K. Stringer, *Border Liberties and Loyalties: Tynedale and Redesdale, c. 1200–c. 1400* (Edinburgh, 2010), pp. 231–9.

[32] SC 8/331/15584; SC 8/10/492.

The nature and extent of the two jurisdictions was the subject of discussion at both national and international level.[33] Across Europe, the nature of secular and ecclesiastical authority, and the appropriate relationship between them, was defined and disputed in the twelfth and thirteenth centuries, not only practically in clashes between rulers and churchmen but also through the study and development of Roman and canon law.[34] But in a context where matters were unresolved, these rival jurisdictions provided fuel to inflame disputes not just at diocesan and archdiocesan level but also at the local level within parishes, when different factions might see the uncertainties of the law as providing opportunities to push their own claims to the right to choose parish clergy.

It was in such disputes that *de vi laica* was most often used, as individuals sought either to exploit the ambiguities at the boundary between the two forms of law or to protest against those who were using these uncertainties to their own advantage. Most frequently, these writ requests were related to the rights of presentation to a benefice, or advowson. One of the key matters of dispute was the legal nature of the advowson. In common law the advowson was a piece of property, and could be inherited, bought, sold and leased (however much the Church protested). Like any property, its income was divisible. In canon law, however, the advowson was conceived of as so intrinsically connected to the cure of souls – that is, to the spiritual welfare of parishioners – that debates over the right to present clergy were claimed as under ecclesiastical jurisdiction. Cases about advowsons appeared then in both the secular and the ecclesiastical courts, although by the mid-thirteenth century the assize of Darrein Presentment (an investigation to demonstrate who had presented the incumbent previously) in the royal courts was increasingly common.[35] What constituted an advowson dispute was also a difficult issue. When was a dispute over two rival claimants to a church, each one promoted by a different party claiming the right of presentation, about the individual clergy, and so definitely under the authority of the bishop, rather than about the advowson, which the royal courts might claim?[36] Resolving

[33] See P. Hoskin, 'The Church and the King: Canon Law and Kingship in England 1257–61', in *The Growth of Royal Government under Henry III*, ed. D. Crook and L. J. Wilkinson (Woodbridge, 2015), pp. 196–211.

[34] For fuller discussion see J. Canning, *A History of Medieval Political Thought 300–1450* (London, 1996), pp. 84–124; A. Black, *Political Thought in Europe 1250–1450* (Cambridge, 1992), pp. 152–5.

[35] Helmholz, *The Oxford History of the Laws of England I*, pp. 477–81; R. A. R. Hartridge, 'Edward I's Exercise of the Right of Presentation to Benefices as shown by the Patent Rolls', *Cambridge Historical Journal* 2 (1927), 171–7; P. Heath, *Church and Realm 1272–1461: Conflict and Collaboration in an Age of Crises* (Oxford, 1988), pp. 124–5.

[36] Gray demonstrated that it was not always possible to draw clear lines between these types of case: J. Gray, 'The *ius presentandi* in England', *English Historical Review* 67 (1952), 481–509.

disputes about the payment of tithes to parish clergy was also an area where jurisdictions might collide: ordinarily such cases belonged to the ecclesiastical courts, although cases that involved more than a sixth of a parish's tithes were thought potentially to affect the ownership of the advowson and were, therefore, claimed by the king.[37] Those cases which involved clerks serving royal free chapels, who could claim exemption from ecclesiastical authority, could also be taken by the royal courts.[38] So although disputes which involved two different clergymen, both claiming the incumbency of the same parish, and appointed by two different claimants to an advowson, should have appeared in the ecclesiastical courts, there were many ways in which one party or the other could seek to complicate matters by involving secular law. Individuals and institutions used these competing and overlapping jurisdictions to their own advantages, sometimes bringing legal process to a standstill.[39] Faced with such impasses, or with an unsatisfactory conclusion in a court to which they had been unwilling to go, the laity could take the law into their own hands.

The writ *de vi laica* was called for when parties had done just this and might, on occasion, involve the bishop directly as a party. When, in 1299, Bishop Sutton of Lincoln ejected William le Graunt from the church of Hulcott (Buckinghamshire) for failing to be ordained priest within a year of his institution, William responded by turning out his replacement, Simon, with the help of an armed band.[40] Other cases were a response by dissatisfied parties following hearings in the Church courts. In the 1290s Hugh de Cresingfield's response to losing a case concerning a mediety of the advowson of Pakefield (Suffolk) was immediately to occupy that church and the sheriff had to be called upon.[41] In 1329 Edmund de Neville's lay force in the church of Great Horkesley (Essex) was said to be preventing the rector,

[37] *Select Cases from the King's Court 1272–1307*, ed. D. Millon, Selden Society 126 (London, 2009), p. lxx.

[38] J. H. Denton, *English Royal Free Chapels 1100–1300: A Constitutional Study* (Manchester, 1970), pp. 151–2; W. R. Jones, 'Patronage and Administration: The King's Free Chapels in Medieval England', *Journal of British Studies* 9 (1989), 6–7, 10–11, 14–15.

[39] B. Bombi, 'The Role of Judges-Delegate in England: The Dispute between the Archbishops of Canterbury and St. Augustine's Abbey in the Thirteenth Century', in *Legati e delegati papali: Profili, ambiti d'azione e tipologie di intervento nei secoli XII–XIII*, ed. M. P. Alberzoni and C. Zey (Milano, 2012), pp. 221–60; for writs of prohibition to halt cases, G. B. Flahiff, 'The Use of Prohibitions by Clerics against Ecclesiastical Courts in England', *Mediaeval Studies* 3 (1941), 101–14; G. B. Flahiff, 'The Writ of Prohibition in the Court Christian in the Thirteenth-Century', *Mediaeval Studies* 6 (1944), 262–96; R. H. Helmholz, 'The Writ of Prohibition to Court Christian before 1500', *Medieval Studies* 43 (1981), 297–314; *Select Cases from the King's Court*, ed. Millon, pp. xxi–lix. For the prior of Eye's payment for such a writ in the regnal year of 1260–1, see *CFR Henry III, 1260–61*, no. 88.

[40] *Reg. Sutton*, ed. Hill, vol. VI, pp. 175, 179; SC 8/235/11725.

[41] SC 8/235/11734.

John de Coule, entering his church, in defiance of a sentence from the court of Canterbury.[42] More frequently, though, it seems that there had been no prior legal hearing in the dispute, and that one party in a dispute had taken the law into their own hands rather than seek legal remedy. At Pillerton (Warwickshire) in the diocese of Worcester in 1309, in Leigh in the diocese of Coventry and Lichfield in 1389, and at Ecton (Northamptonshire) in the diocese of Lincoln in 1340 lay forces were said to be preventing the holding of divine service by the clergy with apparently no previous recourse to the courts.[43]

Requests for the writ signalled the Church's failure to provide enforceable legal resolutions to advowson disputes. Not only could it not uphold its own sentences, needing to ask for secular force to do so, but on some occasions the writ was used when the courts had been bypassed altogether. Violation of Church property automatically invoked major excommunication, and a formal declaration of this would subsequently have been made in public. It was in situations where this excommunication had been no deterrent that the secular arm had to be invoked. In 1291 the archdeacon of Lincoln was instructed to excommunicate those who had invaded the church of Great Hale.[44] In 1293 a sentence of excommunication was issued against all those involved in the seizure of the church and manse of Brixworth.[45] In 1282 the lay force who needed to be removed from the church of Carlisle were said to be already, and ineffectively, excommunicated.[46] Like another more commonly used writ, *de excommunicato capiendo*, the request for *de vi laica* was an admission that the Church's immediate censures of excommunication had failed and that secular aid was needed.[47]

[42] TNA, C 255/22/2/22.

[43] SC 8/237/11818, SC 8/235/11729, SC 8/236/11789.

[44] *Reg. Sutton*, ed. Hill, vol. VI, p. 149.

[45] *Reg. Sutton*, ed. Hill, vol. VI, pp. 173–4.

[46] SC 8/236/11760.

[47] The two sorts of episcopal request could be confused. In 1238 a request by the bishop of Rochester for the intervention of the secular arm to end the intrusion of the monks of Bermondsey into the parish church of Birling is said to have been to the prejudice of the rights of the bishop and church of Rochester, implying a form of trespass, and asks the king to have the force removed, while the rest of the document focuses on the monks' contumacy for more than forty days in the face of excommunication, a phrase borrowed from *de excommunicato capiendo*. The two writs were also used together; Archbishop Pecham requested both of them in documents of 7 November 1280 and 7 and 12 May 1281: TNA, C 85/3/24, 32 and 35; F. D. Logan, *Excommunication and the Secular Arm* (Toronto, 1980), p. 83. By the fourteenth century, when they were clearly distinct, their similarity was recognised by their appearance together in registers of writs: Oxford, Bodleian Library, MS Rawlinson C 292, fols 9a–104a (1318–20), edited in *Early Registers of Writs*, ed. de Haas and Hall. The writ *de vi laica amovenda* is found at p. 140. For the register's dating see pp. lix–lxi.

Yet *de vi laica* could never have been invoked lightly. A request for the writ was not an admission that violence needed to be met with violence. Although a number of lay invasions clearly did use weapons,[48] no sheriff was allowed to shed blood or attack an obstinate layman within the church,[49] and lay forces could prove difficult to remove, but not because they resorted to actual violence. One sheriff reported that he had been unable to remove a lay force because they had played cat and mouse, moving backwards and forwards between the church and the rectory, making them impossible to track down, but he makes no mention of violence.[50] Nevertheless, the writ led to secular authority being exercised on Church property. Although the enforcement of the Church's law by the State was mutually beneficial in settling local disorder and restoring pastoral care, asking for secular help also made the Church particularly vulnerable, since it bought to the fore awkward questions about the relationship between ecclesiastical and secular authority. While the bishops of the thirteenth and fourteenth centuries claimed that they should be able to obtain the use of the secular arm – the issuing of royal instructions to the sheriff through a writ – by right, and in so doing maintain their authority, the king's position was that he acted only through grace.[51] In addition, while the most commonly claimed writ by bishops, *de excommunicato capiendo*, was a writ of caption, requesting the arrest of an individual to be held in a secular prison, *de vi laica* actually gave permission to secular authority to intrude upon ecclesiastical property. The situation was in some ways an inversion of sanctuary. Rather than an individual using the church as a safe place where the intervention of secular authority on Church property was a violation, *de vi laica* actively instructed the sheriff to enter that ecclesiastical property in order to remove men who were seeking judicial protection from the Church.

[48] At Claybrooke in 1295 the laymen invading the church and manse there, who wounded the chaplain, Roger de Wykheye, used arrows and constructed a 'hostile machine' (*machinam hostilem*) in the bell tower. Events at Thame in the same decade involved physical wounds from arrows. The case at Gosberton is another instance when weapons were certainly used: *Reg. Sutton*, ed. Hill, vol. III, pp. xxix–xli, vol. IV, pp. 44–9, 64, 67, 70–1, 104–5, 107–9, 117, vol. V, pp. 112–14; *Select Cases in the Court of King's Bench under Edward I, Volume III*, ed. G. O. Sayles, Selden Society 58 (London, 1939), pp. 11–18; *CIM, 1219–1307*, pp. 459–60; *CPR, 1292–1301*, p. 109.

[49] In the case of Harewood (1307) the returned writ notes that the sheriff failed because he could not use force to remove the laity, and where one layman, John de Helles, working for the sheriff of Kent, was instructed to fulfil such a writ across a number of churches in the diocese of Canterbury in 1303 he did attempt to use force and found himself summoned before the archbishop's court for his actions: TNA, C 225/22/2/6, SC 8/237/11848, KB 27/166, membrane 4; London, British Library, MS Hargrave 375, fol. 109r.

[50] C 255/22/2/4.

[51] *Councils and Synods II*, ed. Powicke and Cheney, vol. II, pp. 1057–8.

The Boundaries of Property

While in many cases the identity of the person who had the right to choose the next incumbent for a parish church was clear and uncontested, and the transition between one clergyman and the next passed without trouble, such was the value of the advowson, which effectively allowed the owner to give a maintenance for life to a relative or associate, that where there was any doubt as to the identity of the owner of the advowson it was worth rival claimants making a case. Among lay patrons, disputes between heirs, particularly during minorities, when there was no strong head of a family, could involve rival claims for ownership of advowsons. The case that began this paper – that of Gosberton – is probably an instance of such a dispute. In 1295 the rector of the church, Thomas Rye, had died. Soon after his death a new rector was appointed.[52] The patronage was in the hands of the Rye family, but the head of the family, who should have held it, was a minor at this time and in November 1295, Ranulph de Rye, guardian of the heir, took it upon himself to appoint a new rector, perhaps not the person who would have been the choice of the rest of the family, who may have felt that Ranulph was overstepping his authority.[53] Disputes about who had the right to appoint clergy were not always, however, limited to direct claims of patronage. Papal presentation to benefices – papal provision – could interfere with patronage rights and could also be protested about by the parishioners themselves. In the 1230s there were riots against foreign rectors in English churches, and their property – particularly the tithes stored on their behalf – was seized and damaged. In 1236 such opposition to the presentation of Master Martin, the pope's legate, at Wotton in Gloucestershire culminated in the seizure of the church by the local laity.[54] At the end of that century the bishop of Lincoln wrote to request the king's intervention at Clopton because the parishioners there were specifically protesting at the provision of a papal candidate.[55] In both instances there were established, monastic patrons of long standing whose rights were infringed, who had little other recourse than to seize the property whose possession by the clergy was at the centre of the dispute, and who were joined in this not just by lay-servants of the religious houses but by the parishioners themselves.

The physical seizure of a parish church by the laity was a way not just of actively resisting the services of a newly appointed clergyman or of

52 *Reg. Sutton*, ed. Hill, vol. V, p. 168, vol. VI, p. 20.
53 *Reg. Sutton*, ed. Hill, vol. I, p. 202, vol. IV, p. 4.
54 *CCR, 1234–1237*, p. 215. Master Martin was, according to the chronicler Matthew Paris, known for his greed for English property. He was in England in 1236, but it is unlikely he attended the church for his institution. See Matthew Paris, *Chronica majora*, ed. H. R. Luard, 7 vols, Rolls Series 57 (London, 1872–83), vol. IV, pp. 416–23, 443–4.
55 SC 8/236/11783.

preventing the sentences of courts being upheld, it was also the seizure of a property that was central to local life and had symbolic value. Occupying a church was a way of contesting the ownership of an incorporeal property, in which the building was an embodiment of the intangible right of advowson. There were a number of good, practical reasons to take physical possession of the building. Not only was a church easy to fortify (possibly the only such building in small communities) but, by physically occupying it, it was possible to prevent a newly appointed incumbent from completing those acts legally necessary for him to take possession of his benefice.[56] In the seventeenth century the necessity for a new clergyman to 'read in' – that is, to read a service within his parish church – within three months of his institution was introduced, but medieval clerics also needed to be present in a church to take complete possession of the benefice.[57] Thirteenth-century episcopal mandates instructing the archdeacon to induct a newly appointed clergyman into a benefice talk of putting the clergy into 'corporeal possession' of the church: the ecclesiastical equivalent of seisin, the legal ritual involving physically standing on a property, necessary when taking possession of land.[58] Without taking physical possession of a church its incumbent could not claim the temporal income there.[59] In preventing a clergyman from completing those steps necessary to take full legal possession a lay force could powerfully assert the interest of their leader in the matter of the selection of clergy.

Even if a lay force could not prevent a clergyman taking legal possession of a church they could certainly prevent him fulfilling his duties and exert a considerable amount of influence over daily parish life. Seizure prevented not only the daily round of the liturgy (unless, of course, the rival incumbent favoured by the lay force was permitted to enter), but also interfered with those offices necessary to everyday life, such as baptisms and burials, and disrupted the holding of markets and the teaching of children. Seizure of a church could not be overlooked and demanded an urgent remedy.

[56] Helmholz, *The Oxford History of the Laws of England, Volume 1*, pp. 101–2.

[57] For canon law on reading in, introduced under King Charles II, see E. Gibson, *Codex Juris Ecclesiastici Anglicani*, 2 vols (London, 1713), vol. II, pp. 898–9. Early uses of *de vi laica* for invasions of secular property make specific mention of the prevention of seisin there: see above.

[58] On corporal possession see G. W. O. Addleshaw, *Rectors, Vicars, and Patrons in Twelfth- and Early Thirteenth-Century Canon Law* (York, 1956), pp. 21–2; B. Kemp, 'Archdeacons and Parish Churches in England in the Twelfth Century', in *Law and Government in Medieval England and Normandy: Essays in Honour of Sir James Holt*, ed. G. Garnett and J. Hudson (Cambridge, 1994), p. 353.

[59] See the bishops of Norwich's statutes of the thirteenth and fourteenth centuries, *Councils and Synods II*, ed. Powicke and Cheney, vol. I, pp. 342, 501.

Conclusion

When the laity occupied a church they took hold of a building over which they had a sense of ownership or rights. More than this, however, they were – at some level – claiming their interest in the operation of the parish, standing on land once given by the laity, often generously endowed, extended, maintained and ornamented both by patrons and the parish in general. It was an embodiment of their community, the space within which their ancestors were buried, and within which they too expected to rest until judgement day.[60] To claim the building of the parish church was also to claim the place in which the Church's judicial processes played out at a local level.[61]

The seizure of a church by a band of laymen could be considered as evidence of anti-clericalism, but only in the very limited sense that a particular local faction took exception to a clergyman chosen by another party, whether a layman, religious house or pope. But never do such disputes seem to have involved complaints about the perceived defects of the individual clergyman. Even those complaints about the clergy imposed on parishes by the pope, while perhaps including some sense of dissatisfaction that their clergyman would inevitably be an absentee, were probably primarily motivated by the fact that the rightful patron had lost a valuable piece of patronage. Those disputes were fundamentally property disputes, not expressions of dissatisfaction with the pastoral ministry or the power of the Church more generally.

While the Church claimed both church buildings and legal authority over the clergy for themselves they could also discover themselves to be in vulnerable situations requiring lay authority. Patrons and parishioners continued to invest heavily in the physical fabric of their churches, and those who were in possession of advowsons only very unwillingly allowed their claims to these to fail. The laity felt a deep investment both in their churches and their ministers, and perhaps perceived the temporal and spiritual concerns of parish life as far more integrated than the theoretical divisions of Church and State allowed for. The lay invasions which led to requests for the writ *de vi laica* were an expression of this lay investment and a way in which their claims of interest could take tangible form.

[60] Attempts to destroy communities, for example following uprisings, could involve the destruction of the parish church. In fifteenth-century Florence, the opposition to secular authority expressed by the village of Pontenano led one councillor to suggest the de-consecration and destruction of the church there so that no-one could ever live there again: Cohn, *Lust for Liberty*, p. 187; S. K. Cohn Jr, *Women in the Streets: Essays on Sex and Violence in Renaissance Italy* (Baltimore, MD, 1996), pp. 123–4, 135.

[61] Uprisings against the Church's secular authority involved invasion of local parish churches, as at Genoa in 1401: Cohn, *Lust for Liberty*, p. 174.

8

The Papacy, Petitioners and Benefices in Thirteenth-Century England*

Thomas W. Smith

Where there are few jobs and many qualified applicants, there will be fierce competition. In the Middle Ages this manifested itself in the struggle for appointment to ecclesiastical benefices. Clerical candidates in want of a living fought bitterly against one another in order to acquire or defend possession of the fruits of churches throughout Christendom, and they employed an ingenious repertoire of legal strategies, tricks and deceptions in order to achieve their ends. The invention of papal provision in the twelfth century, and its widespread use throughout the West in the thirteenth century, was a disrupting influence which changed the face of this competition.[1] Whereas candidates on the make had previously sought collation to Church positions through their local bishop, lay patron or the crown, from the thirteenth century they had a direct route to benefices through the papacy, which issued provision mandates to qualified clergy ordering their appointment to a suitable stipend.[2] Papal provision brought with it advantages and disadvantages to the English clergy. It introduced one new method of appointment that levelled the playing field for those clerics who lacked the backing of a powerful prelate

* I am very grateful to the Leverhulme Trust and the University of Leeds for the award of a Leverhulme Early Career Fellowship (2017–20) to investigate the rise of papal provision in thirteenth-century England, from which this chapter springs, and also to the Royal Historical Society and the Past & Present Society for a generous grant for individual travel to present an earlier version of this work at Leeds International Medieval Congress 2015. My thanks also to the anonymous peer reviewer for helpful comments on this chapter.

[1] On the development of papal provision, see T. W. Smith, 'The Development of Papal Provisions in Medieval Europe', *History Compass* 13 (2015), 110–21.

[2] See below for a fuller explanation of papal provision, as well as: T. W. Smith, 'Papal Executors and the Veracity of Petitions from Thirteenth-Century England', *Revue d'Histoire Ecclésiastique* 110 (2015), 662–83, at 668–70; Smith, 'The Development of Papal Provisions'; T. W. Smith, 'The Italian Connection Revisited: Papal Provisions in Thirteenth-Century England', in *Thirteenth Century England XVII: Proceedings of the Cambridge Conference, 2017*, ed. A. M. Spencer and C. Watkins (Woodbridge, forthcoming).

or lay patron, but it also brought with it new, Italian competitors for English benefices without increasing the number of such church livings available. Thus it intensified competition for benefices and also led to Italian immigration and the alienation of wealth from the English Church, which contemporaries such as Matthew Paris deplored.[3] Modern scholars, following Matthew Paris, have tended to adopt a dim view of the papacy's intervention in the allocation of benefices across the face of the West, portraying it as an abuse of papal authority to intrude Italian favourites into far-away benefices.[4] A more sensitive reading of the sources, however, reveals that papal intervention in the localities was far more complex than simple exploitation, and that the key period of expansion of the system in the thirteenth century was driven by native petitioners as well as papal kinsmen.[5] The topic demands more detailed research if we hope to understand better this central aspect of the medieval Church.[6] The present chapter goes some way towards this by exploring how petitioners made use of the papal supplicatory system as part of legal strategies to secure ecclesiastical benefices in thirteenth-century England, as well as how the papacy responded. Its broader significance lies in the new light it sheds on the strengths and shortcomings of the papal supplicatory system as well as the character of Anglo-Papal relations in this period.

Petitions for Benefices and Dispensations

With the introduction of the system of papal provision in the twelfth century, and its exponential growth in the thirteenth, clerics could acquire

[3] Matthew Paris, *Chronica majora*, ed. H. R. Luard, 7 vols, Rolls Series 57 (London, 1872–83), vol. IV, pp. 419, 441–4, vol. V, pp. 256–7, 355.

[4] G. Mollat, *La collation des bénéfices ecclésiastiques sous les papes d'Avignon (1305–1378)* (Paris, 1921), pp. 1–2, 322; H. MacKenzie, 'The Anti-Foreign Movement in England, 1231–1232', in *Anniversary Essays in Mediaeval History by Students of Charles Homer Haskins*, ed. C. H. Taylor (Boston, MA, 1929), pp. 183–203, at pp. 186, 188, 189; B. Guillemain, *La Cour pontificale d'Avignon (1309–1376): Étude d'une société* (Paris, 1962), pp. 104, 106; W. Ullmann, *A Short History of the Papacy in the Middle Ages* (London, 1972), pp. 245–6; C. Harper-Bill, 'The Diocese of Norwich and the Italian Connection, 1198–1261', in *England and the Continent in the Middle Ages: Studies in Memory of Andrew Martindale*, ed. J. Mitchell (Stamford, 2000), pp. 75–89, at p. 87; P. Montaubin, 'L'administration pontificale de la grâce au XIIIe siècle: L'exemple de la politique bénéficiale', in *Suppliques et requêtes: Le gouvernement par la grâce en occident (XIIe–XVe siècle)*, ed. H. Millet (Rome, 2003), pp. 321–42, at p. 342.

[5] G. Barraclough, *Papal Provisions: Aspects of Church History Constitutional, Legal and Administrative in the Later Middle Ages* (Oxford, 1935); Smith, 'The Development of Papal Provisions'; Smith, 'Papal Executors and the Veracity of Petitions'; Smith, 'The Italian Connection Revisited'.

[6] This is the focus of my project as a Leverhulme Early Career Fellow at the University of Leeds (2017–20).

benefices through a number of different routes, or 'vendors', conceptualised as the *Pfründenmarkt* ('benefice market') in the German scholarship.[7] Papal provision was a system through which the pope could appoint clergy to benefices through the issue of a provision mandate, ordering an executioner (usually a local bishop) to seek out a suitable stipend and induct the candidate to it (hedged around by conditions such as an examination of the suitability of the cleric in question and similar papal grants to others). But provision was not the only, or indeed always the best, means of acquiring a church stipend. Candidates seeking a benefice could turn to a number of other patrons in their attempts to secure a living such as their local bishop, the king and queen, or a lay patron. If he had connections through family or friendship to a local bishop or lay patron, he might decide that he had a good chance of acquiring a benefice through their patronage. If he was employed in royal service, he might turn to the crown. But if he had benefited from a university education or was a poor cleric without any of the previous connections, the candidate's best option was probably to submit a petition to the papacy, rather than to rely on the traditional methods of collation. Each 'path' had its own advantages and difficulties, and it was up to the cleric to decide which method of collation he would pursue. They were by no means mutually exclusive, however, and the sources reveal clergy who crossed over between the different collators, taking advantage of the best 'vendor' available at the time.[8]

There were a number of ways in which a cleric in want of a living might utilise the papal supplicatory system. The first, and most obvious, was to petition for appointment to a benefice, or for dispensation from some defect hindering his appointment. Poor supplicants had to submit their petitions, couched in the correct *stilus curie*, at an office of the papal chancery known as the *data communis* (also called the *recepta communis*).[9] From the middle of the thirteenth century a curialist would then perform an examination of the

[7] A. Meyer, 'Der Weg zur eigenen Pfründe im Spätmittelalter', in *Die Stiftskirche in Südwestdeutschland: Aufgaben und Perspektiven der Forschung*, ed. S. Lorenz and O. Auge (Leinfelden-Echterdingen, 2003), pp. 159–69, at pp. 162–3; A. Meyer, 'Der deutsche Prfründenmarkt im Spätmittelalter', *Quellen und Forschungen aus italienischen Archiven und Bibliotheken* 71 (1991), 266–79, at 267; T. Willich, *Wege zur Pfründe: Die Besetzung der Magdeburger Domkanonikate zwischen ordentlicher Kollatur und päpstlicher Provision, 1295–1464* (Tübingen, 2005), p. 532.

[8] See below, for instance, the example of Richard of Bamfield.

[9] P. Zutshi, '*Inextricabilis curie labyrinthus*: The Presentation of Petitions to the Pope in the Chancery and the Penitentiary during the Fourteenth and First Half of the Fifteenth Century', in *Päpste, Pilger und Pönitentiarie: Festschrift für Ludwig Schmugge zum 65. Geburtstag*, ed. A. Meyer, C. Rendtel and M. Wittmer-Butsch (Tübingen, 2004), pp. 393–410, at pp. 400–1; P. Herde, *Beiträge zum päpstlichen Kanzlei- und Urkundenwesen im 13. Jahrhundert*, 2nd edn (Kallmünz, 1967), p. 152; H. Bresslau, *Handbuch der Urkundenlehre für Deutschland und Italien*, 2 vols, 2nd edn (Leipzig, 1912–31), vol. II, p. 9; T. W. Smith, *Curia and Crusade: Pope Honorius III and the Recovery of the Holy Land, 1216–1227* (Turnhout, 2017), pp. 86–7.

candidate's suitability for a benefice, adjudged from his character, his ability to sing and speak clearly, and his knowledge of Latin and the liturgy – essentially the ability to perform his office.[10] This was a test of his *conversatio*, as the papal documents put it. If the examiner was impressed by what he saw, then the pope might grant a provision mandate *in forma pauperum* – that is, for poor clergy – ordering that the applicant be appointed to a suitable benefice. Such was the case for Roger 'the chaplain' (*capellanus*), a poor clerk of Salisbury diocese, who successfully petitioned Pope Urban IV for a provision mandate in 1263.[11] Urban's letter, addressed to the executor, Walter de la Wyle, bishop of Salisbury, explained that Master Peter, archdeacon of Brulie, in the diocese of Agen, had examined Roger and found him to be sufficiently learned to be appointed to a benefice ('in litteratura competenter ydoneus ad beneficium ecclesiaticum obtinendum') with or without cure of souls.[12] Urban ordered the bishop to check Roger's life and morals (his *vita*) and, if found to be satisfactory, the pope charged the bishop to provide the poor clerk to a benefice in the gift of the abbot and convent of Abingdon and to impose the requirement that Roger reside in the place of his benefice.[13]

The acquisition of a provision document was only the first step on the road to provision, however. The cleric would then have to complete the long journey back home before presenting the document to the appointed executor, who, no doubt, would hardly have leapt for joy at the receipt of another provision request entangling him in additional administrative duties and litigation and probably depriving him of a source of patronage.[14] While the test of the applicant's *conversatio* had already been carried out at the papal curia, the executor would have to verify the facts of the case presented by the petitioner and would often perform his own check of the candidate's learning *in partibus*. It was also left up to the executor to examine the *vita* of the candidate – that is, his life, character and morals – to see if he was suitable to act as shepherd of a flock of souls. This test completed the examination of the providee's *vita et conversatio*. If his character was not found wanting by

[10] W. J. Dohar, '*Sufficienter litteratus*: Clerical Examination and Instruction for the Cure of Souls', in *A Distinct Voice: Medieval Studies in Honor of Leonard E. Boyle, O.P.*, ed. J. Brown and W. P. Stoneman (Notre Dame, IN, 1995), pp. 305–21, at p. 311; K. Salonen and J. Hanska, *Entering a Clerical Career at the Roman Curia, 1458–1471* (Farnham, 2013), p. 196; Montaubin, L'administration pontificale de la grâce', p. 338.

[11] Vatican City, Archivio Segreto Vaticano, Reg[istra] Vat[icana] 29, fols 88v–89r; *Les Registres d'Urbain IV (1261–1264)*, ed. J. Guiraud, 4 vols (Paris, 1892–1904), vol. III, no. 1185, pp. 138–9; *Calendar of Entries in the Papal Registers relating to Great Britain and Ireland: Papal Letters, Vol. I, A.D. 1198–1304*, ed. W. H. Bliss (London, 1893), p. 407.

[12] Reg. Vat. 29, fol. 88v.

[13] Reg. Vat. 29, fol. 89r.

[14] On executors, see K. Hitzbleck, *Exekutoren: Die außerordentliche Kollatur von Benefizien im Pontifikat Johannes' XXII.* (Tübingen, 2009) and Smith, 'Papal Executors and the Veracity of Petitions'.

the executor, if no fault was found in the applicant's learning and everything was as the supplicant had claimed it to be in his papal petition, then the executor was supposed to seek out a suitable benefice. This could be a long and drawn-out process. Often, executors simply ignored provision mandates in order to preserve their own rights of collation.[15] The executor, probably a bishop, also had his own personal queue of followers to collate to benefices. The urgency with which he fulfilled papal provision mandates and his ability to subvert papal orders was almost certainly dependent upon the status of the providee. Those with strong connections to the papal curia or the crown had better chances of a timely execution of their mandates than poor clerks, because there would be political repercussions for non-fulfilment.

Because the papacy functioned in a predominantly responsive fashion – that is, issuing documents in response to petitions without being able to check the facts on which the cases were based – it was quite a straightforward affair to acquire the issue of a provision mandate. The papacy, after all, was not giving away anything in its own possession in any tangible sense. It could issue as many provision mandates as it wished, as it was not the pope who had to find matching benefices for all the documents. There are cases where holders of provision mandates were inducted into possession only after years of waiting and legal strife, or who died before their mandates were carried out.[16] Thus, when studying the intervention of the papacy in the benefice market of Europe, what really matters is not the number of provision mandates granted, but the physical possession (*in corporalem possessionem*) of a benefice and its fruits – a completely different proposition.

In order to speed up this process and increase their chances of success, petitioners with powerful connections often sought intercession in support of their cause from influential lay figures. The kings and queens of England regularly acted as intercessors on behalf of the clergy in their service, and traces of their many interventions litter the papal registers.[17] A provision mandate issued by Gregory X in 1275 ordered the archbishop of Canterbury to find a benefice for William de Alpibus, clerk and physician of Eleanor of Provence, and emphasised to the executor the importance of the queen and her personal interest in the affair ('nos volentes ei huiusmodi exigentia meritorum et obtentu predicte Regine nobis pro ipso cum instantia supplicantis gratiam facere specialem').[18] If presented with two competing provision

[15] See, for example, the example from 1218 when the bishop-elect ignored Pope Honorius III's request to provide his kinsman, Master James, to a benefice: Reg. Vat. 9, fol. 251v; *Regesta Honorii papae III*, ed. P. Pressutti, 2 vols (Rome, 1888–95) vol. I, no. 1307, p. 216; *Calendar of Entries in the Papal Registers*, ed. Bliss, p. 54.

[16] Barraclough, *Papal Provisions*, p. 35.

[17] On the roles of queens as vital intercessors in royal petitionary processes, see Helen Lacey's chapter in this volume.

[18] Reg. Vat. 37, fol. 232r; *Les Registres de Grégoire X (1272–1276)*, ed. J. Guiraud (Paris, 1892–1906), no. 620, p. 263; *Calendar of Entries in the Papal Registers*, ed. Bliss, p. 450.

documents, one from a humble cleric and another with the backing of the queen, it is clear which an executor would fast-track. Like the queen, the king of England also involved himself in the acquisition of provision mandates for his followers, but not all clerics aspiring to a benefice enjoyed such royal connections and favour. There were, however, other options available. Those with closer ties to high-ranking nobles might rely on support from this quarter. In 1289 Gerard de Wippens, a canon of York and nephew of Odo de Grandison, a Savoyard knight in the service of Edward I, did just that, acquiring a reservation to a vacant benefice in the church of York from Pope Nicholas IV partly on the strength of his familial connection to Odo.[19] Like William de Alpibus's connection to Eleanor of Provence, Odo's intercession is cited in the *narratio* section of the document (meaning that it was included in the original petition, since the wording of the supplication was recycled in the *narratio* of the resulting papal document) and it was probably an influential factor in the pope's decision to accept the petition given that Gerard was already a pluralist with benefices and reservations in a portfolio of other English churches. Others exploited connections with cardinals of the curia. John of Godley, rector of the church of Holsworthy in the diocese of Exeter, for instance, managed to secure the intercession of both Gentile, cardinal-priest of St Martin's in Montibus, and Queen Margaret of England in support of his petition for dispensation to hold an extra benefice, which Pope Boniface VIII granted in 1302.[20] The frequency with which we find such documents preserved in the papal registers is testament to the influence wielded by these intercessors in the successful acquisition of papal provision mandates and dispensations. But that influence did not stop at the papal curia. Because chancery scribes copied parts of the text of petitions into the *narratio* clause of papal documents, supplicants bearing such documents enjoyed the influence of such intercessors again when they presented the letters to their appointed executor back in the localities. Thus, petitioners with powerful backers enjoyed considerable advantages over humble clergy at the two key stages of the papal provision process.

[19] Reg. Vat. 44, fol. 262; *Les Registres de Nicolas IV*, ed. E. Langlois, 2 vols (Paris, 1887–93), vol. I, no. 1795, pp. 331–2; *Calendar of Entries in the Papal Registers*, ed. Bliss, p. 507. On Odo de Grandison, see 'Grandson [Grandison], Sir Otto de', in *Oxford Dictionary of National Biography* <https://doi.org/10.1093/ref:odnb/37827> [accessed 9 December 2017] and M. Vale, 'England, France and the Origins of the Hundred Years War', in *England and her Neighbours, 1066–1453: Essays in Honour of Pierre Chaplais*, ed. M. Jones and M. Vale (London, 1989), pp. 199–216, at p. 212.

[20] Reg. Vat. 44, fol. 166r; *Les Registres des Boniface VIII*, ed. G. Digard, M. Faucon, A. Thomas and R. Fawtier, 4 vols (Paris, 1884–1939), vol. III, no. 4515, col. 408; *Calendar of Entries in the Papal Registers*, ed. Bliss, p. 600.

Petitions for Redress regarding Benefices

Clergy did not use the papal supplicatory system merely to acquire papal graces; they also utilised it when seeking redress against aggressors who infringed their rights. In 1237 Master Robert of Gloucester petitioned Pope Gregory IX for justice regarding his right to the church of Eynsford.[21] Master Robert had held Eynsford by papal provision until the official of Canterbury inducted a royal favourite, William de Plessi, a pluralist without dispensation. This injustice, however, was not the end of the story. The archbishop of Canterbury, Edmund of Abingdon, then ousted William de Plessi and installed Master William of Charney of illegitimate birth and also without dispensation. At first, Master Robert attempted to resolve the problem using the local justice system rather than turning immediately to Rome. Yet this came to nothing when King Henry III obstructed the process and the messengers entrusted with the citation of William of Charney were wounded in the process.[22] Subsequently, the archbishop of Canterbury denied Roger access to his court regarding an unconnected transaction with Jewish money lenders.[23] Thus cheated by the ecclesiastical justice system *in partibus*, Master Robert had no choice but to petition the papacy for redress, as Gregory's document recounts ('Unde cum nequeat in partibus illis de pari contendere cum archiepiscopo et intruso predictis nobis humiliter supplicavit, ut super hoc providere sibi misericorditer dignaremur').[24] This case is instructive because it demonstrates that, even as a cleric who had benefited from papal provision and who held the title of *magister* (something which held great currency at the papal court in the allocation of benefices), Robert first attempted to deal with the problem using local ecclesiastical courts. Only after that had failed did he decide to elevate his case to the papal court. The decision to seek papal justice, after all, was expensive and time-consuming, even more so than pursuing cases in England, and potential supplicants, even those who had acquired benefices through the papal supplicatory system, clearly weighed up their chances of success against the cost involved. In this case, however, Robert was left with no other choice, having exhausted his other options.

Because their affairs were of close personal interest to the pope and his cardinals who administered the papal judicial system, Italian curialists and their kin could expect the diligent expedition of their cases at the pope's court. The judicial system, however, remained open to all, and, because the

21 Reg. Vat. 18, fols 213v–214r; *Les Registres de Grégoire IX*, ed. L. Auvray, 3 vols (Paris, 1890–1910), vol. II, no. 3419, cols 528–30; *Calendar of Entries in the Papal Registers*, ed. Bliss, pp. 158–9.

22 Reg. Vat. 18, fol. 214r.

23 Reg. Vat. 18, fol. 214r.

24 Reg. Vat. 18, fol. 214r; *Les Registres de Grégoire IX*, ed. Auvray, vol. II, no. 3419, col. 530.

papacy mostly appointed native judges *in partibus* to deal with litigation in England, the system was not entirely rigged in favour of Italians.[25] One of the highest-ranking curialists to find this out the hard way was Marinus, papal vice-chancellor and canon of Salisbury, who lost his case in England against Master Robert de Cardevill over the treasureship of Salisbury in 1246, despite the fact that one of the three judges was a fellow Italian, Master Laurence de Sancto Martino, canon of Chichester.[26] Although the outcome of such legal cases was far from certain for Italian litigants, what they could be sure of was decent financial compensation as one of the terms of the settlement, and, often, the exertion of some form of financial pressure from the curia to ensure that they received a different benefice as consolation. Thus Marinus, although denied the treasurership, received a stipend of 100 marks from its income under the terms of the settlement.[27] In Pope Innocent IV's confirmation of this settlement, however, he went a step further to protect his vice-chancellor's interests by adding the extra requirement that this stipend be paid until Marinus secured an annual sum from his other benefices of 200 marks. Innocent also issued a pair of documents to the bishop of Worcester, Walter de Cantilupe, ordering him to protect Marinus following his legal defeat and to enforce the payment of the stipend and the requirement that he eventually receive benefices totalling 200 marks per annum.[28] Similarly, in 1218, when a legal challenge from a Master Adam Aaron threw Pope Honorius III's provision of Master Alexander, papal acolyte, to the church of Exminster into uncertainty, Honorius charged Stephen Langton, archbishop of Canterbury, not only to decide the case but, at the same time, to find another suitable benefice for the papal acolyte.[29] Honorius wrote that he did not wish his plan to reward Alexander with a benefice to be frustrated and ordered Langton to provide him ('nolentes ipsum ulterius nostra liberalitate qua se dignum exhibuit sub expectatione frustrari, cum de te specialiter confidamus, ei per te volumus provideri').[30] This pressure from Honorius loaded the die as far as the outcome of the legal case was concerned. But even if papal candidates did

[25] The classic study is J. E. Sayers, *Papal Judges Delegate in the Province of Canterbury, 1198–1254: A Study in Ecclesiastical Jurisdiction and Administration* (Oxford, 1971).

[26] Reg. Vat. 21, fols 332v–333v; *Les Registres d'Innocent IV*, ed. É. Berger, 4 vols (Paris, 1884–1911), vol. I, no. 2169, p. 323; *Calendar of Entries in the Papal Registers*, ed. Bliss, p. 228. On Robert de Cardevill, see J. le Neve, *Fasti Eccesiae Anglicanae, 1066–1300*, ed. D. E. Greenway et al., 10 vols (London, 1968–2005), vol. IV, p. 22.

[27] Reg. Vat. 21, fol. 333r.

[28] Reg. Vat. 21, fol. 333v; *Les Registres d'Innocent IV*, ed. Berger, vol. I, nos 2170, 2171, p. 323; *Calendar of Entries in the Papal Registers*, ed. Bliss, pp. 228–9.

[29] Reg. Vat. 9, fol. 284v; *Regesta Honorii papae III*, ed. Pressutti, vol. I, no. 1525, p. 253; *Calendar of Entries in the Papal Registers*, ed. Bliss, pp. 56–7; Reg. Vat. 9, fol. 285v; *Regesta Honorii papae III*, ed. Pressutti, vol. I, no. 1517, p. 251; *Calendar of Entries in the Papal Registers*, ed. Bliss, p. 57.

[30] Reg. Vat. 9, fol. 285v.

not prevail in their legal tussles with English clergy, the backing of the popes, who issued documents and exerted leverage over powerful prelates on their behalf, meant that the acquisition of a good benefice was just a matter of time. Therefore, we see that, although the papacy's judicial system was loaded with checks and balances, such as the appointment of native and Italian judges in cases between English clergy and Roman curialists and the right to appeal, the papacy still found ways to promote and further the careers of its kinsmen over and above those of humble English supplicants.

We must be careful, however, not to portray the competition for benefices simply as a binary struggle between Italian and English clergy. Aliens also prosecuted each other at the papal court, as the case in 1257 between Master Peter de Camberiaco (Chambry or Chambéry in France), papal chaplain and canon of St Martin's le Grand, London, and Ralph de Montibus, canon of Lausanne, over a prebend of St Martin's demonstrates.[31] From the thirteenth century, English, Italian and French clergy competed against each other for stipends in a benefice market that played out on an international, rather than a provincial, scale. From the perspective of the churches to which these benefices belonged, it seems that opposition to papal provision was more firmly rooted in anger about the loss of traditional powers of collation and patronage than in the fact that many of the clergy appointed through the system were foreigners (see, for instance, the dispute between Master Robert of Gloucester and the papal providee, Henry of Tilton, below). Xenophobia undoubtedly played a significant part in determining English responses to the appointment of papal providees, as the chronicler Matthew Paris vociferously relates, but we need to adopt a more nuanced approach to the material. It appears that opposition to provision had a stronger foundation in the fact that, by petitioning the papacy for provision mandates, English and foreign-born clerics were negating the traditional systems of collation and parachuting into valuable ecclesiastical benefices.

Furthermore, a number of cases give lie to the assumption that Italian providees, and the papacy's administration of the provision system in general, were wholly insensitive to local concerns. In 1264 Pope Urban IV issued a document to Master Hugh de Cantilupe, papal chaplain and archdeacon of Gloucester, and to the treasurer of Salisbury, ordering them to make provision of a benefice in London to Master John de Ebulo, a papal subdeacon and chaplain.[32] Urban's letter recounts that, despite John de Ebulo being next in line for collation to a prebend in London through virtue of provision, when two prebends became vacant John's right was

[31] Reg. Vat. 25, fols 61v–62v; *Les Registres d'Alexandre IV*, ed. C. Bourel de la Roncière, J. de Loye, P. de Cenival and A. Coulon, 3 vols (Paris, 1895–1959), vol. II, no. 2080, pp. 638–40; *Calendar of Entries in the Papal Registers*, ed. Bliss, p. 348.

[32] Reg. Vat. 29, fols 289r–290r; *Les Registres d'Urbain IV*, ed. Guiraud, vol. III, no. 2454, p. 414; *Calendar of Entries in the Papal Registers*, ed. Bliss, p. 417.

ignored and the benefices went to Master Thomas de Cantilupe, nephew of the bishop of Worcester, and Amalric, son of Simon de Montfort.[33] Out of respect for these two clerics, with whom Master John had dealt with in a friendly manner (*amicabiliter*), he did not want to engage in lengthy and costly litigation against them, and sought a remedy from the papacy that did not involve removing either of them and installing him in one of their places ('et litigancium sustanciam super vacuis exauriri sumptibus contingeret desiderat evitare').[34] Of course, John's placid response to his rights being infringed must be read in the context of the political influence of the de Cantilupe and de Montfort families. John clearly did not want to prosecute these two clerics who had such powerful support behind them. He was presented with a situation in which he stood no chance of an easy victory. Either he relinquished his (pretty solid) legal right to the benefice, which had even been reconfirmed by the papacy after a question arose between John and the chapter of London, thus losing his longed-for prebend, or he pursued damaging litigation, which, despite John's legal right, was by no means a foregone conclusion given the powerful families of Thomas and Amalric. The latter course of action would also have earned John dangerous enemies who would seek to thwart any attempts at career advancement in the future. Had the intruders been humble clergy installed on *in forma pauperum* mandates, then it seems plausible to suggest that John would have reacted more aggressively and pushed his case. Unfortunately for John, however, his conciliatory approach did not bear fruit – he is not recorded to have taken possession of any other benefice in London.[35]

The approach pursued by John de Ebulo was not an isolated incident. In 1300 Pope Boniface VIII recommended a similar course of action in a dispute over the deanery of York.[36] In this case, Francesco Caetani, cardinal-deacon of St Mary's in Cosmedin, had a papal reservation to the deanery, but, upon its voidance, York chapter, with the consent of the archbishop, elected Master William of Hambleton to the position.[37] This blatant infringement of the papal reservation set the chapter at odds with the cardinal and the pope, but Boniface not only recommended that Francesco resign from the position in order to avoid litigation ('ad evitanda litigia super hiis') but even went so far as to provide York chapter's candidate, Master William, to the position.[38] As for Francesco, the pope ordered that he be appointed to the next free dignity in the church. In effect, Boniface was pursuing a *Realpolitik* orientated

[33] Reg. Vat. 29, fol. 289v.
[34] Reg. Vat. 29, fol. 289v.
[35] *Fasti ecclesiae Anglicanae*, ed. Greenway et al., vol. I, pp. 7, 93.
[36] Reg. Vat. 49, fol. 285; *Les Registres des Boniface VIII*, ed. Digard et al., vol. III, no. 3481, cols 644–6; *Calendar of Entries in the Papal Registers*, ed. Bliss, p. 586.
[37] *Fasti ecclesiae Anglicanae*, ed. Greenway et al., vol. VI, pp. xxv, 13, 36, 105.
[38] Reg. Vat. 49, fol. 285r.

towards securing benefices for his curialists as smoothly and swiftly as he could and ruffling as few feathers as possible in the process. That is why he adopted a very soft approach to dealing with the usurpation of his cardinal's claim and the very legitimacy of the right of papal reservation. It is clear that English clergy were far from powerless to oppose papal provision and that they used litigation as a weapon by entangling providees in costly and lengthy legal battles. This proved so effective because it was the antithesis of what some Italian providees were seeking, which was a stable and easy cash stream. The two cases presented here reveal that even the mere prospect of litigation could be enough to deter providees from enforcing their legal rights. Italian providees sought to avoid litigation as far as possible, confident in the knowledge that the pope would seek to collate them to another benefice elsewhere. What these two cases also make clear is that papal provision was just one method of collation operating alongside, and jostling against, traditional forms of episcopal collation and lay patronage, and that it did not always trump these other systems.

Petitions for Exemption from Papal Provisions

Although some popes and providees displayed surprising sensitivity to the concerns of the English Church, as revealed by the judgement of Boniface VIII directly above, this was not always the case, and many English prelates also used the supplicatory system to petition the pope to halt further provisions to their churches. A number of such grants can be found in the papal registers. In 1237 Edmund, archbishop of Canterbury, successfully petitioned Pope Gregory IX for exemption from having to provide any clergy with provision mandates to benefices in his gift, unless those mandates made special mention of the exemption document ('nisi expressam de hac indulgentia rescriptum nostrum fecerit mentionem').[39] Sometimes the papacy made these grants in response to complaints from English churches about the number of Italians they had to support through provision grants. In 1240 the abbot and convent of St Mary's, York petitioned Gregory IX that, when vacant, they might convert the church of Kirkby Lonsdale to their own uses.[40] The convent claimed in their petition that they were supporting no fewer than twelve Roman clerics, liberally appointed ('liberaliter est provisum') by Gregory, his predecessor, Honorius III, and an unnamed papal legate.[41] The resulting impoverishment was so bad, the convent reported, that, embarassingly, new recruits were

[39] Reg. Vat. 18, fol. 285v; *Les Registres de Grégoire IX*, ed. Auvray, vol. II, no. 3645, col. 644; *Calendar of Entries in the Papal Registers*, ed. Bliss, p. 162.

[40] Reg. Vat. 20, fol. 14v; *Les Registres de Grégoire IX*, ed. Auvray, vol. III, no. 5209, cols 259–60; *Calendar of Entries in the Papal Registers*, ed. Bliss, p. 190.

[41] Reg. Vat. 20, fol. 14v.

forced to purchase their own habits ('quare iidem de proprio vestes emere').[42] On these grounds, Gregory granted their petition. Such grants appear to have been quite common up until the time of Alexander IV (1254–61). The reason why such graces seem to have petered out after the middle of the thirteenth century requires further research, but it could point to initial widespread opposition to papal provision in the first half of the century (when it was still something of a new phenomenon) followed by grudging acceptance after it became common, or to the effect of the codification of the right of the papacy to provide in the encyclical *Licet ecclesiarum* of 1265.[43] Again, the willingness of the papacy to grant such petitions for exemption displays sensitivity to English concerns about papal provision, especially where the appointment of Italian clergy had gone off the rails, as was the case with St Mary's, York. But, crucially, the papacy retained the upper hand by building workarounds into these grants. If the pope or his successors later needed to provide a Roman cleric to a church in the gift of Canterbury, for instance, all they needed to do to override it was simply to refer to the papal register and make special mention of the exemption document in question. The value, then, of such exemption documents had its limits, especially when the pope sought to provide one of his kinsmen, but they probably represented an effective defence against poor clergy in possession of provision mandates which lacked the valuable *non obstantibus* clauses at the end necessary to supersede previous papal documents. There is also evidence that the papacy took into account the burdens that they were placing on particular churches, especially the highly sought-after cathedral chapters, when deciding where to try and install Roman clergy in the first place. In the document ordering the provision of Master John de Ebulo, examined above, Urban IV specifically exempted the churches of Lincoln, York and Salisbury on the grounds that they were already shouldering heavy burdens through the provision of Italian clergy ('provisione gravata Lincolniensis, Eboracensis et Saresbiriensis ecclesiis dumtaxat exceptis').[44] All of this demonstrates that the papacy was careful not to push English churches too far, but, as the petition from St Mary's, York makes clear, the churches in question that were suffering from too many provisions had to voice their concerns at the curia through the supplicatory system to gain exemption. If they remained silent they were liable to have to fulfil further provision mandates issued by successive popes (and their legates), who were probably unaware of the burden that every church was shouldering and the actions of their predecessors. This was, after all, how responsive papal government functioned: most of the papacy's knowledge about the localities came from information brought to the attention of its curia in the form of petitions, oral messages and diplomatic letters. While popes

[42] Reg. Vat. 20, fol. 14v.
[43] Barraclough, *Papal Provisions*, p. 155.
[44] Reg. Vat. 29, fol. 289r.

would probably be aware of roughly how many Italians the great English cathedrals were supporting, because their prelates were transacting regular business at the papacy and enjoyed close contacts with the cardinals and other curialists through friendship networks, they did not keep track of the burdens borne by smaller institutions. The papacy was issuing documents in a responsive manner – that is, granting petitions that were acceptable according to canon law but without being able to check the veracity of the cases. The responsibility lay with the churches in the localities to complain about high levels of provision and to be able to protect themselves with exemption documents in the event that the curia forgot about, or did not check, the number of providees currently beneficed there.

Problems with the Papal Supplicatory System

There were a number of problems with the papal supplicatory system that motivated English clergy to seek justice through other channels. First, the expenses involved in travelling to Rome to present one's case at the papal curia could be enormous. For example, papal documents issued in 1259 record loans of 1,000 marks and 1,532 marks, contracted by the abbots of Westminster and Glastonbury respectively, to settle expenses incurred in furthering the affairs of their monasteries at the Roman court.[45] This money was needed to pay for the costs of professional proctors who drafted the supplications in the correct form and acquired the resulting papal documents; advocates who argued legal cases on behalf of their clients; the production of the papal documents in the chancery (the taxation of letters); gifts for cardinals and bribes for papal doormen; and travel to and from Italy and accommodation and sustenance while at the curia. Pursuing legal cases in England was also expensive – as we have seen above, English clergy used it as a weapon against Italian providees – but it was a cheaper and more attractive alternative for native supplicants. Papal kinsmen, of course, favoured their local court, which was the papacy.

The papal supplicatory and judicial system could also grind to a halt without resolution through successive, sometimes deliberately frustratory, appeals, leaving litigants in limbo and deprived of income. In 1288, for example, Pope Nicholas IV was finally able to issue confirmation of the judgement in a case between Stephen 'Surdus', papal chaplain (nephew of the late Richard, cardinal-deacon of St Angelo's), and Isabella and Ydonea, daughters and heirs of the late Robert de Vipont, over the church of Kirkby Thore in Carlisle diocese

[45] Reg. Vat. 25, fol. 199v; *Les Registres d'Alexandre IV*, ed. Bourel de la Roncière et al., vol. III, no. 2846, p. 26; *Calendar of Entries in the Papal Registers*, ed. Bliss, p. 364; Reg. Vat. 25, fol. 212v; *Les Registres d'Alexandre IV*, ed. Bourel de la Roncière et al., vol. III, no. 2914, p. 51; *Calendar of Entries in the Papal Registers*, ed. Bliss, p. 365.

that had rumbled on for twelve years.[46] Patronage of the church – which had been under interdict for the duration of the case – was confirmed to belong to Isabella and Ydonea, and Stephen was forced to resign, having intruded to the rectory after the death of Master Peter de Piperno, ignoring the fact that the right of presentation belonged to Isabella and Ydonea's family ('non obstante si predicta ecclesia ad presentationem laici pertinetur').[47] Thus, the right of the papacy to provide to this benefice was faulty from the beginning, but Isabella and Ydonea had to wait twelve years for redress and, even then, it was still something of a pyrrhic victory for their candidate, who was ordered to pay Stephen a pension of forty marks per annum until the end of the Italian's life. Again, this is a good example of how papal providees might lose their legal cases but still extract financial compensation from their defeats.

There were also papal grants that themselves circumvented the papacy's own supplicatory system. In 1259, for example, Pope Alexander IV issued a confirmation to John Maunsel the elder, papal chaplain and treasurer of York, of all the dignities and benefices that he held with or without papal dispensation, making good any defect in his acquisition of those positions, and awarding him any dispensation required to retain these possessions.[48] This suggests that John had not acquired all his benefices and dignities strictly by the book, but managed to keep them anyway.[49] Even more damningly, the pope's own nephew did not bother to seek the proper dispensation in order to acquire benefices. In 1260 Alexander IV granted his nephew, Raynald de Sarmineto, the right to retain two churches, that of St Mary, North Walsham, in the diocese of Norwich, and that of SS Peter and Paul, Tring, in the diocese of Lincoln, despite the fact that he had accepted the latter without dispensation.[50] But the papacy did not always treat such cases with such leniency. Master Geoffrey de Sancta Agatha, a chaplain of Ottobon, cardinal-deacon of St Adrian's, had accepted the rectory of Houghton in the diocese of Durham despite already being in possession of the church of Lazonby in the diocese of Carlisle without dispensation.[51]

46 Reg. Vat. 44, fol. 27; *Les Registres de Nicolas IV*, ed. Langlois, vol. I, no. 211, p. 34; *Calendar of Entries in the Papal Registers*, ed. Bliss, p. 492.

47 Reg. Vat. 44, fol. 27r. See J. Sayers, 'Centre and Locality: Aspects of Papal Administration in England in the Later Thirteenth Century', in *Authority and Power: Studies on Medieval Law and Government Presented to Walter Ullmann on his Seventieth Birthday*, ed. B. Tierney and P. Linehan (Cambridge, 1980), pp. 115–26, at p. 125.

48 Reg. Vat. 25, fol. 192r; *Les Registres d'Alexandre IV*, ed. Bourel de la Roncière et al., vol. III, no. 2811, p. 11; *Calendar of Entries in the Papal Registers*, ed. Bliss, p. 363.

49 *Fasti ecclesiae Anglicanae*, ed. Greenway et al., vol. VI, pp. 25, 109, 113.

50 Reg. Vat. 25, fols 248v–249r; *Les Registres d'Alexandre IV*, ed. Bourel de la Roncière et al., vol. III, no. 3133, pp. 115–16; *Calendar of Entries in the Papal Registers*, ed. Bliss, p. 373.

51 Reg. Vat. 25, fol. 155r; *Les Registres d'Alexandre IV*, ed. Bourel de la Roncière et al., vol. II, no. 2675, p. 821; *Calendar of Entries in the Papal Registers*, ed. Bliss, p. 360.

In response to Master Geoffrey's petition, in 1258, Alexander IV ordered the abbot of St Agatha's, in the diocese of York, that, after freely resigning the church of Lazonby and making restitution for the proceeds accrued from that church, Geoffrey was to be reappointed to Lazonby and hold both with papal dispensation by special grace.[52] The outcome for the papal chaplain Geoffrey was a good one, but the fact that he had to repay the fruits garnered without dispensation makes this markedly less generous treatment than that meted out by Alexander to his own nephew in the case above. Those without any connection to the curia, however, were treated even less favourably. A document issued by Pope Innocent IV to Lawrence of St Martin, bishop of Rochester, in 1253 sheds lights on a strategy of partial disclosure adopted by some of the clergy in his diocese, and the resulting papal orders.[53] Already in possession of many benefices with cure of souls, the supplicants in question concealed this fact ('hoc tacito'), and successfully petitioned the pope for dispensations to obtain yet more benefices.[54] Since these clergy were of insignificant status (they are not mentioned by name), Innocent charged the bishop to carry out his office ('Quocirca mandamus quatenus circa tales officii tui debitum exequari') – that is, presumably, to punish them, although the lack of clarity in the papal order provided the bishop with some wiggle room if he was minded to exercise clemency.[55] These cases therefore reveal clerics simultaneously using and abusing the papal supplicatory system. The difference between the clergy from Rochester diocese, then, to whom the papacy did not offer full dispensations, and the papal kinsmen and those with the status of papal chaplain appears to be the quality of connections they held to the papal court (or lack thereof). It was a strategical decision by some clerics not to seek proper dispensation from the papacy and not to disclose the full extent of their benefice portfolios, only attempting to make good their possession of these positions much later. By waiting, they could save the time, money and effort required to present petitions at the Roman curia, all the while enjoying the fruits of multiple benefices which the papacy might decide to confiscate. But this only appears to have worked for those who were close to the papal court or those with powerful lay supporters. The nature of selective registration of documents at the curia, combined with the fact that unsuccessful petitions were not recorded, could mean that the papacy refused many more requests for retrospective dispensation than it accepted. The very grant of such petitions for retrospective dispensation from influential clergy actually weakened the supplicatory system because it deterred supplicants from

52 Reg. Vat. 25, fol. 155r.

53 Reg. Vat. 22, fols 233v–234r; *Les Registres d'Innocent IV*, ed. Berger, vol. III, no. 6239, pp. 159–60; *Calendar of Entries in the Papal Registers*, ed. Bliss, p. 283.

54 Reg. Vat. 22, fol. 233v.

55 Reg. Vat. 22, fol. 234r.

using it and demonstrated that it could be circumvented without, or with very little, punishment as a result.

The vexatious appeal represented a more serious problem with the papal judicial system. The right of appeal was inherent to papal justice and it rested on the principle that, as the head of the universal Church and the highest ecclesiastical court in Christendom, anyone could appeal to the pope at any time regarding judgements made by lower Church courts. Since the papacy was located so far away from England, the submission of an appeal with no other object than to frustrate the litigation process was a powerful weapon in the arsenal of the medieval clerk. It took around six weeks to send a message to Rome (or the other papal residences) seeking the appointment of judges delegate, plus the time needed to submit the appeal and wait for it to work its way through the curial system, then another six weeks for the return journey, on top of which one could add however long it took for the papal documents to be transmitted within England to the nominated judges and for those judges to examine the case. This was an easy way to buy at least six months' breathing space, during which one could continue to collect the fruits of one's benefice.[56] This was a game at which one Robert Travers, priest, was skilled. A document issued by Pope Honorius III in 1226 recounts that Robert, who was not called to the office by God but by Aaron ('non vocatus a Domino tanquam Aaron'), managed to use lay influence in order to intrude himself as archdeacon of Killaloe.[57] This being brought to the attention of the pope, Honorius charged the archbishop of Tuam and his colleagues to investigate the veracity of the case. In order to frustrate this, Robert lied by claiming that he had appealed to the papacy ('ad nos appellasse mendaciter').[58] On investigation, James, papal legate, penitentiary and chaplain, decided against Robert, imposing silence on him. This judgement must have taken place between 1220 and 1221 – the documented dates of James's legation.[59] But Robert did not give up, and continued to pervert the course of justice for years. Despite the case against him having been proven and the imposition of silence, Robert nevertheless managed to acquire further papal documents addressed to the bishop of Bath and his colleagues ordering them to intervene in his case ('Cumque iam dictus sacerdos ut quocumque modo effectum posset impedire iustitie ad venerabilem fratrem nostrum … Bathoniensi episcopum et collegas suos quasdam a nobis litteras obtinuerit').

[56] On the related issue of disputes over advowson and lay invasion of churches, see Philippa Hoskin's chapter in this volume.

[57] Reg. Vat. 13, fol. 127r; *Regesta Honorii papae III*, ed. Pressutti, vol. II, no. 5921, p. 420; *Calendar of Entries in the Papal Registers*, ed. Bliss, p. 110.

[58] Reg. Vat. 13, fol. 127r.

[59] On his legation, see H. Zimmermann, *Die päpstliche Legation in der ersten Hälfte des 13. Jahrhunderts: Vom Regeriugsantritt Innocenz' III. bis zum Tode Gregors IX. (1198–1241)* (Paderborn, 1913), pp. 93–4.

Once Honorius realised what had happened, he revoked the letters and cited Robert to appear before him in Rome ('et postea reliquus ad nostram presentiam accessisset nos revocatis predictis litteris peremptorie citavimus dictum Robertum nostro se conspectu personaliter presentandum'), but Robert did not present himself for over a year ('per annum et amplius').[60] Honorius therefore ordered the archbishop of Tuam to remove Robert and see that he was replaced by a suitable candidate. Robert's use of the supplicatory system cannot be described as anything other than cynical. He was clearly aware of exactly how the system worked and what its weak points were, and exploited this knowledge at every turn in order to cling onto the archdeaconry by his fingernails. His strategy was quite simple: to frustrate the course of papal justice for as long as possible so as to maximise his income from the position. That Robert was able, surreptitiously, to acquire new papal letters dragging the bishop of Bath into a closed case demonstrates another weakness of papal government: that it was overwhelmed with business and could not easily keep track of all its judgements and letters.[61] Robert managed to acquire rescripts appointing the bishop of Bath because he lied in his petition. As mentioned above, the responsive nature of papal government meant that if such supplications *appeared* to be acceptable according to canon law, the papacy would issue letters in response ordering investigation and judgement. In order to root out such false appeals, the popes relied upon the reports of other parties and the investigations of local judges delegate because they did not have the time or resources available at the curia in Italy to be able to perform these checks themselves. In the example of Robert, justice was eventually served, but his case demonstrates how little effort was required to cheat the system through the submission of frustratory petitions.

A letter of Pope Martin IV from 1283 recounts the injustice perpetrated by a Master Robert of Gloucester (a different Master Robert of Gloucester from the one discussed above), who adopted the same strategy as Robert Travers when he intruded, with the connivance and support of the abbot and convent of Gloucester, into the rectory of Wraysbury in the diocese of Lincoln.[62] Master Robert exploited the papal supplicatory system in order to retain his ill-won fruits for as long as possible. The rectory had been in the possession of one Master Silvester until his death at Anagni. Thereupon, the

[60] Reg. Vat. 13, fol. 127r.

[61] D. d'Avray, *Medieval Religious Rationalities: A Weberian Analysis* (Cambridge, 2010), pp. 142–6.

[62] Reg. Vat. 41, fol. 155; *Ut per litteras apostolicas* database, Pope Martin IV, no. 596 <http://apps.brepolis.net.001377n30932.emedia1.bsb-muenchen.de/litpa/Search.aspx> [accessed 15 December 2017] – n.b. this letter is omitted from the printed calendar *Les Registres de Martin IV (1281–1285)*, ed. Les Membres de l'École française de Rome (Paris, 1901); *Calendar of Entries in the Papal Registers*, ed. Bliss, p. 471. On this Master Robert of Gloucester, see *Fasti ecclesiae Anglicanae*, ed. Greenway et al., vol. VIII, p. 86.

pope issued letters ordering executors in England to collate Henry of Tilton to the church, but the abbot and convent of Gloucester presented Master Robert to the rectory ('contra collationem provisionem investituram et decretum') before the executors could carry out their duties.[63] When an attempt was made to execute the papal mandate and induct Henry to the rectory, Master Robert appealed to the pope in order to prevent the provision ('frustratorie ad sedem apostolicam appellavit').[64] The reason for his appeal is stated in the papal document: he retained the church for the time it took for his appeal to work its way through the system ('et tali pretextu dictam ecclesiam detinuit') and, with it, the fruits of the rectory ('et adhuc detinet occupatam fructus percipiens ex eadem').[65] Henry of Tilton lodged a petition with the pope to end this injustice, and the pope ordered the archbishop of Canterbury and the dean of London to induce Master Robert and the abbot of Gloucester to hand over possession of Wraysbury within eight days and to pay back to Henry the fruits owed to him during the illegal occupation of the church ('ac de fructibus inde perceptis satifactione plenam et debitam exhiberet'), or else to present themselves at the papal court within two months.[66] The malefactors chose not to appear, again, to buy more time (which meant more fruits from the benefice). Henry, who had been waiting at the papal curia for his enemy to arrive so that justice could be served, publicly accused Robert and the abbot of contumacy ('in ostio palatii apostolici protestatione coram ostiariis nostris permissa dictorum abbatis et Roberti contumantiam accusante').[67] Although the pope appointed Peregrine de Andirano, canon of Aix, as auditor to hear the case at the curia, again Robert and the abbot did not attend. While waiting for his opponent to appear, Henry died at the papal court, never having seen justice done and never having taken possession of the rectory of Wraysbury. Pope Martin therefore awarded the church to Master Edmund of Warfield, chaplain of Hugh of Evesham, cardinal-priest of St Lawrence in Lucina, by papal provision and once again ordered the archbishop of Canterbury, the bishop of Lincoln and the archdeacon of Dorset to cite Master Robert and the abbot of Gloucester to present themselves at the papal curia within two months. This long and drawn-out case illustrates the limits of papal authority as well as those of the papal supplicatory and judicial systems. Importantly, the pope had attempted to do justice regarding the ill-gotten fruits of the benefice and to remove the motivation for such actions in the future by ordering their restitution to the rightful candidate. But, as we have seen, if it was this difficult, and took this long, for legitimate providees to gain possession of their churches, the odds of such victims managing to recover

[63] Reg. Vat. 41, fol. 155r.
[64] Reg. Vat. 41, fol. 155r.
[65] Reg. Vat. 41, fol. 155v.
[66] Reg. Vat. 41, fol. 155v.
[67] Reg. Vat. 41, fol. 155v.

lost fruits on top of this was doubtful. Indeed, when balanced against the aggravation and cost of pursuing further litigation, most probably decided that it was simply not worth it. This explains why malefactors deemed it worthwhile to seize the benefices of others and pursue such vexatious supplicatory strategies. It required very little effort on their part to detain a church and its fruits, but it was an extremely arduous task to remove them from possession. Usually, in the end, justice would be done, so intruders could not hope to retain their target churches indefinitely, but they could rack up a couple of years' income quite easily, a debt that they would probably not have to pay back, especially if their victim was of humble standing.

All of these limitations of papal provision and the supplicatory system led some clerics, even those with papal connections, to seek collation through the traditional methods. In 1278, for instance, Richard of Bamfield, a priest and papal chaplain, petitioned Pope Nicholas III for dispensation to hold the rectory of Rothbury in the diocese of Durham as the result of a contest with a clerk presented to the same church by King Edward I.[68] Nicholas granted the dispensation, which is recorded in the papal register. This dispensation is illuminating because it reveals that Richard was presented to the church not through papal provision but through the patronage of the bishop of Carlisle, despite holding the status of papal chaplain. Obviously, in this case, Richard's chance of collation to the church through the bishop was stronger than through papal provision, and he chose to follow this route to the benefice rather than to petition the pope. This underlines the argument that provision was not always the unstoppable papal juggernaut that overrode all other forms of collation, as it has often been perceived. Instead, it was just one method of appointment available to the clerical consumer on the hunt for benefices. Each cleric chose the route most likely to secure a successful outcome. Thus, although papal provision became one of the main methods of appointment to ecclesiastical benefices in thirteenth-century Christendom, it did not, nor ever could, completely supplant the traditional methods of collation.

Conclusion

The case studies examined in this chapter demonstrate how petitioners, both English and Italian, made use of the papal supplicatory system and reveal its main strengths and shortcomings. The defining element of the system was the distance between the Roman 'centre' and the English 'periphery'. This distance meant that the papacy could not verify the claims and cases presented before its court – it was reliant on the reports of petitioners and the honesty of local

[68] Reg. Vat. 39, fol. 22v; *Les Registres de Nicolas III (1277–1280)*, ed. J. Gay (Paris, 1898), no. 94, p. 27; *Calendar of Entries in the Papal Registers*, ed. Bliss, pp. 454–5; *English Episcopal Acta 29: Durham, 1241–1283*, ed. P. M. Hoskin (Oxford, 2005), p. 248.

deputies involved in the processes, chief among which stood the figure of the papal executor. But the office of executor was a problematic one. In addition to the extra burdens that the papacy loaded onto them, executors were fighting to protect their own collation rights. This meant that they sometimes ignored the legitimate requests of humble supplicants so as to preserve their power of patronage. The distance between England and Rome also meant that the pursuit of papal justice was a long, drawn-out process especially vulnerable to vexatious frustratory strategies and dishonest appeals. The appeal process meant that determined supplicants and litigants with enough money to prosecute their cases to the end could expect to see justice done, but how long would it take? Some, like Henry of Tilton, exhausted of both energy and funds, died without ever managing to enforce their legal right. The appeal process was a double-edged sword in that it guaranteed, as far as was possible, the fairness of the system – intruders to benefices would usually be deprived of their ill-gotten gains and malefactors punished, even if it took years – but it was also left open to easy exploitation simply through the submission of an appeal.

As demonstrated throughout this chapter, the notion derived from Matthew Paris that the English clergy were powerless, downtrodden victims is a fallacy. Rather, they were remarkably successful in fighting papal providees through legal and extra-legal means. The most common and effective approach was simply to drag papal providees through the courts for as long as possible, sapping their will to prosecute their claim to a benefice and pushing them to seek a more peaceful living elsewhere. Moreover, the papal judicial system was not necessarily rigged in favour of Italians: a number of popes showed, on occasion, surprising sensitivity to local concerns, such as in the cases of John de Ebulo and Francesco Caetani. Furthermore, local judges delegate were often English (although it must be remembered that local judges delegate were themselves reliant upon the papal court to expedite their own affairs, and therefore could not afford always to decide against Roman interests). The main difference between the chances of success for English and Italian supplicants was that the papacy was invested in the promotion of the latter and often provided consolation prizes in its judgements so that Italian curialists would not be left out of pocket. Humble English litigants simply did not have access to the pope in the same way.

This chapter also sheds light on the strategies of papal supplicants. Master Robert of Gloucester's case regarding the church of Eynsford demonstrates that many supplicants, especially English clergy, and even those with papal connections and the title of *magister*, relied on local courts first, before deciding to appeal to the papacy. Some, even papal curialists, decided to sidestep the papal supplicatory system entirely and acquired benefices without the necessary papal dispensations, only to seek them retrospectively when it suited them. The role of intercessors was central to the supplicatory strategies of petitioners and appears directly to have affected chances of success. As a result, petitioners emphasised their intercessors in the texts of their petitions, which we can trace in the corresponding papal mandates, such as those issued on behalf of William de Alpibus and Gerard de Wippens following the intercession of Eleanor of Provence and Odo de Grandison, respectively. Supplicants were quite careful in the selection not only of their intercessor but also of their preferred 'vendor' of patronage. The case of the papal chaplain Richard of Bamfield demonstrates quite clearly that even those with enviable links to the papacy would still select other patrons when it suited their cause better; the papacy did not immediately become the undisputed fount of grace after the invention of provision.

The provision system was also more complex than previously thought in that it did not simply pit English clergy against Italian in the struggle for benefices but opened up the collation system and made it even more international, so that the pool of candidates included English, French and Italians. Similarly, this chapter demonstrates that resistance to the *system* of papal provision is not the same as xenophobic hatred of Italians, although this did play a part. The primary cause for grievance appears to have been the principle of the matter: papal provision circumvented traditional methods of collation and directly impacted upon the power of bishops to exercise their powers of patronage. This, more than the fact that the beneficiaries of papal provision were often Italian, seems to have been the biggest source of tension. In many ways, this point typifies the findings from new research into papal provisions. The system, its actors and the supplicatory strategies that they pursued were much more complex than previous research has allowed.

9

Playing the System: Marriage Litigation in the Fourteenth Century

Frederik Pedersen

Medieval English courts have preserved an astounding amount of information. A staggering volume of high-quality summaries of narratives presented in the theatre of the court by witnesses and litigants can be compared with an equally impressive set of procedural documents. The narratives frequently contained exquisitely detailed narratives of apparent verisimilitude and have provided the evidence behind a multitude of studies of medieval everyday life.

Most of these studies have implicitly taken for granted that the court record represents a more or less true image of the events under legal scrutiny.[1] Only a few historians, most notably Natalie Zemon Davis, have attempted to explore these records as part of a fluid and constantly changing narrative strategy intended to further the interests of a particular party in a dispute. In two brief, but eminently readable, studies, Davis has shown that litigants were aware of the need to present their cases in a way that maximised their chances of survival[2] or of the continued success of a loved one left behind.[3] Her careful analysis of the legal choices faced by defendants as cases progressed through the courts shows the importance of a detailed scrutiny of the records in their entirety. Accordingly, in addition to the mere words preserved in the record, a thorough analysis should include, *inter alia*, a consideration of the social circumstances of the litigants, the timing of interventions and the avenues that legal procedure opened (and closed) as a case moved through the legal systems.

Davis's work focused on cases that involved the death penalty and, so far, only a few scholars have successfully integrated Davis's insight into their analyses of less high-stakes types of cases. This is a pity because a more careful reading of

[1] S. M. Butler, *Divorce in Medieval England: From One to Two Persons in Law* (Abingdon, 2013); P. J. P. Goldberg, *Communal Discord, Child Abduction, and Rape in the Later Middle Ages* (New York, 2008).

[2] N. Zemon Davis, *Fiction in the Archives: Pardon Tales and Their Tellers in Sixteenth-Century France* (Stanford, CA, 1987).

[3] N. Zemon Davis, *The Return of Martin Guerre* (Cambridge, MA, 1983).

such cases suggests that a much more complex understanding of the law could be found among ordinary people and should instil a healthy scepticism about the veracity of depositions among those who investigate medieval everyday life. In this chapter I shall investigate the records of four much more mundane cases of litigation in the fourteenth-century consistory court in York: the York Cause Papers, preserved at the Borthwick Institute for Archives. I do so in order to demonstrate how an analysis based on a wider reading of information and of context, both within and without the court's records, can enhance our understanding of the dynamic of litigation, and to caution that medieval litigants had easy access to legal advice, which means that not only did they adjust their narratives to suit the requirements of the law but that, in some cases, their out-of-court behaviours were determined by their strategic aims in litigation.

There were two ways in which cases came to the court's attention: one was at the instance of a plaintiff; the other was pursued *ex officio* by the consistory court. In the latter kind of case a judge summoned defendants to answer an anonymous accusation or a public rumour that a transgression had taken place; in the former, the court acted at the instigation of one of the parties to the case. In many jurisdictions *ex officio* cases continued through the legal system according to inquisitorial procedure, but in England it appears that local legal custom meant that English courts habitually turned *ex officio* cases into instance cases.[4] A case was thus reduced to written form and presented to the court as an adversarial case with a plaintiff and a defendant. This means two things: one, that the record shows an incomplete picture of the level of 'inquisitorial' litigation in the English courts and presents a false picture of the nature of many of the cases (and also that the written records predominantly appear to contain instance cases between a woman seeking to secure a husband and a man eager to avoid marriage); and, two, that from its inception the written record shows only the legal issues the court was able and willing to investigate, which is not necessarily the issues that mattered most to the litigants. The first significant written evidence in an instance case-file is the so-called *libellus*. This was a document that followed an oral presentation in front of a judge in which the plaintiff outlined her/his case. Not until this oral presentation had convinced the judge that a legal case had to be answered did the court assign a proctor (or the plaintiff appointed one themselves) to the plaintiff. A proctor was a member of the court who had trained in law and who would advise and guide his client through the legal system. We can therefore see that, rather than being a reflection of what went on in the real world, the written record is the result of a process of selection and verification guided by legal arguments and supervised by a member of the court who was educated

[4] C. Donahue Jr, 'The Canon Law on the Formation of Marriage and Social Practice in the Later Middle Ages', *Journal of Family History* 8 (1983), 144–58 and C. Donahue Jr, *Law, Marriage and Society in the Later Middle Ages: Arguments About Marriage in Five Courts* (Cambridge, 2008).

or trained in law. Sometimes we also discern that the litigants were themselves well informed about the law or that they were advised by members of their family who were well versed in the law. In other cases, proctors, confessors and the local community in general helped litigants to present their cases in the manner best suited to procure their desired outcome. It is rare (though not unheard of) to find that litigants simply ignored the advice they were given, or that they were not given advice at all, and when that happened it is helpful to investigate the reasons, whether they be economic, cultural or geographical, why such advice was not forthcoming.[5] But, in the main, it was necessary for a successful litigant to present their case in a manner that was consistent with the law and intended to produce an outcome that was pleasing to the client.

This did not mean that court proceedings were simple theatres for the advancement of lies: high ethical standards demanded of the proctors secured that there were checks and balances in place for the proper conduct of the cases.[6] But 'proper conduct' in this connection meant that litigation was conducted in accordance with the rules – the law was not necessarily interested in a representation of true events. It was designed to procure litigants their legal *rights* rather than justice, and the law took a very practical view of what constituted rights, duties and proper conduct within marriage. To mention but one example: when examining whether a marriage should be annulled because of non-consummation (which in practical terms meant 'male impotence' in the English courts), the judge was required to establish whether both parties had known of the impossibility of penetrative heterosexual sex before the marriage, whether the parties had cohabited with the intention of procreation for two full years and whether neighbourhood rumour confirmed the impossibility of sexual congress; as a final step, he was also to establish by the help of expert witnesses the existence of an impediment to penetrative intercourse.[7] Any other information was irrelevant. The law was *only* interested in the parties' procreative intent and their ability to perform intercourse. In the rare instances where information about behaviour outside the bedroom is forthcoming, the record has been preserved because one of the parties behaved in a way that directly affected the value and weighting of evidence regarding the parties' ability to perform their marital duties, for example by forcing their wives to produce a public oath that their husbands had had intercourse with them or that they had the ability to do so.[8]

5 For example, in York, Borthwick Institute for Archives, CP.E.248 and CP.E.256.

6 J. A. Brundage, 'Vultures, Whores, and Hypocrites: Images of Lawyers in Medieval Literature', *Roman Legal Tradition* 2 (2002), 56–103.

7 Donahue Jr, *Law, Marriage and Society*, pp. 19–20, 371.

8 F. Pedersen, 'Motives for Murder: The Role of Sir Ralph Paynel in the Murder of William Cantilupe (1375)', in *Continuity, Change and Pragmatism in the Law: Essays in Memory of Professor Angelo Forte*, ed. A. R. C. Simpson et al. (Aberdeen, 2016), pp. 68–93, at p. 85.

In this short chapter it is impossible to cover all the strategies employed by litigants in such marriage cases, so I shall limit myself to a few examples that illustrate some of the ways in which litigants were familiar with the institutions of law. I shall start by examining two examples of how litigants accessed expert knowledge of canon law, in the first instance among members of their family and in the second instance from their confessors and local community.

Newton and Garth c. Waghen, CP.E.245 (03/04/1391–20/04/1391)

Despite being a somewhat complex case, Newton and Garth c. Waghen (CP.E.245) lasted only seventeen days and showed remarkable economy in the use of witnesses: only three witnesses were heard and two of these were clerics. The case was an unusual multi-party case in which two men, Thomas del Garth and John Newton, competed to have their marriage to the widow Agnes Waghen validated by the consistory court.

As a widow, Agnes Waghen was probably a relatively wealthy woman. But more important for our purpose is the fact that she was the daughter of William Cawod, a proctor in the York consistory court and the vicar general of the archdeaconry of Richmond. William Cawood was an up-and-coming man in York: he held a licentiate in both laws, and a few years later he was appointed official of the archbishop's court in York. From there he rose to become the archbishop's chancellor and one of the most influential members of his household.[9] Though Cawod did not act formally in his daughter's case, his legal training is clearly behind the swiftness and economy of its conduct. The successful plaintiff, Thomas del Garth, was advised by a court proctor, Nicholas Easingwold. On 3 April 1391 he composed a 'foul' copy of the libel, which included the intention to prove that, having exchanged their marriage vows, Thomas and Agnes Waghen had consummated the marriage. However, only a few days later, on 6 April, Nicholas presented the court with a revised 'fair' copy of the libel. This final version of the libel did not seek to prove the alleged intercourse but asked the court to examine only three questions: had there been an exchange of vows? Had the vows been unconditional? Was there neighbourhood rumour to the existence of the marriage? The omission of the claim that the parties had subsequent intercourse is significant and

[9] The chancellor was formally the head of the archbishop's chancery or secretariat, but by the beginning of the fourteenth century at York (as at Canterbury and the other English dioceses), the archbishop's chancellor was mainly an attendant *jurisperitus*, serving the archbishop both as legal adviser and as judicial deputy in the audience and on visitations. See A. H. Thompson, 'The Registers of the Archdeaconry of Richmond, 1361–1477', *Yorkshire Archaeological Journal* 30, 32 (1931, 1936), 1–134, 111–45; K. F. Burns, 'The Medieval Courts', vol. I of 'The Administrative System of the Ecclesiastical Courts in the Diocese and Province of York', unpublished manuscript, Leverhulme Research Scheme (York, 1962), p. 142.

can be interpreted in several ways. One interpretation sees the 'foul' copy of the libel as evidence that Nicholas Easingwold worked to a fixed 'template' in accordance with which he expected to be able to present evidence for consummation of the marriage and that this 'template' was used as a kind of 'exemplar', or might even have been found in a kind of 'formulary book'[10]. The relatively short period – in effect less than two days – between the 'foul' and 'fair' copies indicates that Nicholas met either with Thomas del Garth or with William Cawood when he had composed this draft libel. The existence of a 'fair' copy of the libel indicates that Thomas (or William Cawod) was presented with the 'foul version' (either orally or in writing) and that the opportunity was taken to correct Nicholas's 'stock narrative'. Another interpretation suggests that Thomas del Garth expected to have to prove that consummation had taken place but that he was persuaded by his proctor (and/or his prospective father-in-law) that such an argument was a needless complication of the case. In either case, the existence of two versions of the libel demonstrate that the 'fair copy' version was the result of a consideration by men trained in law of the necessity to present certain kinds of information in order to secure the marriage of Agnes and Thomas and to prevent the marriage of Agnes and John.

The rest of the case demonstrates a similar concern and familiarity with what it was possible to achieve by an economical use of the law. The 'fair copy' of the libel named three witnesses – two clerics and one lay person – to be interrogated regarding Alice and Thomas's marriage vows. Despite the low numbers, the clerical expertise was impressive. William Donnington was the master of the hospice at St Mary's near Bootham – in other words, a worthy and valuable witness to the contract who also happened to live where numerous marriages took place. William Burton was the vicar of the Church of St Mary's, Bishopshill,[11] and would therefore have been thoroughly familiar with the ritual of marriage. But Burton also brought along his clerk. Burton told the court that his clerk was a notary, so we can safely presume that he also would have been familiar with marriage law, even though he was not called as a witness.[12] Donnington and Burton would certainly have had a good knowledge of the liturgical offices and would have been well acquainted with

[10] In proposing this I am aware of Richard Helmholz's warning against using formulary books as a tool in the study of legal practice: R. H. Helmholz, *Marriage Litigation in Medieval England* (Cambridge, 1974), pp. 22–3. I am not sure that such a 'formulary' necessarily would have been a physical object like the later York formulary book mentioned by D. M. Owen, *The Medieval Canon Law: Teaching, Literature, and Transmission* (Cambridge, 2009), pp. 51–2, or the Aberdeen Style book: M. C. Meston and A. D. M. Forte, *The Aberdeen Stylebook 1722* (Edinburgh, 2000). What I am proposing is that Esyngwald was aware of a 'model progression' of this kind of case which made him expect that certain arguments needed to be made to ensure success for his client.

[11] It is unknown whether this refers to St Mary's Bishopshill, *Senior* or *Junior*.

[12] Nor is there any notarised record of the marriage.

the Church's teaching on marriage. They were probably personal friends of William Cawood, the bride's father, and the monastery of St Mary's itself was the setting for many marriage contracts. Thomas del Garth had also invited two other persons to be present at the exchange of marriage vows: Henry Sutton, a spicer, and William Rufford, a butcher. They may have been his personal friends. But, unlike Donnington and Burton, it is unlikely that either had any formal training in the law of the Church. Perhaps it is indicative of the value put on these two witnesses by Esyngwald and Cawod that only Henry Sutton was called to witness, and he proved to be the least informative of the three witnesses examined by the court: he produced only a very vague confirmation of Thomas and Agnes's marriage. However, the expert evidence of Donnington and Burton carried the day and the court ruled that Thomas del Garth and Agnes Waghen contracted marriage according to the rules of canon law.

I have already remarked on the fact that it took only seventeen days to hear the case from beginning to end, but it is also worth noticing that the case involved only three witnesses, all of whom deposed that Thomas and Agnes exchanged the bare minimum of words necessary to create the marriage bond, which was amplified by the clerical witnesses mentioning the exchange of a ring.

The competitor for Agnes's hand, John de Newton, who described himself as an *armiger*, launched a series of objections written in a strong confident hand by someone clearly familiar with legal procedure. The fact that his objections were compiled by a professional scribe whose hand is not otherwise found in the York consistory court suggests that John Newton found it difficult to find a York scribe to present his case, perhaps an indication that the York legal establishment conspired against John Newton's unwanted marriage. The sentence in the case went against John (and mentioned that his witnesses were interrogated, but their depositions have been lost).

Lovel c. Marton, CP.E.18 (18/01/1328–28/11/1328)[13]

When faced with the fact that every case had a plaintiff and a defendant who attempted to prove their opposing view it is tempting to conclude

[13] Following a re-examination of the documents I have corrected the dates of the case: the Borthwick Institute Database <https://www.hrionline.ac.uk/causepapers/causepaper.jsp?id=91635> [accessed 24 August 2017] lists the dates as 18/01/1326–16–30/10/1328. The case contains a memorandum dated 'iiij kln' decembri anno et cetera xxvjto' (i.e. 28 November 1326), which is the only surviving document dated to that year. However, internal evidence demonstrates that the correct year should be 1328: the memorandum says that Thomas swore to having married a woman called Elena de Aneport: 'pendente lite super matrimonio inter Elisabeth' filiam domini Simonis [Lovel militis] pendente indecisa [sic]'. As the earliest exchange of vows between Elizabeth did not take place until January 1328 (which would be 'anno et cetera xxvij' in the Old Style), the scribe must have left out a minim. This error is reflected in the Borthwick Institute Database. Richard Helmholz also overlooked this scribal error in *Marriage Litigation in Medieval England* (Cambridge 1974), p. 213.

that all litigation was adversarial. However, the custom of transforming *ex officio* cases to instance cases makes a close analysis of the contents of some of the surviving cases desirable. It is not difficult to see that litigants may indeed have been cooperating to ensure that the consistory court disallowed a marriage neither plaintiff nor defendant wished to enter.[14] Alternatively, in a time when marriage certificates did not exist, litigants may have worked together to achieve an outcome that not only confirmed the legality of their marriage but also provided written evidence in the form of a copy of the court's sentence. The case Lovel c. Marton (CP.E.18) may be an example of this. The real antagonists in this case are almost certainly the defendant and his father, or possibly someone who did not appear before the court at all, the defendant's fiancé, Elena de Aneport, with whom he confessed to have contracted a marriage before his marriage to Elizabeth Lovel, which was solemnised while the case was pending in York.

In her (undated) libel Elizabeth Lovel claimed that she had conducted marriage negotiations with Thomas Marton in her father's brewhouse,[15] which ended with a betrothal on 31 January 1328, that she and Thomas had contracted a legitimate marriage by exchanging vows *verba de presenti* in Thomas's bedroom on 9 April that year, and that Thomas had sworn to the existence of their marriage at a meeting held in the church of Hovingham, which brought together, among others, Elizabeth's father and aunt and Thomas's father in October 1328. The court's task was fairly straightforward, especially because Thomas did not deny that he had exchanged marriage vows with Elizabeth.

Elizabeth produced the evidence of her two sisters and of Thomas's friend Nicholas Bartelmew, who had been present at two separate exchanges of vows. Elizabeth's sister Agnes deposed that on the Sunday before the Purification of the Virgin just past (that is, on 31 January 1327) she and Nicholas Bertelmew had been present at an exchange of vows which, though intended to create a marriage, had created only a betrothal. The exchange had taken place in Thomas's father's brewhouse in "Drokton" (present-day Draughton) in Rydale, when Thomas had said to Elizabeth, 'behold my oath that I will take no one as my wife except you' and she replied, 'behold my oath that never will I have anyone as my husband except you'.[16] Agnes added that in token of their marriage they held hands and kissed each other in front of her and Thomas's friend, Nicholas Bartholomew, who confirmed her version of events in his deposition.

[14] Cf. CP.E.245, above.

[15] CP.E.18: 'in bracino'.

[16] CP.E.18–5: '"Ecce fides mea quod non ducam aliquam in uxorem nisi te." Et ipsa statim respondebat: "Ecce fides mea quod nullo tempore habebo aliquem in virum nisi te habeam"'.

However, as Thomas explained to Elizabeth on 9 April, they had intended to contract marriage on this occasion, but they had only contracted a marriage *verba de futuro* by their words. This flaw had been pointed out to Thomas by his confessors, the Augustinian friars in nearby Bolton abbey, during his annual confession. Consequently, when Elizabeth visited Thomas in his chamber on the Tuesday morning after Easter 1327, Thomas – lying naked in his bed – expressed his concerns about the validity of their contract to Elizabeth. He did so in the presence of Agnes and Euphemia, another one of Elizabeth's sisters, who had also come to visit Thomas in his bedroom in Draughton. Both sisters confirmed that, using words that Thomas had learned in confession, he and Elizabeth again exchanged vows, this time by using valid *verba de presenti* phrasing. The contract was witnessed by the two sisters, Agnes and Euphemia, and by Richard Hyman, Thomas's servant (who did not testify before the Hovingham tribunal mentioned below).

Sometime before the case was heard in the full consistory court in York, a 'pre-court tribunal' convened to establish whether the court in York needed to examine the case.[17] The meeting took place in the parish church of Hovingham, twenty miles outside York, and those present included Elizabeth's father, her aunt and Thomas's parents. Also present were Edmund Stanley, William de Easingby and two men – William Appleton and William Thornton – who acted as legal advisors to Elizabeth and Thomas.[18] Elizabeth and Thomas confirmed the two exchanges and the words used. The witnesses called made the implicit point that Thomas and Elizabeth contracted their marriage without the knowledge and consent of their parents, and Elizabeth and Thomas were called upon to produce an oath about the exchanges. But when Thomas had finished his oath, something unusual happened: Thomas returned to the small group consisting of Elizabeth, William Appleton and William Thornton, and the four of them held a small conference. Then Thomas returned to address his father, Elizabeth's father and her aunt. He said that, although he verbally consented to the marriage, mentally he had expressed a reservation – he had not wanted to marry Elizabeth unless his friends or family consented to the marriage.[19] In terms of law this was a

[17] F. Pedersen, 'The Legal Sophistication of Litigants in Marriage Cases from Medieval York', in *Proceedings of the Tenth International Conference of Medieval Canon Law, Syracuse, New York, 13–18 August 1996*, ed. K. Pennington, K. H. Kendall and S. Chodorow, Monumenta Iuris Canonici, Series C: Subsidia, Vol. 11 (Vatican City, 2001), pp. 965–84.

[18] The documentation for this period of the court's existence is sparse, but a certain William Appleby was a proctor of the court some thirteen years later. Since the suffix -ton is the English version of the Scandinavian suffix -by, it may be suggested that William Appleton could have been a member of the court in York at this time. William Appleton certainly seems to have been there to advise Thomas and Elizabeth in the canon law of marriage.

[19] CP.E.18–5: 'Et postmodum, dictus Thomas, post huiusmodi confessionem dicte

poor excuse and it would hardly have had any impact in a normal trial, but Thomas's statement in Hovingham appears to have been designed to sow doubt about the validity of his marriage to Elizabeth so that their case would be heard by the consistory court, where it would be settled publicly once and for all. Why this was important to Elizabeth and Thomas cannot be stated with certainty, but we may speculate that it was not unrelated to an event that came to light only after Elizabeth had won the case in York: Thomas had solemnised a marriage with Elena de Aneport in the diocese of Chester, a diocese which fell under the jurisdiction of Canterbury. The case of Elizabeth and Thomas was heard in York, and the fact that the court in York was unlikely to find out about the Chester marriage ceremony may have increased the likelihood that the court would find for Elizabeth and Thomas. In addition, whatever Thomas's ultimate aim may have been, in his mind and in the estimation of his advisers, his admission of mental reservations posed a threat to the legality of the vows between him and Elizabeth. However, Thomas's objections were disregarded by the court in York and a sentence for Elizabeth and for upholding their marriage was passed on 27 October 1328.

This case shows some of the same traits as the Waghen case. One is struck by the economy of effort, particularly in its early phase. Only two witnesses were heard to confirm the exchanges in Draughton: Euphemia Lovel and Nicholas Barthelmew deposed about the first exchange, Euphemia and Agnes Lovel for the second one. A third witness was present at the second exchange – Thomas's servant, Richard Hyman – but, like Donnington's clerk, he was not called to the Hovingham meeting, nor was he summoned to York. At the Hovingham meeting it appears that Thomas and Elizabeth's advisors deliberately calibrated Thomas's surprise plea of mental reservations so that it might sow doubt about the validity of the marriage – not enough to prove that the exchanges did not create a marriage, but enough to convince the Hovingham meeting that the consistory court ought to be called upon to consider the validity of the marriage. The venue and the way in which two of the people present – William Appleton and William Thornton – evidently acted as legal counsel to Thomas and Elizabeth make it clear that Thomas knew what he was doing and that he did so after consultations with his apparent opponent, Elizabeth.

Thomas's actions in Hovingham raise another question about the case: was it really adversarial? The written record shows that Elizabeth Lovel pleaded

Elizabet, parum deliberavit cum Willelmo de Thornton et Willelmo de Appilton. Et statim rediens ad dictum Simonem et alios superius nominatos, fatebatur se talia verba matrimonialia in forma per ipsam Elizabetem recitata eidem Elizabeti dixisse et protulisse. Adiecit tamen idem Thomas quod tempore quo talia verba matrimonialia fecit et protulit dicte Elizabete, in mente et voluntate cogitavit quod dictum contractum non adimpleret nisi adesset voluntas amicorum suorum. Et tunc dicta Elizabet eidem respondebat quod de cogitatione nescit, sed ille contractus fuerat simplex, sine conditione aliquali. Cui asssertioni dictus Thomas nichil in contrarium respondebat.'

in York to have the court enforce her marriage to a reluctant Thomas Marton. However, our examination suggests that neither Elizabeth nor Thomas were averse to the marriage. Instead, it seems that Thomas's father, Robert Marton, had other plans for Thomas. Just how marrying Thomas to Elena of Aneport during the hearing of the case in York fitted into his plans is impossible to say, and the facts of the case present a confusing picture. One would have thought that Thomas Marton's father would have been happy to have Elizabeth, a member of the aristocracy, as a member of his family. But Robert Marton evidently was not: his actions were an unambiguous attempt to pre-empt a decision by the court in York in favour of his son's marriage to Elizabeth Lovel. Indeed, he took extreme measures to protect the marriage to Elena of Aneport: Thomas's marriage to Elena took place after Elizabeth had entered her plea in York and in a diocese outside the jurisdiction of the northern province, where the reading of the banns was unlikely to attract attention. Thus, despite initial appearances, this case is not simply a case of a teenager who spoke too soon and later regretted his words: it is a manifestation of teenage insistence on marrying against the parents' wishes. It has already been argued above that the laity had a good grasp of the basic Church rules of marriage, but Thomas's surprising action at the meeting in Hovingham suggests that, even in 1328, members of the laity knew how to use the courts, including being able to present sufficiently vague protestations at pre-court hearings to ensure that a case would be heard by a 'proper' legal tribunal.

Paynel c. Cantilupe, CP.E.259 (15/03/1368–01/04/1369)

The situation of the 26-year-old Nicholas Cantilupe, who defended his marriage to Katherine Paynel against an accusation of impotence in 1368, was more complex than those of either Agnes Waghen or Elizabeth Lovel. Nicholas's wife, Katherine Paynel, alleged that he 'did not have organs suited for intercourse' and was 'unable to emit semen'. His best defence, therefore, would be to appear before the court to demonstrate that he was potent and that his genitals functioned normally. Not only was this his best hope of preserving his marriage: canon law required that his condition be confirmed in all of three ways: by cohabitation (nominally for three years, but in practice until the beginning of the third year); by neighbourhood rumour; and by an examination of his ability to perform sexually. But it is also very likely that he would fail such an examination.[20]

Nicholas Cantilupe was a member of a family with a proud legal tradition and he traced his lineage back to several prominent canon lawyers – among them the thirteenth-century bishop Walter Cantilupe of Hereford and St Thomas of Hereford (who was his great-uncle) – and to the diplomat and

[20] The canon law says three years, but it is clear that this was interpreted as having completed two years of cohabitation. I examine the case in greater detail in 'Motives for Murder'.

royal justice who shared his name. Upon his death in 1355, Nicholas's grandfather had bequeathed him extensive lands which, when he came of age, made Nicholas one of the largest landholders not just in the North but in England as a whole. However, because he held these lands in fee tail, a public acknowledgement of his inability to produce an heir would be a serious setback. His actions to avoid this outcome of the case show an awareness of both lay and ecclesiastical legal systems and a willingness to use this knowledge (and one presumes, any influence at the papal curia which his sainted great-uncle might have provided) to further his case.

Nicholas's fundamental problem was that his wife's allegation was probably true. It was therefore imperative for Nicholas to avoid a physical examination, and Nicholas used every means at his disposal to perform a delicate balancing act between being found out and staying within the (canon) law. Nicholas had several reasons to be circumspect in his use of the law: his prime concern would have been to preserve the claim of his heirs – however they might have been conceived – to the lands which Nicholas held in fee tail. Should he be shown to be impotent his claim on his extensive lands would be void. His responses to the threat of losing his bequest therefore included extra-judicial violence, litigation at the king's bench, subterfuge and eventually an appeal to what must have appeared to him to be a more sympathetic court, the papal curia. Thus, before the case was introduced to the York consistory court in March 1368 (but after his wife made her original complaint to the 'proper' jurisdiction, the diocese of Lincoln, three years earlier), Nicholas tried to settle the case by extra-judicial means. In a desperate attempt to forestall the case he abducted his wife from her parents' manor in Caythorp in Lincolnshire in October 1367. In his stronghold, Greasley castle in Nottinghamshire, he threatened her with perpetual incarceration unless she publicly swore an oath that he was capable of intercourse. She did swear the oath, but even then he did not allow her to leave Greasley. In February 1368 his father-in-law 'attacked' Greasley and carried away goods to the value of 2,000 pounds, most likely made up of the contents of his daughter's dowry.

Nicholas must have been aware that the only way that he could get restitution for this loss of goods was by seeking the help of the royal courts. He complained to the king's bench about the attack and procured an indictment of his father-in-law and three of his servants. In actual fact, the 'attack' was probably an ill-tempered argument that took place when Nicholas met Katherine's aggrieved parents inside Greasley castle, an encounter that ended with the Paynels seizing Katherine's dowry and liberating her from captivity. The king's bench record alleges that the attack was performed by five people: Nicholas's father- and mother-in-law (i.e. Ralph Paynel and his wife Katherine), Ralph Paynel's chamberlain, John Hevore 'from Lincolnshire' and Margaret Halton, the nurse/confidante of Nicholas's wife. The composition of this group of allegedly violent attackers who allegedly not only 'ravished' and 'abducted' Nicholas's wife but also robbed him of 2,000 pounds' worth of goods is unusual, to say the least.[21]

But if Nicholas had hoped for a quick restitution of his wealth (and his wife) by pleading for the king's justice he was mistaken. He had not taken into consideration that the king's bench would not make a decision while a marriage case was pending, a procedural fact that meant he had to wait for the ecclesiastical court in York to make a decision in his wife's case against him. That decision would depend on the outcome of a court examination of Nicholas's sexual potency.

On 5 August 1368 the court publicly summoned Nicholas to appear for a physical examination in York on 13 September. This left Nicholas in a difficult situation: if he did not appear before the court he would be liable to excommunication and to the loss of his case, and if he failed the examination he would also lose the case. The way in which he solved the problem of demonstrating to the court that he was willing to go through with a physical examination in York, while at the same time avoiding it, was simple and possibly also intended to allow him to appeal his case to the apostolic see: on the appointed date he presented himself to be examined in Lincoln rather than York. Whether this was a conscious subterfuge is impossible to establish. But it is suggestive of his intention to avoid censure that there are no preserved documents in the case between the letter that recorded his appearance for a physical examination dated 13 September 1368 and the York sentence for Elizabeth dated 21 April 1369.

Immediately following the York decision the king's bench resurrected Nicholas's complaint about the attack on his castle and eight days later, on 29 April, it interrogated three witnesses about the events. The king's bench fixed another meeting to take place in September 1369. Nicholas must have realised that his chances of a successful trial before the king's bench were increasingly slim when Ralph Paynel took on a commission to travel to the Continent on business for the king's brother, John of Gaunt, during that summer.

[21] TNA, KB 27/434: 'Robertus Raufchaumberlayn Paynel, Johannes de Hevore de comitiva Lincolnensis et Margareta de Halton de Holland attachi fuerunt ad respondendum Nicholo de Cantilupo de placito quare ipsi sunt cum Radolpho Paynel, milite, et Katarina, uxore eius, vi et armis Katerinam uxorem dicti Nicholi apud Greseley rapuerunt et eam cum bonis et catallis eiusdem Nicholi abduxerunt et ea adhuc detinent et alia enormia etc, ad grave dampnum etc, et contra pacem etc, ac contra formam statuti etc … [et] vi et armis, scilicet gladiis, baculis, arcibus, sagitis etc Katerinam uxorem ipsius Nicholi apud Gresley rapuerunt et eam cum bonis et catallis eiusdem Nicholi scilicet anulis aureis et argentis serculis cum petris preciosis, discis plateris et saltaris de argento abduxerunt et ea ei adhuc detinent et alia enormia etc et contra pacem etc, et unde dicit quod deterioratus est et dampnum habet ad valorem duarum mille Librarum' accessed via <http://aalt.law.uh.edu/AALT2/E3/KB27no434/aKB27no434fronts/IMG_0117.htm> [accessed 8 January 2018].

Nicholas had also approached the court in York with a request for an appeal to the papacy. The court granted this appeal on 2 May 1369, a fortnight after its decision, presumably in recognition of the fact that the case had not followed all the procedural steps necessary in canon law (i.e. that Nicholas had not undergone a physical examination of his genitals). Towards the end of the summer of 1369 Nicholas put his things in order by appointing a caretaker for his estates in England. When Nicholas appeared before the king's bench in September 1369 Ralph Paynel's chamberlain presented a letter from Edward III excusing Paynel from litigation because of his absence abroad on business for John of Gaunt. The case was therefore abandoned and Nicholas took up his other option: the appeal to the papal curia. We must assume that Nicholas had every reason to hope for a favourable outcome of litigation in Avignon; he was, after all, the great nephew of a recent saint. However, at only 27 years of age, Nicholas died while in Avignon, and with his death the case ended.

CP.E.259 illustrates several ways in which a knowledge of the law and of the procedure of the court influenced litigants' behaviours. Most importantly, though, it demonstrated how Nicholas Cantilupe tried to avoid the legal consequences of his condition and illustrated how he employed his understanding of not only canon but also secular law to achieve this aim of preventing the case going forward. His abduction of Katherine Paynel was intended to stop her pursuing her case in York, and when he presented himself for examination in Lincoln he opened a significant opportunity: the absence of a physical examination of his body meant that the York consistory court reached a decision in his case without following proper procedure and this allowed him to appeal the case to the papacy, where he presumably expected a more sympathetic hearing.

Palmer c. Brun and Southburn, CP.E.25 (01/03/1333–19/10/1333)

Agnes Waghen was a widow who had the help of her father and her case was a standard one: her successful suitor alleged that marriage had been contracted in the simplest form and backed this position with the evidence of two strong witnesses (and one less convincing). Thomas Marton and Elizabeth Lovel were teenagers who, having run foul of parental marriage plans, received legal advice in confession and during the process of litigation to force the court to acknowledge their marriage. Nicholas Cantilupe drew on his own knowledge of the law and may have hoped for a more favourable hearing at the papal curia because of his family connections. The Waghen and Lovel cases stayed firmly within the boundaries of the canon law, while in the Paynel c. Cantilupe case we moved towards the outer limits of what that law would permit. But what could a litigant do if they simply did not have a case that fitted within the boundaries of law? What could a party do to pursue a case successfully in which they were quite simply in the wrong and where the defendant, for reasons of their own, might want to collude in the dissolution of their unhappy marriage?

The case of Palmer c. Brun and Southburn (CP.E.25) is a confession to perjury: six years after successfully petitioning for an annulment of her marriage to Geoffrey Brun because of her alleged precontract with a certain Ralph Fouler, Alice Palmer returned to the consistory court to confess her perjury in early March 1333. In her confession she outlined how she had procured the annulment of her marriage to Geoffrey Brun by perjured evidence, which she had purchased at a price of five shillings from Ralph Fouler. For that price Ralph had organised the requisite two witnesses to swear before the court that he had contracted marriage with her prior to her exchange of vows with Geoffrey Brun. Now, six years later, she wished to confess to her crime.

Alice Palmer's story is a sad one: a tale of an unhappy marriage and domestic abuse that culminated in her (unsuccessful) attempt to murder her husband by feeding him arsenic. What is interesting from our perspective is the way in which it appears that she was inspired (and possibly helped) by a previous encounter with the law to make her claim of precontract and that a number of circumstantial details suggest that Alice made her successful plea aided and abetted by the local parish priest. In his turn the priest may have been instructed by the archdeacon of the East Riding of Yorkshire, under whose jurisdiction Alice had originally been called to answer for the marital discord between herself and her husband Geoffrey.

Geoffrey and Alice had married in the village of Folkton sometime before 1327, but their marriage went spectacularly wrong. Two witnesses confirmed that Geoffrey often assaulted and beat Alice badly. A third witness – William, the vicar of Scalby, who had officiated at their marriage – reported to the court that although public violence was committed only by Geoffrey, Alice had threatened to kill Geoffrey in his sleep and tried to kill him by poisoning him with arsenic. The marriage was clearly a public scandal that called for the *ex officio* investigation by the archdeacon's court. In his 1333 deposition William explained that, after the case had been heard by the archdeacon, Alice sought the advice of her father. It was her father (now conveniently deceased) who suggested that they find someone to pass himself as her husband in an earlier marriage. Together Alice and her father paid Ralph Fouler, who lived in a neighbouring village, five shillings to appear before a court to swear that he had contracted marriage with Alice before she contracted with Geoffrey. This stratagem gained Alice and Geoffrey an annulment of their marriage. Geoffrey subsequently married Johanna Southbrunne, and William Scalby blessed their nuptial bed. Despite this non-liturgical, but doubtless common, involvement in Geoffrey and Johanna's wedding, William Scalby was careful to point out that he had not been present at the solemnisation of the marriage. Had he been, and had he known about a possible impediment to the marriage, he faced the penalty of suspension from office for three years. The York court, however, accepted, at the suggestion of her father, Alice had obtained the annulment by perjured witnesses and there is no record of any action against William Scalby.

But the sequence of events also suggests an additional level of complicity between Alice and the archdeacon of the East Riding in coming up with the idea to use perjury to end Alice's unhappy and conflict-ridden marriage. In his deposition William Scalby outlined the sequence of events leading to the idea of using perjured witnesses: this had come to Alice after she had appeared before the court of the archdeacon of the East Riding, who demanded that she answer questions about her constant quarrelling with Geoffrey and their public threats to do each other harm. We cannot say for certain that Alice Palmer colluded with the court or with the local priest William Scalby, but we may suggest that the following was the sequence of events. When he examined Alice Palmer and Geoffrey Brun's marriage the archdeacon of the East Riding could not annul the marriage on canonical grounds because Alice and Geoffrey were publicly married and could not hope to procure an annulment by canonical means. Instead, the archdeacon and his assistant subsequently approached William Scalby to discuss the case and to hint at what the court needed to be told. William Scalby then advised Alice how to proceed, or at least someone with a good knowledge of canon law did. Alice then knew how to go about obtaining her annulment with maximum efficiency and the minimum amount of fuss. She hired a man to pass himself off as her husband. He, in his turn, provided two witnesses to secure the annulment. Between them, Alice, Ralph and the two witnesses presented a convincing case for the existence of a pre-contracted marriage to the court of the archdeacon of the East Riding – who may already have been in on the plan to annul the marriage.

In this case I can only speculate about the *fons et origo* of Alice's decision to procure an annulment. There is no concrete evidence for direct clerical interference. The aiding and abetting of a miscarriage of justice by a cleric, then as now, carried a heavy penalty and William Scalby may have been covering his tracks when he claimed that Alice's dead father had put her up to procuring an annulment. When he told the court in York that he did not solemnise Geoffrey and Johanna's marriage William Scalby was making sure that he could not subsequently be accused of having withheld his knowledge of an impeding marriage at the solemnisation of the marriage of Geoffrey to Johanna. There is additional, though weak, evidence that something unusual took place in this case. At its outset the court in York appointed Richard de Grimston, the rector of the church of Settrington, and Thomas de Wyte, the rector of the church of Weng, to hear the case, but they had their appointments withdrawn soon after the beginning of the case 'for certain reasons'. Perhaps it is not too mischievous to suggest that Richard and Thomas were compromised in this case, too?

Conclusions

The records of medieval litigation must be approached with caution. To a surprising degree fourteenth-century litigants were well informed and their knowledge about the law was bolstered by their interaction with the personnel of the courts. In this chapter I have analysed four cases that illustrate the entanglement of the courts and the litigants in four different ways. In the case of Newton and Garth c. Waghen we saw the way in which the defendant's family was crucial to the outcome of the case. The successful party presented a variety of evidence with economy and knowledge. It was not necessary to produce the evidence of a notary (though he had been present). We also saw how the unsuccessful party appears to have used a scribe with no York connection to draw up his case, which may be seen as evidence that litigants could easily find legal expertise outwith the York Consistory Court. The Lovel c. Marton case demonstrated how a little knowledge of the law could go a long way and how a young couple was able to use the law to thwart the wishes of a parent who made alternative marriage arrangements for his son. The Paynel case shows a defendant who appears to have done everything he could to avoid the far-reaching consequences of the discovery of his gender, while the Palmer case as presented here was conducted in a complex interaction between court and lay persons who jointly wanted to alleviate an unbearable situation.

Davis's work has shown us that when the stakes were high litigants had little difficulty in selectively presenting the facts of their case, and that they presented them in such a manner that they increased their chances of a pardon or, failing that, in a manner which secured the continued prosperity of family and kin. Davis presented evidence of these strategies in action, but her evidence did not allow her to go into detail about how litigants and those who pleaded for mercy found the knowledge that allowed them to organise their narratives in such a manner that their pleas for pardons had the maximum impact. For that kind of analysis a different kind of text is needed. That can be found in the much more mundane case files in York, which preserve both the arguments and the procedural progression of a comprehensive corpus of marriage litigation. In this analysis of a small proportion of the York Cause Papers we have examined a selection of petitions and case files. The analysis has shown that there existed a legal culture that allowed litigants to avail themselves of a wide range of legal expertise which was both easily accessible and used with surprising sophistication. Litigants approached the courts for a variety of purposes: to repel an unwanted suitor, to enforce the right to choose one's own spouse, to protect an estate or to dissolve a marriage to an abusive husband. In all these cases litigants successfully accessed legal expertise, and, using strategies suggested by these experts, presented the York court with a convincing case. In other words, this was a supplicatory culture characterised by a willingness to use the full arsenal of the law. Sometimes that use went beyond what the law allowed, but, as we saw in the case of Alice Palmer, even then litigants were keen to pretend that they had remained within the bounds of the law. The written records of these cases demonstrate that a process of selection and verification guided by legal arguments and supervised by a member of the court who was educated or trained in law took place. Though this means added complications for the student of medieval social history, a closer analysis of the surviving cases in their legal, social and cultural context will not only provide us with numerous stories of everyday life but also show us a popular, flexible and useful medieval culture of supplication and petition.

10

Killer Clergy: How did Clerics Justify Homicide in Petitions to the Apostolic Penitentiary in the Late Middle Ages?

Kirsi Salonen

Violence in its many forms – warfare, murder, manslaughter or assault – was an omnipresent phenomenon in medieval society. It was especially linked to lay society, but members of the clergy were not immune to it either.[1] Medieval sources – court records, annals, treatises and many others – tell about clergymen involved in violent events. In these sources clergymen are typically victims of a violent act committed by a layperson. But, even though the ecclesiastical legislation strictly forbade members of the clergy from acting violently, medieval sources also contain a lot of information about clergymen who committed violent crimes. Particularly good source material for the study of clerical violence comes from the register series of the apostolic penitentiary, which contains numerous petitions from clergymen all over Christendom asking for pardon because of violent behaviour.

The aim of this chapter, which is based on the late fifteenth- and early sixteenth-century penitentiary documentation, is to examine what kinds of strategy the clergymen who turned to the penitentiary applied in order to get their consciences cleansed. In particular, it analyses the wording that the clients of the penitentiary accused of homicide used in their petitions in order to convince papal officials of their innocence.[2]

Canon Law and Violent Clergy

According to the principle of the fifth commandment ('Thou shalt not kill', Ex. 20:13), the ecclesiastical norms did not tolerate any form of violence or killing.

[1] P. Clarke, 'The Medieval Clergy and Violence: An Historiographical Introduction', in *Violence and the Medieval Clergy*, ed. G. Jaritz and A. Marinković (Budapest, 2011), pp. 3–16, at p. 3.

[2] Vatican City, Archivio Storico della Penitenzieria Apostolica (henceforth: APA), Reg. Matrim. et Div.

Since members of the clergy were supposed to act as models for laypeople, the ecclesiastical norms required clergymen to abstain from violence. In order to protect the peaceful clergymen from lay violence the Second Lateran Council (1139) stipulated in its constitution no. 15 – known as *Si quis suadente* – that anyone who laid violent hands on the members of the clergy or on men or women in monastic vocation incurred automatic excommunication, which could be lifted only by a papal absolution.[3] This constitution became part of what is now known as *privilegium canonis* and refers to the special protection of clergymen against any kind of assault. As Peter Clarke has pointed out, this was not the only way the Church tried to protect its officials. The Church introduced also another privilege, *privilegium fori,* according to which only a clergyman could judge the misdeeds of another clergyman. In practice, this privilege meant that the crimes committed by clergymen had to be judged in ecclesiastical tribunals. For the members of the clergy this meant immunity from lay justice, which used much harsher sentences, such as the death penalty.[4]

One of the main principles of the Church in promoting the idea of non-violent clergy was the prohibition on carrying weapons. According to canon 20 of the ecclesiastical council of Naples (1120), which was later included in the *Liber Extra,* the collection of canon law promulgated by Pope Gregory IX in 1234, clergymen were not allowed to carry any kind of weapon. The only exception to this rule was a small knife necessary for daily use, such as cutting bread.[5]

Despite its protective hand, the Catholic Church and its legislation were not lenient towards those of its officials who acted against the most significant ecclesiastical principle of non-violent behaviour. Indeed, the regulations of canon law severely punished clergymen who committed violent acts. If a clergyman was involved in a violent act he incurred immediately, *ipso facto,* an automatic excommunication from which he could be released only by an absolution granted by the pope. In addition to this, clergymen guilty of violent behaviour were also considered irregular because of the defect of perfection of leniency of heart (*ex defectu perfectae lenitatis*). Being irregular meant that the person in question was not allowed to carry out any ecclesiastical functions – which in practice meant that he lost his job and thereby his means of income – and, if he did, he made his situation even worse by committing an excess

[3] R. H. Helmholz, '"Si quis suadente" (C.17 q.4 c.29): Theory and Practice', in *Proceedings of the Seventh International Congress of Canon Law,* ed. P. Linehan, Monumenta Iuris Canonici, Series C 8 (Vatican City, 1988), pp. 425–38. Constitution 15 of the Second Lateran Council is edited in *Decrees of the Ecumenical Councils,* ed. and trans. N. Tanner, 2 vols (Washington, DC, 1990), vol. I, p. 200.

[4] Clarke, 'The Medieval Clergy and Violence', pp. 8–9.

[5] X 3.1.2., *Corpus Iuris Canonici, Pars Secunda, Decretalium Collectiones,* ed. E. Friedberg, 2nd edn (Graz, 1959), p. 449. On the regulations concerning the use of knives by clergymen, see G. Jaritz, 'The Bread-Knife', in *Violence and the Medieval Clergy,* ed. Jaritz and Marinković, pp. 53–65, at p. 57.

(*excessus*). The only way to remove the burden of irregularity was to receive a papal dispensation. Thus a clergyman who had acted violently had to turn to the papal curia and ask for both absolution and dispensation before his conscience was cleansed and he could return to his ecclesiastical functions.

However, a papal absolution and dispensation did not necessarily restore all clerical rights to clergymen who had acted violently. The ecclesiastical norms stipulated that a priest who had participated in bloodshed was suspended from altar service forever and deposed from his office and income. The Church was even stricter with clergymen who killed their closest ones. The regulations of canon law state that such priests were to be deposed from the clerical stand – and thus from the protection of the *privilegium fori* – and handed over to secular authorities for capital punishment.[6]

The ecclesiastical norms did not differentiate between different levels of violence, but considered all kinds of violent act – from an angry blow to a premeditated murder – as an offence against the regulations of the Church and punished the culprits with the same punishment: that is, excommunication. Hence, the ecclesiastical norms did not draw any distinctions between persons who were guilty of dealing a blow without bloodshed (*percussio*), causing a bloody wound (*vulneratio*) or causing a permanent injury (*debilitatio, mutilatio, truncatio*) to their victim. In case of homicide (*homicidium*), canon law did not distinguish between murder and involuntary manslaughter, as civil legislation typically already did in the Middle Ages. According to the Church it was the result, the death of someone, which counted. Thereby, any violent act that resulted in the death of the victim was considered as homicide, even if the perpetrator had no intention to kill. Therefore, a person who had been present – even if only casually – in a place where a violent act had led to someone's death was considered guilty of the death of the victim. This meant that clergymen who had been present on the battlefield or participated in court sessions in which someone was sentenced to death were considered guilty of the death that followed. The same principle was applied to those who provoked someone to violence, even if they did not personally participate in the violent act. The penitentiary to which the popes had delegated – from the 1360s onwards at the latest – the powers to pardon violent clergymen, however, took these differences into account in its decision-making, as the entries in the registers of the penitentiary demonstrate.[7]

[6] X 5.12.24., X 5.25.1., *Corpus Iuris Canonici, Pars Secunda*, ed. Friedberg, pp. 803–4, 825. On the penitentiary and regulations of canon law regarding clerical violence, see L. Schmugge, P. Hersperger and B. Wiggenhauser, *Die Supplikenregister der päpstlichen Pönitentiarie aus der Zeit Pius' II. (1458–1464)* (Tübingen, 1996), pp. 98–103; K. Salonen, *The Penitentiary as a Well of Grace in the Late Middle Ages: The Example of the Province of Uppsala 1448–1527* (Helsinki, 2001), pp. 128–9, 136–7; K. Salonen and L. Schmugge, *A Sip from the 'Well of Grace': Medieval Texts from the Apostolic Penitentiary* (Washington, DC, 2008), pp. 30–3.

[7] Schmugge et al., *Die Supplikenregister*, pp. 99–100, 115; Salonen, *The Penitentiary*,

The Apostolic Penitentiary

The apostolic penitentiary, which is often called 'the supreme tribunal of conscience', was one of the most important papal offices. Its main task was to deal with sins and crimes that were reserved for papal authority. The penitentiary functioned under the guidance of a cardinal called the major penitentiary, who, together with his second-in-command, the regent, could make decisions on behalf of the pontiff. With powers received from various popes, the penitentiary could grant to its clients four different types of grace: 1) absolutions for those who had broken the regulations of canon law;[8] 2) dispensations that allowed Christians to act against the regulations of the Church;[9] 3) licences that allowed Christians not to observe ecclesiastical norms regarding the exercise of one's faith;[10] and 4) official declarations.[11]

The best source for understanding the great variety of issues entrusted to the office is the medieval penitentiary registers, which are divided internally into seven sections: *de matrimonialibus* (marriages); *de diversis formis* (different types of cases); *de declaratoriis* (declarations); *de defectu natalium* (illegitimacy); *de uberiori* (holding more than one benefice while being of illegitimate birth); *de promotis et promovendis* (ecclesiastical ordinations); and *de confessionalibus* (the right to choose one's confessor).[12] Two of these sections, the *de diversis formis* and the *de declaratoriis*, contain petitions related to the violent behaviour of clergymen and are relevant to this chapter.

pp. 130, 136; L. Schmugge, 'Kanonistik in der Pönitentiarie', in *Stagnation oder Fortbildung? Aspekte des allgemeinen Kirchenrechts im 14. und 15. Jahrhundert*, ed. M. Bertram (Tübingen, 2005), pp. 93–115.

8 The powers of the penitentiary allowed it to absolve Christians even from sins reserved for papal authority.

9 The dispensations granted by the penitentiary allowed Christians, for example, to marry a close relative, to become a priest despite an impediment of illegitimacy, minority or bodily defect, or to continue in an ecclesiastical career after becoming irregular because of a severe sin or crime.

10 This category includes issues such as confessing to a priest other than one's own parish priest, consuming meat and dairy products during Lent, carrying a portable altar or transferring from one monastery to another.

11 The penitentiary could grant declarations testifying that a cleric was not guilty of murder or mutilation despite (unjust) accusations or that a forced marriage or monastic profession was void.

12 There is a certain variation of the number of sections in the penitentiary registers. For example, in later volumes, the *de defectu natalium* and *de uberiori* sections are united in a single section called *de illegitimiis*, and the *de diversis formis* and *de declaratoribus* sections are combined in the single section *de diversis materiis*. On the archival material of the penitentiary and the medieval penitentiary registers, see Salonen, *The Penitentiary*, pp. 425–6; Salonen and Schmugge, *A Sip from the 'Well of Grace'*, pp. 3–9; K. Salonen, 'The Curia: The Apostolic Penitentiary', in *A Companion to the Medieval Papacy: Growth of an Ideology and Institution*, ed. K. Sisson and A. A. Larson (Leiden, 2016), pp. 259–75, at pp. 265–7.

The *de diversis formis* section is one of the largest petition categories in the penitentiary registers and contains a number of different types of grace: absolutions, dispensations and licences related to behaviour contrary to the regulations of canon law. One of the largest groups of offences recorded in this section was violent behaviour: murder, manslaughter or assault in which priests were involved either as victims or perpetrators. Other petitions deal with monastic issues, simony, sacrilege, sexual crimes or the breaking of oaths or solemn vows, as well as licences to deviate from dietary regulations during Lent, for example.[13]

The petitions regarding the competence of the penitentiary to grant official declarations are in their turn recorded in the *de declaratoriis* section. The majority of petitioners in this section were clergymen asking for an official declaration stating that they were not guilty of homicide and thus could continue in their ecclesiastical careers without problems, even though they had participated in events that resulted in someone's death. This section also includes petitions for an official testimony annulling a forced monastic profession or an illegal marriage.[14]

In these two groups we find traces of two different kinds of petition from clergymen guilty of violent crimes. In the *de diversis formis* section are recorded those petitions in which the petitioner had recognised his guilt and asked for absolution and dispensation so that he could cleanse his conscience and remove the irregularity which impeded him from acting in his office. But, as noted above, a papal absolution and dispensation in a standard form (*in forma*) was not enough to restore the full priestly rights for a person guilty of taking someone's life, since the regulations of canon law stipulate that a priest (*presbyter*) who was guilty of bloodshed lost his right to act in altar service and hear confession for life. In practice this meant that the guilty person was no longer allowed to act as parish priest, for example, but only in lower offices without the cure of souls. In certain circumstances, however, the penitentiary had the powers to restore the full status of a priest, despite the fact that he had been involved in bloodshed or homicide.

For petitioners who were ordained only to the lower ecclesiastical orders and did not want to be promoted to the three higher orders, receiving a papal absolution and dispensation in the standard form was not a problem, but men ordained to priesthood risked the loss of their job and income with only the standard papal pardon. For those men, who wanted to be sure that they could continue in their priestly order, or in case of clerics in lower orders who hoped to be promoted to the higher orders at some point, there was another option: receiving a papal letter of declaration stating that the perpetrator was not guilty of homicide or assault. Petitions for such letters are recorded in the

13 Salonen and Schmugge, *A Sip from the 'Well of Grace'*, pp. 28–49.
14 Salonen and Schmugge, *A Sip from the 'Well of Grace'*, pp. 49–56.

penitentiary registers in the *de declaratoriis* section. In order to receive such a letter, the petitioners had to be able to demonstrate that – on the basis of certain extenuating circumstances stipulated in canon law – they should not be considered guilty of homicide. The need to justify their innocence in the text of the petition explains the numerous details in the petitions registered in the *de declaratoriis* section. The petitions in this section are much longer than those found in the *de diversis formis* section (which are often laconic)[15] and include a detailed *narratio* – an explanation of all relevant facts with numerous small details intended to underline the innocence of the petitioner.[16]

Requirements for Obtaining a Declaration in the Case of Homicide

A person who was clearly guilty of homicide could not receive a letter of declaration from the penitentiary. However, if a petitioner who had been involved in events during which he had killed someone could demonstrate that certain extenuating circumstances took place during the events, he could petition for such a letter. But his case had to fulfil three requirements. He had to be able to show: 1) that he acted in self-defence; 2) that he used only the minimum amount of violence necessary; and 3) that he used a legitimate instrument as a weapon. In addition to this, the penitentiary could grant declarations of innocence also to petitioners who could demonstrate that there had been a pure accident or that they had only been present in the place where someone had been killed, without having anything to do with the events.[17] In the following are described how these different extenuating circumstances are reflected in the wordings of the penitentiary petitions and what they mean.

The regulations of canon law permitted the members of the clergy to use violence only in situations when they were in imminent danger of death. The right to self-defence is a Roman legal maxim (*vim enim vi defendere omnes leges omniaque iura permittunt*),[18] from which it has been adapted to canon law.[19] Thousands of penitentiary petitioners guilty of having caused someone's death

[15] One of the shortest descriptions of a murder case in the *de diversis formis* section is as follows: 'Paulo Petri diocesis Aboensis; interfecit clericum' (Paul, son of Peter from the diocese of Turku, killed a cleric): APA, Reg. Matrim. et Div. 3, fol. 152. The document is edited in *Auctoritate Papae. The Church Province of Uppsala and the Apostolic Penitentiary 1410–1526*, ed. S. Risberg and K. Salonen, Diplomatarium Suecanum, Appendix, Acta Pontificu, Suecica II, Acta Poenitentiariae (Stockholm, 2008), no. 28. The petitions in the *de declaratoriis* section instead are often several pages long.

[16] Salonen, *The Penitentiary*, pp. 119–20.

[17] Schmugge et al., *Die Supplikenregister*, pp. 176–7.

[18] Dig. 9.2.45. All laws and all rights permit persons to repel force with force.

[19] Clem. 5.4.un., *Corpus Iuris Canonici, Pars Secunda*, ed. Friedberg, p. 1184. K.

profited from this legal principle. They applied for a letter of declaration, basing their supplication on the fact that they should not be considered guilty for a homicide as they acted only in legitimate self-defence. But in order to receive a declaration of innocence based on the principle of acting in self-defence the petitioners had to explain carefully the events that led to the death of their adversary and to be able to demonstrate that their life really had been in danger.

In the petition texts this requirement is reflected in various formulations in the long and detailed *narratio*. Typically the *narratio* describes how the adversary had first attacked the petitioner and how the clergyman had then been obliged to defend himself in order to avoid a certain death. In these cases the penitentiary petitioners always use the phraseology referring directly to the respective wording in Roman law: *vim vi repellendo* or *vim vi repellendo et se defendendo*. The wordings used may vary slightly, but the reference to the legal principle of one's right to self-defence is always clear.[20]

Since the use of violence should have been the last resort for the person under attack, the stressing of self-defence was not always sufficient to receive a declaration of innocence. It was important for the penitentiary petitioners to underline the fact that the situation at the moment when they had been attacked had been so serious that they could not escape. Sometimes the petitioner tells explicitly how he had first escaped from the attacker, who eventually caught him, and how, in this situation, the only solution was to act in self-defence. The majority of penitentiary petitioners emphasised their difficult situation by using a phrase stating that they could not have avoided the danger of death in any other way (*aliter mortem evadere non valens* or *aliter evadere mortis periculum non posset*).[21]

Another important point that the penitentiary petitioners had to be able to demonstrate was that they had used the minimum force necessary to escape from the dangerous situation. This was a reference to the principle of *moderamen inculpatae tutelae*, from Roman law (latterly translated to ecclesiastical legislation). This principle refers to the right of a person to use a controlled amount of blameless force to repel violence, but according to it the defender should not be stronger than the attacker.[22]

In order to fulfil this requirement the clients of the penitentiary had to underline in their petitions that they were in a weaker position than

Pennington, 'Moderamen Inculpatae Tutelae: The Jurisprudence of a Justifiable Defense', *Rivista Internazionale di diritto commune* 24 (2013), 27–56.

20 Schmugge et al., *Die Supplikenregister*, pp. 104–5; Salonen, *The Penitentiary*, p. 129; T. Jørgensen, '"... Killings, unfortunately, take place more often here than anywhere else": Civil and Clerical Homicide in the Late Medieval Norway', in *Violence and the Medieval Clergy*, ed. Jaritz and Marinković, pp. 29–45, at p. 39; Salonen and Schmugge, *A Sip from the 'Well of Grace'*, pp. 52–3.

21 Schmugge et al., *Die Supplikenregister*, p. 104; Salonen, *The Penitentiary*, p. 129.

22 Jørgensen, 'Civil and Clerical Homicide', pp. 39–40; Pennington, 'Moderamen inculpatae tutelae', p. 27.

their adversaries. This could be explained in many ways. Sometimes the petitioners related that their adversary had entered their homes after they had already gone to bed or while they were eating. With such a statement the petitioner could show that he was totally unprepared to face a violent attack, and thus totally defenceless. Similarly, many petitioners explained that their adversaries arrived with a group of friends and thus had superior force on their side.

An important factor in the description of the moderate use of violence is the type of violence. According to the principle of moderation, the victim should not act more violently than the assaulter. For example, if one had received an angry blow with an open hand, it was not legitimate to hit back with a fist or to use a weapon. Similarly, if the attacker had hit the victim on his arm, the victim should not respond by striking the assaulter about the head. In addition, the amount of violence used in the moment of self-defence had significance when the penitentiary made its decision. The main principle for moderate self-defence was that the defender should not hit the assailant more times than necessary for him to knock the other down so that he could flee. This fact is reflected in the petition phraseology by statements such as 'he hit only once' (*unico ictu percussit*) or 'he hit him lightly and only once' (*unico ictu leniter percussit*).[23]

Another extremely significant factor for the penitentiary petitions in referring to the principle of *moderamen inculpatae tutelae* was the ability to demonstrate the moderate use of a weapon in self-defence. Here, the regulations of canon law prohibiting clergymen from carrying weapons played a central role. Since the norms of the Church allowed clergymen to carry only a small knife for daily use, ecclesiastics who had defended themselves with any other type of weapon needed a very good explanation if they wanted to plead innocence. Otherwise the use of a weapon other than the small knife was automatically held against the petitioner.[24]

The regulation about the small knife can be seen in the penitentiary petitions in the form of a very common phrase: 'he hit him with a small knife' (*cum parvo cultello percussit*). Those clients of the penitentiary who had used another type of weapon had to give a very good explanation for its use. A very typical explanation was that the petitioner had received the weapon from someone else present in the situation or that the events took place in a location where other persons' weapons were at hand and thus the petitioner had grasped what he found available. In some cases, the person applying for a declaration referred to a special need to carry a weapon in the particular situation when he had met his adversaries. For example, some men travelling alone claimed they carried weapons to protect themselves against robbers or dangerous animals

[23] See, for example, *Auctoritate Papae*, ed. Risberg and Salonen, nos 79, 234, 316, 418, 417, 451.

[24] Jaritz, 'The Bread-Knife', p. 57.

along their route. Others stated that they were returning from a hunting tour and, therefore, were carrying weapons used for that purpose.

Sometimes the weapons used in self-defence were not really weapons in the strict sense of the word. In one Finnish case, for example, the priest, who had to turn to the penitentiary because he caused a permanent injury to another person during a fight, explained that his adversary was a carpenter. Since the carpenter attacked the priest in the room where he was working, there were various sharp tools to hand, and the priest had just grasped the first implement available when he had to face the rage of his attacker.[25]

In their supplications the petitioners had to explain all these details credibly before they could receive a positive decision from the penitentiary, resulting in formulaic phrases explaining away the guilt of the petitioner, such as: 'when he realised that he was badly injured and could not avoid death in any other way, he hit his adversary once with a small knife, which he carried with him for cutting bred, and wounded him' (*videns se graviter lesum fore cum quodam parvo cultello, quem ipse ad scindendum panem secum deferebat, cum alias mortem evadere non posset, suum adversarium unico ictu percussit et vulneravit*). Additionally, since the contrition was an integral part of confession and absolution, the clients of the penitentiary always explained in their petition that they were very sorry for what had happened (*cum autem dictus exponens de morte ipsius ab intimis doleat*).[26]

The above phraseology is connected to events in which the petitioner had killed in self-defence. But, as already noted, the penitentiary could also grant declarations in other kinds of case. According to the regulations of canon law, the mere presence of a person in a place where someone was killed made that person guilty of the death of the victim. The same guilt fell upon those who instigated others to violent acts or helped or advised the aggressor in some way. The idea behind this regulation, which brought a considerable number of clerics before the penitentiary, was that clergymen should try to bring peace, rather than cause conflict. If a clergyman had been in a place where someone died because of violence he had to be able to demonstrate either that his presence there had been coincidental and that the events at the time of his arrival had already gone so far that he could not stop the violence, or that he had tried to stop the violence but had not succeeded.[27]

[25] APA, Reg. Matrim. et Div. 12, fol. 139. The document is edited in *Auctoritate Papae*, ed. Risberg and Salonen, no. 114. For more about the case, see K. Salonen, 'Träsnidaren Nicolaus öde', *Finskt museum* (2004), 21–7.

[26] APA, Reg. Matrim. et Div, 9, fols 238v–239r, edited in *Repertorium Poenitentiariae Germanicum IV: Verzeichnis der in den Supplikenregistern der Pönitentiarie Pius' II. vorkommenden Personen, Kirchen und Orte des Deutschen Reiches, 1458–1464*, ed. L. Schmugge et al. (Tübingen, 1996), no. 1787. About the *contritio cordis*, see Jørgensen, 'Civil and Clerical Homicide', p. 40; on the different formulas relative to the use of knife, see Jaritz, 'The Bread-Knife', pp. 57–60.

[27] X 5.12.11., VI 5.4.3., *Corpus Iuris Canonici, Pars Secunda*, ed. Friedberg, pp. 797, 1081;

This regulation has also left traces in the penitentiary petitions in the form of an oft-used formulary stating that the petitioner had not given any help, advice or favour in the death of the deceased person (*in morte dicti defuncti non presterit auxilim, consilium vel favorem*). In addition to this, the petitioner had to explain to the penitentiary why he happened to be in the location where the death took place and what he had done in the situation. Many petitioners explained carefully how they had just been enjoying a pleasant evening with friends, perhaps eating and drinking, when persons in the company or in the same room had begun to quarrel. Typically, the petitioners state that they had tried to calm the situation down, but it then escalated so much that reconciliation became impossible.

The last possible way of obtaining a letter of declaration from the penitentiary was to demonstrate that the petitioner had caused someone's death, but that it had happened accidentally; according to the ecclesiastical norms, an unintentional act could not cause guilt.[28] These cases included real accidents, such as a case from Germany in which the petitioner, Tiellemannus Waethkenfeidde, a cleric and school rector from Braunschweig, had built a stage for a school feast. During the event the stage could not bear the weight of the many people standing on it and collapsed, causing the death of some children, after which Tiellemannus was accused of causing their deaths.[29] In these cases the petitioners underlined the fact that the cause of death was unintentional with the phrase 'this petitioner is not guilty of his death in any other way' (*dictus exponens de morte ipsius aliter culpabilis non sit*), or similar.

The petition of a Finnish priest, Stephanus Petri, the deputy of priest Olavus Magni in the parish of Tuulos, is a good example of how petitioners explained various details in their supplications to the penitentiary in order to convince the office of their innocence in events that caused the death of adversaries. The petition begins by relating how one day Olavus had entered his cellar and realised that his beer had been stolen. He informed Stephanus about this unfortunate event and asked him to make inquiries about the theft. Stephanus remembered seeing Katarina, the wife of a certain Peter, who was one of Olavus's servants, carrying a vessel of beer from the cellar and told his superior about this. When Peter heard that Olavus had subsequently

Schmugge et al., *Die Supplikenregister*, pp. 102–3; Salonen, *The Penitentiary*, pp. 130, 134–5; Salonen and Schmugge, *A Sip from the 'Well of Grace'*, p. 53.

28 *Nullo modo peccatum sit, si non sit voluntarium* is a phrase from St Augustine, which was later included in the ecclesiastical regulations by Petrus Lombardus and Gratian. See S. Kuttner, *Kanonistische Schuldlehre von Gratian bis auf die Dekretalen Gregors IX. systematisch auf Grund der handschriftlichen Quellen dargestellt* (Vatican City, 1935), pp. 133–4.

29 APA, Reg. Matrim. et Div. 13, fols 356v–357r; edited in *Repertorium Poenitentiariae Germanicum IV*, ed. Schmugge et al., no. 1834. Schmugge et al., *Die Supplikenregister*, pp. 102–3; Salonen, *The Penitentiary*, p. 130; Salonen and Schmugge, *A Sip from the 'Well of Grace'*, p. 53.

reprimanded his wife he became angry and decided to provoke discord between the two priests.

After giving this more general background information, the petition goes into a more detailed description of the events that eventually led to the death of Olavus and Peter. On one Sunday, at the hour of Vesper, Stephanus asked for Olavus and was told by the housemaid that he had already gone to bed. Stephanus found it strange that Olavus had gone to bed at this time, without having said Vespers or without supper, but asked the maid to give him a drink before he would go to bed too, and the maid did that. At the same moment, Olavus appeared. He slapped the maid's face and said to Stephanus: 'What are you doing? Do you want me to toast you to hell?' Olavus then tried to attack Stephanus with a sword he grabbed from a young servant, Henrik. At this point, the unarmed Stephanus tried to escape the furious Olavus, who, along with his servant, followed him with drawn sword as if to kill him. Stephanus pleaded for mercy, took hold of the point of Olavus's sword with his hand and was seriously wounded. Seeing no other way to escape, Stephanus took out a small knife and struck Olavus in his left side, of which blow Olavus died on the following day. Stephanus then tried to escape the furious servant, Peter, who was hitting him on the back and head with his sword, and he struck Peter on the shoulder with the knife, wounding him lethally.

After having explained all this the petitioner states that he was not guilty of the death of these two men in any other way than that, that he truly regretted their deaths and still did, and that he wished to minister in his orders and to be able to act in altar service. However – Stephanus continued in his petition, using a very typical phraseology for the penitentiary petitions – many simple people who did not know the law and were also, perhaps, his enemies claimed that he had incurred excommunication and irregularity because of the events and therefore should not be allowed to act in his orders or to hold a benefice. In order to close their mouths he now petitioned for a declaration of innocence, which would state that he had not incurred excommunication or become irregular and that he could continue in his orders, altar service and benefice. The regent of the penitentiary agreed upon the case in November 1498 but asked one of the lawyers in the papal curia to check that the content of the petition was legally correct, after which the final solution of the case was referred to the bishop of Turku, who was supposed to investigate that the events described by Stephanus corresponded to the truth and especially that he had had no chance to escape.[30]

In this case we find all the essential elements for explaining that the petitioner – who had personally killed two men – was not guilty of homicide

[30] APA, Reg. Matrim. et Div. 47, fols 439r–440r; the document is edited in *Auctoritate Papae*, ed. Risberg and Salonen, no. 360.

according to the regulations of canon law due to the extenuating circumstances. The petitioner could tell how he had been caught by surprise, how the adversaries – having superior power – attacked him first with heavy weapons (a sword), how he feared for his life in a situation in which there was no escape, and how only at that point, already wounded, did he take his small knife and defend himself. The petitioner also explains that Olavus did not die immediately of the wound caused by Stephanus – stressing the fact that the Stephanus had not used too much power – and that he had hit Peter on his shoulder, while Peter had hit him on his back and head. All these details support clearly the claim of Stephanus that he acted only in self-defence and used moderate violence and a legitimate weapon. In addition to this explanation come the usual phrases about his regret over what had happened and his wish to continue in his ecclesiastical career. Since Stephanus could support his request with all these details, the penitentiary could do nothing but grant him the grace he wanted – as it did in so many other similar cases.

Use of Proctors

As the number of details required in supplications demonstrates, it was not simple to compose a petition to the penitentiary and to choose the right words that would lead to the desired result. The composition of a petition was not particularly difficult if the client of the penitentiary only wanted to confess his guilt and to receive absolution and dispensation. But if he desired a declaration of innocence it was much more important to know how to formulate the supplication in the correct way. This leads us to the central question: who formulated all the petitions presented to the penitentiary?

It is impossible to know how the penitentiary petitioners composed their supplications, since there is no written evidence of this. Scholars of the penitentiary have assumed that only a few clients of the penitentiary would have had the necessary profound knowledge of the regulations of canon law or the *stilus curiae*, according to the rules of which the petitions had to be composed, that would have allowed them to act alone. Since it is well known that the penitentiary employed a certain number of proctors who offered their services – against payment – to the clients of the office, it is evident that these proctors must have taken care of the composition of the petitions on behalf of the clients.[31] Further evidence that the wording in the petitions must originate from the pens of professional proctors is that the phrases used are always very formulaic and are repeated in the same form over and over again. Had each petitioner freely written his or her petition, the variation in wording

[31] On penitentiary proctors, see Schmugge et al., *Die Supplikenregister*, pp. 41–8; Salonen and Schmugge, *A Sip from the 'Well of Grace'*, p. 70.

would have been much larger and the petition texts much less professionally composed.

The penitentiary registers also offer direct evidence for the use of proctors, since the names of the proctors responsible for each petition are recorded in some register volumes. This information cannot be found in all register volumes, but occur in two of the earlier ones (volume nos 7 and 8 from the years 1459 and 1460) and again from the year 1507 (volume no. 55) onwards.[32] Of course, such a reference to a proctor in connection with a petition is not a guarantee that the proctor composed the text of the supplication, but, taken with the other evidence, this points strongly to the conclusion that petitions were written by professionals.

The division of labour between the professional proctors and the petitioners was apparently clear. The proctors, who knew the regulations of canon law and the curial writing style, were experts in composing the petitions in the right way so that the result would have been profitable for their clients. Thus it was their job to take care of the right formulations. But they needed to get the principal information from the petitioners. When the proctors had heard the whole story, they could present to the client all the possible alternatives, after which they could decide together which strategy to follow.

Did the Petitioners Lie? The *veritas precum*

Scholars of the penitentiary have generally agreed that the office typically approved all petitions presented to its competence if the petition was phrased according to the correct formulations and there were no formal mistakes.[33] Especially with the more complicated *de declaratoriis* petitions, this raises the inevitable question of veracity: if the penitentiary was merely a rubber stamp and the petitions were composed by experienced professionals who knew what one should say in a successful petition, could petitioners simply lie in order to receive their grace? This is a legitimate and important question and needs to be addressed.

The answer is, in principle, negative. No, the petitioners could not simply tell lies to the penitentiary and get away with their sins and crimes so easily. Especially in the cases of the *de declaratoriis* petitions the penitentiary always granted a positive answer, but it did so conditionally. In these cases the guilt of the petitioner was not simply removed when the letter of grace was granted; the case had to be submitted to a further investigation before it could be closed. Therefore, the penitentiary did not expedite the letter of grace directly to the petitioner, but instead to an executor, who was a local

[32] APA, Reg. Matrim. et Div., 7, 8, and from 55 onwards.

[33] K. Salonen and J. Hanska, *Entering a Clerical Career at the Roman Curia, 1458–1471* (Farnham, 2013), pp. 33–4.

ecclesiastical person – often the bishop of the petitioner. The task of the executor was to investigate more closely the details of the case, the so-called *veritas precum*, for example by interviewing witnesses. If the executor found out that the petitioner had told the truth, he could declare the petitioner not guilty. If, instead, he discovered that some details given by the petitioner did not match the truth, the executor would declare the grace granted by the penitentiary void.[34]

Since it was neither easy nor cheap to obtain a letter of declaration from the penitentiary,[35] it seems more probable to suggest that petitioners tried to stick to the truth, at least regarding the most important details. But this remains a mere assumption, unless we find a concrete case showing that this was actually true. There is at least one case which supplies good testimony to the assumption that the petitioners must have told the truth to the penitentiary, even if they wanted to conceal the sordid details from others. This case concerns one of the late medieval canons of the Roskilde chapter in Denmark, Jens Tetzen Rosengård, who, according to the information in local sources, killed his brother Jørgen in April 1532 in unclear circumstances that have been interpreted as a hunting accident. Since priests guilty of homicide needed to apply to the papal curia to cleanse their consciences, Jens did just this. He turned to the penitentiary in the spring of the following year, 1533, because he needed a declaration as official proof of his innocence so that he could continue serving the Church. As evidence of this, we have a copy of his petition in the registers of the penitentiary. But, surprisingly, the text in the penitentiary register does not describe a hunting accident, as the local sources relate, but tells a totally different and much more violent story.

According to the text of his petition, Jens Rosengård's brother Jørgen had attacked the canon and hit him hard about the head with a silver vessel (*vasa argentea*) and thereafter threatened him with a sword. In this situation, Jens explained, he feared for his life and could not do anything else but to defend himself by force, and so he hit his brother once, wounding him lethally so that Jørgen died immediately.

Since the details in this case support the fact that there was a question of self-defence in imminent danger of death, Jens Rosengård requested from the penitentiary a declaration of innocence, which he received in May 1533. The declaration guaranteed that Jens could continue in his ecclesiastical vocation. He had travelled personally to Rome to ask for the declaration and the penitentiary document states that the handling of his case was committed to

[34] On the petitioning process in the penitentiary, see Salonen and Schmugge, *A Sip from the 'Well of Grace'*, pp. 69–83, esp. pp. 73–4.

[35] On the fees of the penitentiary, see W. P. Müller, 'The Price of Papal Pardon – New Fifteenth-Century Evidence', in *Päpste, Pilger, Pönitentiarie: Festschrift für Ludwig Schmugge zum 65. Geburtstag*, ed. A. Meyer, C. Rendtel and M. Wittmer-Butsch (Tübingen, 2004), pp. 457–81.

one of the minor penitentiaries in Rome because Jens was personally present in the Roman curia and had brought all necessary evidence with him.[36]

But which story is the true one? Did Jens lie to the penitentiary? In my opinion, the local story about a hunting accident must be fictitious version of the events that the family may have used to try to hide the true situation. If so, the penitentiary document – with much more aggravating circumstances – must be the true version of the events. The first point in support of this argument is that the details told to the penitentiary are much more aggravating for the petitioner than a hunting accident would have been. It would have been much easier to receive a declaration in the case of an accident than in a case of self-defence. So if the story about the hunting accident had been true, why would Jens have invented the other story? Secondly, canon Jens Rosengård was the nephew of the local bishop, Lage Urne, who would have been the person deciding whether Jens could continue in his ecclesiastical career or not. It is extremely unlikely that the bishop would not have known the truth about the fate of his nephews and would have accepted a letter of declaration from the penitentiary based on incorrect details. Thus, in this case, the story told to the penitentiary must be correct and the story about a hunting accident must be an invented one.

Conclusion: Supplicatory Strategies?

The penitentiary material offers a lot of information about what kinds of possibility the clients of the penitentiary had when they turned to the office in cases in which they were accused of causing someone's death. The examples above demonstrate that it was of crucial important to know the regulations of canon law and especially the different extenuating circumstances so that one could successfully petition for a declaration of innocence from the apostolic penitentiary.

But, as the texts of the petitions directed to the penitentiary were composed by professional proctors, who mastered – in addition to the regulations and loopholes of canon law – the successful writing style of the papal curia, can we really talk about petition strategies if the only task left to the supplicant was to tell the proctors what had happened? I think we can. The proctors could give much good advice, but they could not decide on behalf of their clients what they should do and how, and the petitioners always remained responsible for the content of the petition.

Because we cannot check the facts in the penitentiary petitions it is not possible to say whether the petitioners told the truth or whether they dressed

36 APA, Reg. Matrim. et Div. 81, fols 489v–490r; 'Slægten Rosengaard', *Danmarks Adels Aarbog* (1912), 393 a.) and b.).

up the story in their favour. If we draw a parallel between the penitentiary cases and late medieval court cases, in which the parties tried everything possible in order to reach a favourable solution for themselves, we could assume that many clients of the penitentiary must also have embellished the stories in their favour, although they must have done this skilfully in order to achieve the desired outcomes.

The veracity of the details in the *narratio* was crucial for a successful petition. As the wording in the letter of declaration was based on the information in the original petition, any inaccuracies in the petition would end up in the letter of declaration as well. And, as the penitentiary appointed a local executor to investigate the *veritas precum*, the details had to be correct if the petitioner wanted to get his grace approved locally. Thus it was left for the petitioner to decide what kinds of detail they wanted to stress in the petition and what perhaps was better left out. If they made decisions that were strategically wise and pressed the right buttons, so to speak, they stood to save both their soul and their career.

Index